Peter Bayne

Two Great Englishwomen, Mrs. Browning & Charlott Brontë

With an Essay on Poetry

Peter Bayne

Two Great Englishwomen, Mrs. Browning & Charlott Brontë
With an Essay on Poetry

ISBN/EAN: 9783337140984

Printed in Europe, USA, Canada, Australia, Japan

Cover: Foto ©Thomas Meinert / pixelio.de

More available books at **www.hansebooks.com**

TWO GREAT ENGLISHWOMEN

MRS. BROWNING & CHARLOTTE BRONTE

WITH AN

ESSAY ON POETRY,

ILLUSTRATED FROM

WORDSWORTH, BURNS, AND BYRON.

BY

PETER BAYNE, M.A., LL.D.,

Author of "*Chief Actors in the Puritan Revolution*," "*Lessons from My Masters*," &c., &c.

London:
JAMES CLARKE & CO., 13 & 14, FLEET STREET.

1881.

NOTE.

THE Essay on Poetry is published for the first time. Those on Mrs. Browning and the Brontë sisters are founded on Studies which appeared in *The Literary World*, and have now been carefully revised, greatly modified, and considerably extended.

CONTENTS.

ESSAY ON POETRY.

Criticism by Sample—Mr. Arnold's Test of no use to ordinary readers—Poetry not criticism, but creation—Observation and Imagination—The Poetic Glow—Metrical Form—The Song-element—Wordsworth—Burns—Byron—Mrs. Browning—The Brontë Sisters ix

ELIZABETH BARRETT BROWNING.

CHAPTER
I.—Her Earliest Verses 3
II.—The Seraphim and Drama of Exile . . 7
III.—A Vision of Poets, and The Poet's Vow . . 27
IV.—The Romaunt of Margret, and other Poems . 38
V.—Her Philanthropic Poetry 48
VI.—Lyric Pencillings 55
VII.—Lady Geraldine's Courtship . . . 60
VIII.—The Rhyme of the Duchess May . . . 72
IX.—Poems of Affection 81
X.—Her Love Sonnets 87
XI.—Poems of Patriotic Sympathy . . . 97
XII.—Aurora Leigh.—Conclusion . . . 107

CHARLOTTE BRONTË AND HER SISTERS.

I.—General Impression of Charlotte Brontë—Thackeray's opinion of her—Mrs. Gaskell and Mr. Wemyss Reid—The Moors—The Mother of the Brontës—The Father's Poems 157

CHAPTER	PAGE
II.—Branwell Brontë—Charlotte's Correspondence with Southey.	168
III.—The Poems of the Sisters—Emily Brontë	180
IV.—Wuthering Heights	196
V.—Heathcliff and Cathy—Old Joseph—Isabella—Linton Heathcliff	207
VI.—Heathcliff and Cathy—Emily Brontë and Mr. G. H. Lewes	221
VII.—Charlotte and Emily in Brussels—Belgian Scenery—The Professor—Villette—The School Scenes in Jane Eyre	233
VIII.—Jane Eyre—Thornfield Hall—Meeting with Rochester	247
IX.—Jane and Rochester—Jane's Pictures—The Mermaid—Rochester's Plea	262
X.—Charlotte Brontë's Defence of Jane Eyre—Rochester an egotist	278
XI.—Women's Rights—The Ethics of Abnegation—Mr. Meredith on Egotism—Thackeray's moral analysis	291
XII.—M. Paul Emanuel—The Brontë lovers	299
XIII.—Mr. Donne's Exodus—Shirley the author's most characteristic book—Mercenary Marriage—A Day with Shirley—The Duty of Endurance	311
XIV.—The Brontë genius—The Yorkshire School of Literature—The Deaths of the Sisters	326

ESSAY ON POETRY.

POETRY

WITH

ILLUSTRATIONS FROM WORDSWORTH, BURNS, AND BYRON.

I DON'T know that criticism wants any other vindication than that good critical writing is very pleasant reading. Mr. Ruskin and Mr. Arnold have of late used words so dainty, bright, and expressive in instructing us as to what true poetry is that, apart from the value of the lesson (which I estimate highly), we like the receiving of it. These eminent critics have laid stress mainly upon the selection of examples, not indeed excluding system and formula, but, on the whole, choosing rather to *show* what poetry is than to say. The method is a delightful one for the pupil, and the examples quoted by Mr. Ruskin and Mr. Arnold are, with hardly an exception, so apt and beautiful, that I wish they could be indefinitely extended. But it is a method that obviously belongs of right only to those who have a great and just confidence in themselves. To such it is given by the acclamation of their contemporaries, and the acquiescent consciousness of genius, to wield the sceptre of the realms of admiration; to touch, with golden authority, this, that, and the other poetic gem, and to say, " These are admirable; admire what are like these." I shrink from the presumption of adopting this imperial method.

Sooth to say, however, there is another objection to this mode of teaching the art of poetical criticism. The samples, though chosen with infallible tact, can consist, severally, of but a few lines, and can bear no proportion to the works from which they are taken. If these are by great poets, the probability is that, for every line quoted, its author has written at least a thousand. A poem is an organised thing. That is self-evident and indisputable. From the lyric of three stanzas to the epic of four-and-twenty books, every true poem is a unity of many parts. Its organisation is fine and complex, so fine, complex, and mysterious that Mr. Ruskin does not scruple to pronounce a true poem a living thing, and that not in mere metaphorical illustration, but with aim at clear scientific precision. Now, a handful will tell you the quality of a quarter of wheat, a tumblerful will tell you the quality of a cubic league of sea-water, a chip will tell you the quality of a block of granite weighing a thousand tons; but people have been very properly laughing for more than two thousand years at the man who carried about a brick as sample of a house, and a brick may give you much more information about a house than a line, or a couple of lines, or even a stray stanza, about a poem. If we add, what is again indisputable, that the greatest poets have weak, flat, bombastic passages, and that very little poets occasionally strike a lofty note, we shall have the more reason to distrust the critical method which depends upon selected lines or stanzas. Two critics, equally adroit and equally well read, would have no difficulty in bombarding each other with separate lines, to prove, in the one case, that Shakespeare was a great, in the other that he was not a great, poet; and the simple hearer, unacquainted with Shakespeare's works, might find himself utterly unable, at the end of an hour, to decide as to the place he deserves to occupy among poets.

But it is the simple reader, not the man whose born instinct and disciplined and cultured skill enable him to dispense with rules, that requires to be assisted to discriminate between excellent poetry and such as is not excellent; and, in his interest, we may ask whether it is not possible to define the characteristics of true poetry generally, in such a way that he may intelligently assign a reason for considering one poet, on the whole, greater than another. In endeavouring to arrive at a comprehensive and at the same time practically useful criterion of excellence in poetry, I shall continue to avail myself of the pleasant help of Mr. Matthew Arnold, though not in a spirit of too servile pupilage.

Poetry, as Mr. Arnold first and fundamentally conceives it, is "a criticism of life." More particularly it is "a criticism of life under the conditions fixed for such a criticism by the laws of poetic truth and poetic beauty." This addition, however, only seems to help us; for it is clearly a truism to say that poetry is criticism under poetical conditions. We do not define an island when we call it land situated under insular conditions. The question is, What are the conditions which distinguish that criticism of life which is poetical from that criticism of life which is not poetical? To have poetical value, he explains from Aristotle, criticism of life must have high truth and high seriousness—it must, in both respects, be higher than history; and excellent poetry is such as involves "the noble and profound application of ideas to life."

Let us apply these principles to a passage quoted by Mr. Arnold from Wordsworth.

> Oh, for the coming of that glorious time
> When, prizing knowledge as her noblest wealth
> And best protection, this Imperial Realm,
> While she exacts allegiance, shall admit
> An obligation, on her part, to *teach*
> Them who are born to serve her and obey;
> Binding herself by statute to secure,
> For all the children whom her soil maintains,
> The rudiments of letters, and inform
> The mind with moral and religious truth!

These lines accord well with Mr. Arnold's main conception of poetry. They are manifestly a criticism of life. No criticism could be more serious, and I do not see that any criticism could be more true. Does the passage not embrace, also, a "noble and profound application of ideas to life"? What form of life could be presented to the imagination more august than that of a mighty nation? And what idea bearing upon national life could be nobler than that all the children belonging to a nation ought to be instructed? Applying Mr. Arnold's test, then, to these lines—inquiring whether they exemplify a noble and profound application of ideas to life—we are shut up to the conclusion that they are excellent poetry. To our surprise, however, on turning to him for that confirmation of our decision which we have a right to expect, we are greeted with this estimate of the passage: "Wordsworth calls Voltaire dull, and surely the production of these un-Voltairian lines must have been imposed upon him as a judgment. One can hear them being quoted at a Social Science Congress; one can call up the whole scene. A great room in one of our dismal provincial towns; dusty air and jaded afternoon daylight; benches full of men with bald heads and women in spectacles; an orator lifting up his face from a manuscript written within and without to declaim these lines of Wordsworth; and, in the soul of any poor child of nature who may have wandered in thither, an unutterable sense of lamentation, and mourning, and woe!"

In other words, Mr. Arnold thinks Wordsworth's lines exceedingly bad poetry, so bad that only such persons as are worthy of bitter contempt would listen to them. Why the members of the Social

Science Congress should be selected for anointing from the phials of Mr. Arnold's scorn, it is not easy to see. About the practical operations that precede pleasant results there is apt to be a certain dinginess, dreariness. Follow a gardener as he digs about and dungs young apple-trees, a school inspector as he examines stupid classes, a Florence Nightingale as she looks into the details of hospital work, and you will meet with matters as unromantic as the "dusty air and jaded afternoon daylight" in which "men with bald heads and women in spectacles" do their best to broaden the thin margin of white on the page of life, and find some anodyne for human pain. But it is not our present business to inquire into Mr. Matthew Arnold's view of the contemptibility of trying to bring scientific precision of thought and knowledge into the operations of benevolence. What we are concerned with is the discovery that Mr. Arnold's quotation, himself being witness, is very defective poetry, although, to the best of our judgment, it is admirable criticism of life. It happens that I agree with Mr. Arnold that Wordsworth's lines are not of high poetical value; but I hope to be able to assign a better reason for thinking so than is touched upon by Mr. Arnold's test.

Let us take another example from Mr. Arnold. The poet is again Wordsworth.

>   One adequate support
> For the calamities of mortal life
> Exists—one only;—an assured belief

> That the procession of our fate, howe'er
> Sad or disturbed, is ordered by a Being
> Of infinite benevolence and power;
> Whose everlasting purposes embrace
> All accidents, converting them to good.

Could any criticism of life be higher in its seriousness, nobler in its tone, than this? Those who disbelieve in the existence or providence of God will say that, for them, it is untrue criticism; but it is difficult to see how any one should deny that, from the poet's standpoint, it is profound criticism. Were we treating of the poet of a vanished civilisation, an extinct religion, we should be constrained to admit that lines into which he condensed the quintessence of that consolation which all races and tribes of men accepting the religion in question had derived from it were, as criticism of life, both noble and profound. Here, too, however, Mr. Arnold holds that the lines are not good poetry. They fail, he says, to exhibit "the characters of *poetic* truth." We have a fair smile at Mr. Arnold for his italics, and remind him that he has been teaching us that criticism of life, qualified by a few adjectives—true, serious, profound, noble, each taken in a very high degree—is excellent poetry. He was bound to show either that the lines *are* shallow and ignoble as criticism of life, or that they are *not* inferior as poetry. I do not think the poetical quality of Mr. Arnold's second quotation so poor as that of his first; but I do not think it is poetically worth much. And again I think I can assign a reason for this estimate more tenable than its worth or worthlessness as a criticism of life.

Once more I take a sample from Mr. Arnold. It is now Shakespeare that is the poet, the lines occurring in Henry the Fourth's expostulation with sleep.

> Wilt thou upon the high and giddy mast
> Seal up the ship-boy's eyes, and rock his brains
> In cradle of the rude, imperious surge?

Can it be alleged that, in any practical, tangible, not fantastic sense, these lines contain any criticism of life whatever? They are an exceedingly imaginative—a most picturesque and powerful—description of the influence of sleep in lulling into unconsciousness all sense of danger, all capacity of joy or pain; but as a criticism of life they can scarcely be weighed or measured, and no one could aver that, in seriousness or profundity of meaning, they excel a grave summing-up of the consolation mankind has derived from the consciousness of God. Yet Mr. Arnold tells us that these lines are unsurpassably fine poetry. I agree with him for reasons that will presently appear; but in the meantime I reiterate the question, What profit can be had of a test of poetic quality that fails so egregiously? Mr. Arnold's criterion is like the Bank Act—made to be suspended exactly in those emergencies which it was intended to provide against. We should want Mr. Arnold always at our elbow to apply, or rectify, or suspend his own test. His intuitive perception of what is excellent in poetry, and what is not excellent, may be so trustworthy that it enables him to dispense with his own formula; but less gifted or cultured persons are driven to inquire whether it cannot be replaced by a better.

Mr. Arnold goes astray at the outset in seeking a definition of poetry by reference to the judging faculty. Criticism of life is not primarily or distinctively the function of the poet. If it were, mankind would have been wrong in placing Aristotle, Plato, Epicurus in one category, and Homer, Sophocles, Pindar in another. There is no criticism of life better than that of Bacon's Essays, yet these are not poetry at all. Professor Huxley was right, on the other hand, when, one day lately at Birmingham, he claimed for science a place of importance in the criticism of life. Doubtless—and the remark is of moment—criticism of life is involved in poetry, but it is not distinctive of poetry, it belongs to prose as well as to poetry.

The fundamental idea on which a sound and a practically useful definition of poetry may be based will be found indicated by Wordsworth himself. In the beginning of his sonnet to the painter, Haydon, are these words:

> High is our calling, Friend!—Creative Art
> (Whether the instrument of words she use,
> Or pencil pregnant with ethereal hues).

Poetry is that branch of creative art which works in and with harmonious words. The essential characteristic of all art is that it makes something; the arts distinctively called useful serving the body, the arts distinctively called fine serving the soul. Science looks upon the universe and asks what is the relation between its parts, what are its processes of change, what is going on beneath its surface. Art looks out upon nature and upon man, rejoicing in the vision; essays to imitate, to *re-present it*; and, from its materials, visions forth a world of man's own, the world of music, sculpture, painting, poetry. A simple and adequate principle of classification and distinction between these is obtained by reference to the materials with which they work. Poetry is the most spiritual and the highest of the arts; by the more than magical spell of words, she makes all other arts her vassals.

Aristotle traces poetry to imitation; Bacon, in dealing with the same subject, lays stress upon imagination. There is beyond question, as Professor Masson has pointed out, a certain antithetic opposition in their ways of viewing the matter; but there is, I submit, a still deeper agreement. Aristotle himself affords the hint on which a reconciliation between their views can be effected. The poet, he says, may imitate in one of three ways—showing men *better* than they are, *worse* than they are, or *as* they are. The first of these—Homer's way—he describes as producing the noblest poetry; and this is obviously what Bacon would have called the imaginative, the improving, the idealising poetry.

I discussed this matter very carefully a good many years ago, and I may be permitted to quote from myself some sentences relating to the importance of the instinct of imitation, as *giving the initiative* in art. " It was characteristic of the unimpassioned and comprehensive observation, the strong sense, and the masculine simplicity of Aristotle, to make this instinct his starting-point in his theory of poetry. In so doing, he virtually recorded the suffrages of the great mass of mankind. I once had an opportunity of observing the play of the great human instinct of imitation in a fresh and interesting manner. I was in conversation with a mechanic, on board a steamer, in one of the most magnificent estuaries of our island. My companion was a rough-hewn, sturdy, hard-working man, thoroughly read, as very many of our mechanics are, in the political history of the day, but who had probably reflected little, or not at all, on theories of art. The time was summer, and the general tone of the landscape was that of still grandeur and majestic calm. The atmosphere, though cloudless, was suffused with faint vapour, and bathed the prospect in a pale brilliancy of light. From right and left the mountains stooped undulating to the bay, the tint of their green, softened by the pearly veil of air, melting into the amethystine floor of sea. One or two yachts, slim and graceful, cleft tenderly the glistening ripples, amid the general serenity of radiance, like maidens stepping delicately in the dance to the mild music of the breeze. The combination of splendour with a certain faintness and pallor in the aspect of the scene —as if nature, oppressed with light, had grown languid in this hour of Pan—was somewhat remarkable. My admiration was awakened, and I called the attention of my fellow-passenger to the beauty of the prospect. He expressed sympathy with my feelings, but passed instantly to another emotion, which was called forth more vividly in his own breast. He spoke of the keen desire, instantly experienced by the beholder, to copy such a picture. The pleasure he had in possession, arising from his sensibility to the beauty of the scene before him, was evidently slight in his estimation, compared with that pleasure at which he conceptively grasped in reproducing it for himself."

The artist is, first of all, the man who, awakening to the world of nature in his youth, is stirred by irrepressible longing to take some copy of it, to reproduce its sights or its sounds, to express the feelings and thoughts it calls forth within him, to fashion, produce, create from its materials a something, be it a statue, be it a landscape, be it an epic poem, be it a lyric song, which he can call his own, a something on which his spirit shall look with unique and ravishing gladness, as a man looks upon his first-born son. It is this impulse that makes the future Mrs. Browning flood her father's parsonage with her singing before she is eight years old. It is this impulse that sends the idle boy from the noisy crowd of his playfellows up into the still pavilion of a leafy tree, where, literally like a bird among the boughs, he may pour forth reams of puerile verse. It is this impulse which sets the keen-eyed, nimble-fingered child,

William Turner, to scratch copies of everything he sees, if only with a pin on a pewter plate, and which, when power has yielded to age, and the eye is becoming filmed, makes him still insist on having, by the bed on which he lies dying, the pigments and the pencils that remind him of the glorious sovereignty of his art.

In seeking, therefore, a practically useful criterion of greatness, of excellence, of degree of merit in poetry, we are not to ask, in the first place, how the poet in question criticises life, but how much of nature and life he reproduces, and whether he reproduces greatly or not greatly; only in the second place, as having a highly important bearing on the general character and quality of his poetry, are we to inquire into his criticism of life.

This criterion has the advantage of exceeding practicality. It is derived from a broad view, first of all art and then of poetry. Any one can apply it. Glance, for example, at those whom the world has decided to enthrone as the greatest of poets. Homer embodies in the *Iliad* a whole form of civilisation, a long since vanished type of manners, usages, beliefs, feelings, relations. From Olympus, where the upper ten, or rather the upper twelve, of heaven sit on their golden three-legged stools, and Zeus keeps the universe with ease, and his wife with difficulty, at bay, and the celestial meal is enlivened by inextinguishable laughter at the limping Hephaistos, to the shore where the black ships of the Achaians are drawn up, and dogs and vultures are feeding on the pestilential corpses that taint the camp, and the king of men and the prince of heroes are engaging in a fierce brawl about a stolen girl, and Thersites is railing, and Nestor is praising the past, and Chryses is harping on his daughter, all that stirring world is vividly present to us. It is ideal, visionary, painted on the mind's retina by the miracle-working power of Homer's imagination; and yet the personages in the scene are intensely real, the human character, whether seen under Olympian conditions or those of mortality, is utterly true to the human character of to-day.

Dante is another of the poets whose work is universally acknowledged to be of sovereign excellence. His great poem represents a succession of regions peopled with human creatures, displaying an immense variety of character and passion. The mediæval age is almost as comprehensively, almost as graphically, portrayed in the *Divine Comedy* as the heroic age of Greece is portrayed in the *Iliad*. Once more, Shakespeare brings to the actual world of his time a more subtle and penetrating observation, a more comprehensive sympathy, a mightier imagination than either Homer or Dante, and the world of his art embraces a still larger number of typical characters, a still wider vision of human affairs and human life than theirs.

It is interesting, and can hardly be uninstructive, to observe that Keats, himself a fine poet and critic, instinctively contemplates the work of poets from the point of view I have been suggesting. Excellent poems are, for him, " goodly states and kingdoms," " islands," " which bards in fealty to Apollo hold." He had heard of the spacious realm that owned the sway of Homer; but he had not really known it till Chapman revealed it to him. Was it then a new " criticism of life," or a new world bodied forth to the eye of imagination, that he was aware of?

> Then felt I like some watcher of the skies,
> When a new planet swims into his ken.

In applying our test, it will be conducive to intelligence and perspicuity to distinguish the two elements which it embraces, to wit, what the poet *takes from* nature, and what the poet *gives to* nature. The spirit of man creates nothing out of nothing, and it will be found that the quality and value of what a poet produces depend upon the power with which he can observe, and upon the richness of the materials which are used by his imagination in its constructions. In the actual exercise of the poetic gift, the two processes—observation, imagination—may go together in the same moment of time, and the exact relation between the two, in any case of high and original production, is too subtle for analysis; but both are necessarily present, and very useful suggestions as to the order of greatness in which poets are to be classified may be derived from simply considering what they chiefly observe, what supremely interests and delights them.

Poets of one class observe the beauties of nature with exquisite accuracy, but have, comparatively speaking, no hold upon the interests, passions, thoughts, activities of men. These poets love colour for its own sake, form for its own sake, and are consummate in execution. With the warring, the working, the passionate loving, of the dusty throng around them, they have little sympathy; from humanity they ask only such lovely tints and hues as may afford play to their artistic skill. Their highest name, perhaps, is Keats. In delicate felicity of execution his work will challenge comparison with any the world ever saw. Shakespeare himself cannot excel him in his own walk. But he cares little for common interests, common feelings, common life. A hundred generations of fighting men have thrilled to the harp, or to echoes from the harp, of Homer. The greyhaired farmer, as he harnesses his old mare, thinks of the genial notes of Burns. The furnaceman, as he groans and sweats, is happier because Schiller sang the song of the bell. But what ploughman or blacksmith ever heard the name of Keats? what carpenter, as he plied adze or hammer, what fisherman, as he furled his sail, ever murmured a ditty of the London School? They are experts writing for experts.

But the power of fresh and vivid delineation of beautiful objects in nature is a true mark of poetical genius. If, indeed, we might venture on any one assertion respecting the poets of all climes and periods, it would be that they had a sense of keen enjoyment in the beauties of nature. Homer did not describe particular flowers, or dwell upon the features of a landscape for their own sake; but there is a pervasive feeling of the open air in his poetry, and he is constantly referring to the sea, or to starry nights, and knows better than any London or Lake poet the proper office of flowers to heighten, by gush of sympathetic radiance, the impassioned joy of lovers. In modern poetry, however, this gift of graphic presentation of the beauty of nature plays a much more important part than in ancient poetry; and, though it may be in excess, and may thus offend a masculine taste, its presence must be pronounced indispensable to all poetry that will satisfy the demands of modern readers. The more artificial society becomes, the more we are pent up in smoke-darkened cities, the more enchanting, probably, will be those talismanic touches whereby the poet suddenly wafts us into far-away woods, or places us again on the hillside or the river-brink where we played in childhood.

Nature being, to all practical intents, infinite, the secret of freshness in describing her beauties lies in the habit of first-hand observation. If you watch the breakers as they crash on the shore when the scour of the receding wave suddenly takes their feet from under them, if you try to count and name the colours of the stranded foam in full sunlight, while the breeze passes over it, fluttering its myriad emeralds and rubies and amethysts and topazes, if you note the characteristic groupings and humours of the clouds in any one locality, you will find that no poet or painter can exhaust nature's variety. It would not be easy to find a better example of that kind of description by which modern poets bring nature's facts not only to the eye, but to the ear, than we have in Mr. Arnold's admirable poem on Dover Beach.

> Come to the window, sweet is the night air!
> Only, from the long line of spray
> Where the ebb meets the moon-blanch'd sand,
> Listen! you hear the grating roar
> Of pebbles which the waves suck back, and fling,
> At their return, up the high strand,
> Begin, and cease, and then again begin,
> With tremulous cadence slow, and bring
> The eternal note of sadness in.

We may be sure that no man who has not this eye for nature will obtain recognition and honour among modern poets; it is more, perhaps, from the deadness of their sense on this side than from any other characteristic that Dryden, Pope, Johnson are firmly and unanimously denied the distinctive glory of poets by the present generation. The lilies of the field are in array against them. They have said no tender, heartfelt things, instinct with music, about the birds and the brooks. Not one of those splendidly clever, keenly intellectual men, felt about a daisy like Chaucer or like Burns. I do not believe that any one of them had such delight in the sea, and the stars, and in green meadows, as old Homer. It has become second nature with us to exact from our poets, as an indispensable pledge of tenderness, sweetness, melodiousness, that they shall take us with them to the country.

Poetry, viewed in relation to the poet, is language uttered under the influence of that *glow* of the spirit which renders it picture to the eye and music to the ear. The poetic product may be a little thing or a great thing, a lyric or an epic, a single vase or a town with all its towers; but now, as in the days of Orpheus and Amphion, it arises before the eye, and it arises to strains of music. The poet rejoices in his work. No word is truer than this:

> What poets feel not, when they make,
> A pleasure in creating,
> The world, in *its* turn, will not take
> Pleasure in contemplating.

Mr. Matthew Arnold gives this as *a caution to poets;* I respectfully suggest that it may be useful also as a caution to critics who are tempted to think that poetry can be defined as criticism of life.

Music is the mother-tongue of joy—nature's mode of expressing rapture in sentient beings. Science has in these last times taught us to compare and connect nature's methods with each other throughout all the families of life; and we now know to be a fact, what might formerly have passed for a mere flourish of rhetoric, that the nightingale illuminating the night of the spring woods with song is a lyric poet, and that, by fundamentally the same law that sets the nightingale singing, the fountains of exultant power, of joyful sympathy, of delight in nature, of affection for man, overflow in the poet in melodious words.

The poetic glow is, of course, like all the most important facts, a mystery. To analyse it into its elements, to understand and classify its methods of operation, may well be beyond us. What criticism, modestly observant of the workings of genius, can do is to distinguish a few of its more notable characteristics.

One of these, first perhaps in the order of importance and distinctiveness, is its tendency to make the poet view all things as alive. If the reader has not remarked this unique quality of poetic genius, he will be surprised to observe its universality, and the sharpness with which it divides the most accomplished versifier from the poet. It is more or less an accident whether the poet writes in the form of verse or the form of prose, but be sure, if he is a poet, that he scatters largesse of life abroad upon creation. If he is not a poet, he cannot do this. He may array his figures with exquisite taste, adorn them with jewels, crown them with gold; but they will be wooden figures after all. He may apostrophise flowers and trees : he may speak very finely about the whisperings of Windsor Forest and the tuneful gliding of the Thames ; but he does not—Pope, for example, does not—in the least believe in his own illusion. Mr. Ruskin, on the other hand, though he unfortunately abandoned the metrical forms which he used in boyhood with richly promising skill, constantly betrays the essentially poetical character of his mind by giving life to all he loves, to all that intensely interests him. The crossing ripples of the tidal wave advancing on the shore are for him children kissing and clapping hands ; the mountain flowers come forth to his eye, " crowded for very love," crushing their leaves into strange shapes "only to be nearer each other;" and the delicate pines "follow each other along the soft hill-ridges up and down." Homer knew perfectly well that the mortality in the Greek camp spoken of in the first book of the *Iliad* was occasioned by disease arising from the heat of the sun, and that dogs and men, dying of plague, are not struck with arrows. He speaks expressly of disease. And yet, with the glow of poetic vision and creative imagination in heart and brain, he sees, and cannot help seeing, Apollo, the angry sun-god, striding along the mountains, the silver arrows in his quiver clanging behind him as he moves, and taking up his position opposite the Greek camp, and bending his bow. Shelley gives life to winter, making it a colossal giant, with the wind for a whip.

> He had torn the cataracts from the hills,
> And they clanked at his girdle like manacles.

Shelley's sensitive plant is as alive as one of Ruskin's pines, and nature becomes beautifully and tenderly alive around her.

> A sensitive plant in a garden grew,
> The young winds fed her with silver dew,
> And she opened her fan-like leaves to the light,
> And closed them beneath the kisses of night.

He who has not this life-giving power is no poet; he who possesses it, appearing from the fact of his possessing it to be either inspired or a maniac, as we interpret his symptoms, is a poet. If he is a great poet, he gives life to men, he dowers his Achilles or his Hector with an immortality that will be fresh when Cheops and his pyramid are "blown about the desert dust;" if he is a true but not a great poet, he cannot, imaginatively, give life to men, but he fancifully gives life to a thousand inanimate things: in all cases, where there is no life there is no poetry, where there is the life of fancy there is true poetry, where there is the life of imagination there is great poetry.

If now we glance back at those lines quoted by Mr. Arnold from Wordsworth, and pronounced by him to be inferior poetry, we shall, I think, find grounds for considering them such without reference to their quality as criticism of life. What they want is not critical depth or accuracy in dissertating on life, but life itself. They have the calculating self-possession of prose; the eye of the writer, as he gravely recites them, is not dilated and inflamed by the ecstasy of poetic vision. England is an "Imperial Realm." A geographical, political, thoroughly prosaic expression! Turn to Milton's prose, often grander in its rhythm than his verse, and note how he gives imaginative life to England, whether, as an eagle mewing her mighty youth, or as a veiled mother weeping for her banished children, and learn the difference between genuine poetic work and those lines which Mr. Arnold quotes from Wordsworth. Applying our principle to the three lines quoted from Shakespeare, we find that they are a vivid picture, the mind's eye of the dullest reader being compelled to see the ship-boy on the giddy mast, rocked in the cradle of the surge, while sleep draws near to him, a subtle, mysterious, living thing, to lull him into fatal slumber. This is faultless poetry, though perhaps it shows Shakespeare in his highest fanciful rather than in his strictly imaginative power; but I do not see how, as a criticism of life, any high value can be attached to the lines.

It will probably be felt, and justly felt, by practical readers, that criticism is bound to give a more precise account than I have yet attempted of the association between poetry and metrical form. Though poetry may occur in the form of prose, it never occurs without cadence, without rhythmic swell and melody, in one word, without tune; and verse is its legitimate, its consummate form. The poet who writes in prose has never succeeded in "beating his music out." Perfect verse, then, is the most precious and enchanting illustrative instance that exists, of that law of modulated continuity, of measured progression, of ordered movement, of living balance and symmetry, which pervades nature. The expansion and contraction of the lungs in respiration, the beat of the pulse, the rise and fall of rippling waves, the succession of leaves on the branch, the lull and swell in gales, are cases in which the law is observed. The earliest dawn of art, in the strict sense, as distinguished from mere compliance with the demands of animal nature, is in law and order. The savage who covers his water-jug with confused scratches, not for any pleasure they give him, but in sheer vacancy of mind, has not made the first step in fine art; but when he draws a steady line round its neck, or two lines parallel to each other, or zigzag lines in a definite order, he is on the threshold of art; and when he puts one broad line in the middle, and two thin lines, one on each side, or remarks that a curved line becomes more interesting from being opposed to a straight line, then he has struck upon that leading principle of all composition, contrast, and is prepared to grapple with the problem that presents itself to artists in every province, the combination of breadth with variety. The earliest efforts in poetry and in music—the two probably went together—were doubtless of a kind corresponding to those rude yet ordered lines and zigzags which we find on prehistoric pottery,—lilts in which the low, sweet monotone was suddenly interrupted by the shrill notes of surprise, delight, or apostrophe. Speech in all races, though custom may have dulled our ears to its apprehension, proceeds with more or less of wave-motion, associated with respiration and the correlated physical conditions; and when there is strong and noble emotion the wave-measure becomes more marked, the tones more full, melodious, and thrilling. Poetry in its purest form—which I agree with Mr. Pater in holding lyrical poetry to be—has always been directly associated with music, and the primeval bard was doubtless a singer. In all impassioned feeling there is pitch, modulation, correspondence between the feeling and the sound. " In the spring a fuller crimson comes upon the robin's breast." That is one of nature's arrangements. In the spring a deeper, clearer, more melodious rapture comes into the nightingale's voice. That again is one of nature's facts. In all the spring-tides of human emotion, in the elevation of intense and noble sympathy with all great human interests, the passion of the feeling announces itself both in the colour and the modulation of the speech,—picture, as I said before, unfolding itself to music.

When, therefore, Mr. Carlyle, in his epoch-making essay on Burns, laid stress upon the test of melody as enabling us to discriminate between prose and poetry, between eloquence and song, he put his finger on one of those truths which ought not to be forgotten or discarded; and Mr. Matthew Arnold, in referring us to true and serious, noble and profound, criticism of life as a criterion of poetical excellence, does not take us beyond the point to which Carlyle conducted us, but back from it. Edgar Poe was very right when he said that a good off-hand way of gauging the poetical quality of verse was to write it in form of prose, and try whether it still forced us to feel that it was poetry. Of lyrical poetry it may, I think, be stated universally that, if the reader does not feel himself under some impulse to sing or chant it—if he can recite it with perfect comfort while taking no account of the division into metrical feet or into lines—it is not good lyric poetry. You feel the song-element in this of Victor Hugo:

> Je suis le Cid calme et sombre,
> Je n'achète ni ne vend,
> Et je n'ai sur moi que l'ombre
> De la main de Dieu vivant.

The attainment of perfect modulation will imply choice of the most picturesque and expressive words, and it is characteristic of a young poet that such words have a charm for him and are hoarded in his memory. Of such precious stones his poetical architecture will be built. The melody and charm of the verse are heightened also, not only by just and powerful thought and by noble feeling, but by every one of a thousand nameless touches and tones of association, by which the poetical fancy and the poetical imagination, working with all the spells of remembered fact and metaphorical enhancement, can suggest pleasant places and happy hours. All nature is a harp for the poetical imagination, and by an apt metaphor, or assemblage of metaphors, the emotion which the poet expresses is suddenly and transcendently excited.

> The pale moon is setting beyond the white wave,
> And time is setting wi' me.

No words can measure the heightening of the impression of sadness wrought by such a tone of nature's music as that.

> The moonshine, stealing o'er the scene,
> Had blended with the lights of eve,
> And she was there, my hope, my joy,
> My own dear Genevieve.

Here it is the serene exaltation of intensest joy that is expressed, and again the power of the metaphoric spell is beyond all measuring. A single line will show that a man has the poet's ear for melodious words,—

> Sweet closes the evening on Craigie-burn wood.

The charm of true poetry is a subtle, complex, and

unique charm, having many elements; but it depends mainly on this, that it combines the intense delightfulness of law with the intense delightfulness of freedom. Law is charming, even in zigzag lines; how much more, then, in the wave-like, star-like movement of perfect verse: freedom is charming, even in the frolic wind or flying cloud; how much more in the bounding ecstasy of lyric song.

Mr. Arnold, illustrating his principles of poetical criticism by an example of their application, undertakes to prove Wordsworth superior to any poet that appeared in Europe between the death of Milton and the rise of poets still living, with the single exception of Goethe. Victor Hugo he specifically includes among the poets to whom Wordsworth is superior. To this decision I by no means assent; and we cannot have better practice in the use of those tests which we have been endeavouring to frame than in examining this claim on behalf of Wordsworth put forward by his adroit and gifted advocate.

Mr. Arnold dwells upon "the extraordinary power with which Wordsworth feels the joy offered to us in nature, the joy offered to us in the simple primary affections and duties," and "the extraordinary power with which, in case after case, he shows us this joy, and renders it so as to make us share it." This is "the cause" of the "greatness" of Wordsworth's poetry. "Here," says Mr. Arnold, "is an immense advantage for a poet."

Without question he is a great poet who shows

the joy of simple affections and duties with extraordinary power, and makes his readers share it; but I dispute the extraordinary power of the Wordsworthian display of simple joy, and I still more strongly dispute the Wordsworthian capacity to make us share that joy. Wordsworth has a comprehensive and honest sense of the pleasantness of nature, and can reproduce with accuracy many of nature's sights and sounds. No one knows or shows the pleasure of a fine day better than Wordsworth. But that exultation which great poets have in human joy, and which certainly is a note of great poetry, is slightly shared by Wordsworth. I do not deny that there are traces of it in his works, but they are few, and there is little depth or vehemence in their joy. The power of music to enrapture a street crowd, the power of reverie to make a country girl in London see a river flowing down the vale of Cheapside, the power of cocks crowing, streams flowing, small birds twittering, cattle feeding, to make a poet, who has nothing to do but to watch them, happy—these, with some glad stanzas about the ethereal minstrelsy of the lark, almost exhaust the joy-producing strains which Mr. Arnold puts into the volume in which he embodies Wordsworth's main achievement in poetry. On the other hand, how profoundly depressing are Wordsworth's poems generally! Mr. Arnold speaks of simple joys, but the pieces he applauds have no gleam of joy in them. *Michael*, *The Brothers*, *Ruth*, *Lucy*, *Margaret*, and I know not how many others, are unutterably mournful. To step into the poetic realms of Goethe or Schiller is to step into a land of abounding life and splendour and joy; but to walk with Wordsworth is to be sad. What poet has said such mournful things? For what poet are "all the ways of men so vain and melancholy"? Here is his own account:

> We poets in our youth begin in gladness;
> But thereof comes in the end despondency and madness.

He writes with pretty fancying, almost mirthful, about the small celandine; but once he takes another tone, and it seems to come from a far deeper region in his soul. He had often noticed the flower muffling itself up when hailstones were falling, and coming out again bright as the sun itself when the storm was over. Once, however, he observed a change, and thus describes what he saw and what he thought:

> But lately, one rough day, this flower I passed,
>   And recognised it, though an altered form,
> Now standing forth an offering to the blast,
>   And buffeted at will by rain and storm.
>
> I stopped, and said, with inly-muttered voice,
>   "It doth not love the shower, nor seek the cold;
> This neither is its courage nor its choice,
>   But its necessity in being old."

The weariness with which man toils along in his pilgrimage, the dumb forces of nature always like invisible enemies bearing him back—the hopelessness of the conflict with old age—the heart-heaviness and desolation that overtake the honest Michaels and Margarets, in spite of their industry and worth—

these are the impressions that remain with one after reading Wordsworth's poems. Of the sunlight of exultation with which poets of more humour, of more jocund and mirthful power, disperse or illumine the mists that shroud the world, there is in Wordsworth singularly little. He does, indeed, rest upon the consolations of religion. With placid faith, that seems never seriously moved by the sorrows he poetically describes, he trusts that the impotence of human grieving will some day be supplemented by Infinite Power, and that God will mend all. This is a very great consolation, and in placing it, as he does, in many impressive lights, Wordsworth is, perhaps, at his best; but this is exactly that part of Wordsworth's "criticism of life" which Mr. Arnold thinks commonplace and homiletical.

Looking more particularly into Wordsworth's poetical workmanship, I submit that he adds less to nature, exercises less of imaginative power, than belongs to great poetry. Mr. Arnold takes a bold course in dealing with this part of his subject, alleging that what I must regard as a fatal defect is a transcendent merit. "Nature herself seems"—these are his emphatic and eloquent words—"I say, to take the pen out of his hand, and to write for him with her own bare, sheer, penetrating power. This arises from two causes—from the profound sincereness with which Wordsworth feels his subject, and also from the profoundly sincere and natural character of his subject itself. He can and will treat such a subject with nothing but the most plain, first-hand, almost austere naturalness. His expression may often be called bald—as, for instance, in the poem of *Resolution and Independence*—but it is bald as the bare mountain tops are bald, with a baldness which is full of grandeur."

Is it imagination too mighty to endure any but the naked majesty of nature, or is it sheer lack of imaginative power, that characterises Wordsworth's poetic method? That is the question. Mr. Arnold tells us that even he cannot read *Vaudracour and Julia*. I beg to ask why. The language of the piece is quite on a level with Wordsworth's usual writing—nay, unusually felicitous.

> Oh, balmy time,
> In which a love-knot on a lady's brow
> Is fairer than the fairest star in heaven!

The following lines, on Vaudracour's love for Julia, are about as good as you will find anywhere in Wordsworth.

> Earth breathed in one great presence of the spring,
> Life turned the meanest of her implements,
> Before his eyes, to price above all gold;
> The house she dwelt in was a sainted shrine:
> Her chamber window did surpass in glory
> The portals of the dawn; all paradise
> Could, by the simple opening of a door,
> Let itself in upon him.

If Wordsworth had often expressed the joy of noble passion with such power, I should not have denied him a place among those poets whose music gladdens the world for us. Nevertheless, *Vaudracour and Julia* is, as a whole, unreadable even by so fervent a Wordsworthian as Mr. Arnold, and I ask the reason why. The secret, I am convinced, lies in this—that it is literal fact—no more. The passion of Vaudracour for Julia, simple, intense, generous, self-forgetting; the locust pride of his family, eating off every green leaf of hope, every opening bud of joy, in his bosom and hers; the dismal end in Julia's being immured in a convent, and Vaudracour's becoming a drivelling idiot—all this is detailed with the literal precision of a transcript from nature. Therefore it is oppressive in the sense in which a description of any hideous calamity, any social horror, drawn out in mere statistical prose, is oppressive—a newspaper account, for example, of a woman found by the police sitting, starved to death, by a fireless grate in winter; a father taking his boy from the house in which he is being cared for, and hanging him up like a dog; a steamer run into on the river, and six hundred persons screeching and drowning in the water. Told in the dreariest prose, these things affect us, but not as art affects us. There is nothing in the bare narrative of them to impart that redeeming spell whereby imaginative handling lends fascination to sorrow, and attracts us again, again, and yet again, to contemplate the woes of Juliet and Romeo, of Othello and Desdemona, of Lear and Cordelia, of the chained and vulture-torn Prometheus.

Now you will find, if you look, that Wordsworth's method in *Vaudracour and Julia* is his habitual method—an unimaginative method. Mr. Arnold admits that a very large proportion of Wordsworth's work is unimaginative. He throws overboard even so Wordsworthian and so extensive a performance as *The Excursion*. But he avers that Wordsworth's imagination, when it does awake, is extremely powerful. "No poet, perhaps," he says, "is so evidently filled with a new and sacred energy when the inspiration is upon him." I am not prepared to deny that the author of *The Affliction of Margaret*, *Laodamia*, several of the odes, a good many of the sonnets, and some other pieces, was possessed of imagination; but what has most deeply impressed me in connection with Wordsworth's imagination is the rarity of its awakenings, and the slow and grave character of its action even when awake. No piece of writing could be more intensely true than *The Affliction of Margaret*; Wordsworth, in that poem, gets into the inmost recesses of a bereaved mother's heart, and only imagination could have brought him there. The fire of imagination burns his own theory of imaginative expression to ashes; and he makes the woman speak to her son in language elevated by passion until it has more of Shakespearean exaltation than of Wordsworthian simplicity.

> Perhaps some dungeon hears thee groan,
>   Maimed, mangled by inhuman men;
> Or thou upon a desert thrown
>   Inheritest the lion's den;
> Or hast been summoned to the deep,
> Thou, thou and all thy mates, to keep
> An incommunicable sleep.

Deeply characteristic of Wordsworth is the utter sadness of the poem—as if his main conception of man's lot were that of painful, hopeless, life-long breathing with a gravestone on the breast. Here, as so often with Wordsworth, there is *no* help; strange to say, in this his mood of deadly earnestness, he permits to his sufferer no glimpse of light from those celestial countries, from that Father's home, to which he so often, and with faith so placid, refers.

> I look for ghosts; but none will force
>   Their way to me :—'tis falsely said
> That there was ever intercourse
>   Between the living and the dead;
> For, surely, then I should have sight
> Of him I wait for day and night,
> With love and longings infinite.

But to give intensely imaginative expression to a single emotion cannot be pronounced one of the higher efforts of poetical genius; and though we admit that Wordsworth has given unsurpassed expression to the *sorrow* arising in connection with the simple primary affections, we have still to ask for proof that he deserves a lofty seat among those poetic sons of the morning who excel in the far higher office of quickening life and increasing joy.

Estimate as you please, however, the occasional imaginative success of Wordsworth, I contend that, as a general rule, his imagination fails expressly at those points where its interposition is required, and that the failure in *Vaudracour and Julia*, on which Mr. Arnold himself lays emphasis, is but a striking instance of what occurs in a great variety of cases. Take *Peter Bell*, take *The Waggoner*, nay, take *Michael* and *Resolution and Independence*, not to mention scores of minor poems,—I maintain that, in each and all of these, imagination fails to give the right, vital unity of art. An artist does not produce a picture by merely beginning at one line on his right and working round to another line on his left. That is a mere strip of country transferred to canvas. The true artist puts an eye, a soul, into his landscape, whether castellated crag, or towered city, or sail on the far horizon; and all his picture centres in that. Wordsworth treats his subject topographically. Some incident or series of incidents has come within the field of his experience, and he chronicles the details, beginning at the beginning and going on to the end. Peter Bell comes to the river-brink, observes the donkey, notes how its long ear rolls round on the pivot of its skull, discovers the corpse in the water, mounts the ass, rides to the hut of the drowned man, and so forth; the waggoner drives his team in the stormy night, has one or two mildly interesting adventures, takes a little too much at the public-house, is dismissed by his master, &c., &c. Michael is an industrious, upright peasant; his only son, who has always been dutiful, goes to the great town and becomes bad; and his father thinks of him with inexpressible sadness as he tries in vain to take interest in the simple industries they used to transact together. The poet sees the leech-gatherer at his work and asks him to tell his story; the leech-gatherer complies, but the poet has gone off in melancholy musings about "mighty poets in their misery dead," and asks the leech-gatherer to go over it all again, which the good soul does; and the poet then tells it to the reader; and it turns out to be no great story after all, though illustrating the resolution and independence of leech-gathering peasants. This, I say, is Wordsworth's manner, and it is *not* the manner of great imaginative poets.

These poems, however, show Wordsworth at his best, or nearly at his best; but it is fair that we should take him also, if in one sample only, at his worst. In *Ellen Irwin, or the Braes of Kirtle*, he displays a degree of imaginative torpor distinctly beyond that which appals Mr. Arnold in *Vaudracour and Julia*. He had a fine subject to deal with, and the old minstrel who treated it before him had shown him how it could be imaginatively treated. Love, death, woman sacrificing herself to save her lover, and the fiery vengeance of the lover overtaking the man to whom her death was due—such was the subject. If that does not awaken imagination, what will? It awakened the imagination of the old minstrel so effectually that it is almost impossible not to feel that he must himself have been a chief actor in this truly dramatic lyric.

> O that I were where Helen lies,
> Night and day on me she cries,
> O that I were where Helen lies,
>   On fair Kirkconnell Lee!

Is that not the very wail of love in agony ? And then the vengeance—

> I hackèd him in pieces sma'.

You see that he could have torn the slayer of his love with his teeth like a tiger. That is imaginative work.

Read now the unparalleled production in which Wordsworth, as I have no doubt, believed himself to have improved upon the rugged work of the old "maker," and shown him how it ought to have been done. With exemplary, gin-horse industry, he begins, *more suo*, at the beginning, and plods on to the end, in tiresome, soporific detail. The name of the one lover was Bruce, the name of the other was Gordon; the one did this, the other did that, &c., &c. So mortally unimaginative is the work, that it becomes untrue even as a transcript of possible fact. One of the lovers—I forget whether it was Bruce or Gordon, and don't care—" launched a deadly javelin " at the breast of the other; whereupon

> Fair Ellen saw it when it came,
> And stepping forth to meet the same,
> Did with her body cover
> The youth, her chosen lover.

Consider that. The writer has evidently no *vision* of what occurred, and writes what, even in prose, would be untrue. Had Ellen " stepped forth to meet the same," the javelin must have reached its goal in her lover's heart before she had completed her arrangements. Even a schoolboy, or the bellman, would have said "springing upward like a flame," or something like that. Hear Wordsworth on the passion of the lovers.

> For it may be proclaimed with truth,
> If Bruce hath loved sincerely,
> That Gordon loves as dearly."

"It may be proclaimed with truth,"—Wordsworth, his mark! Such phrases, even in prose, denote sprawling, nerveless, unimaginative composition. They indicate in Wordsworth an occasional union of lethargic cerebration with perpetual self-consciousness not exhibited, I think, by any other poet who has got a place, as Wordsworth has after all rightfully done, among the true poets of the world. Mr. Arnold speaks of the "new and sacred energy" of Wordsworth's inspired moments. But how frequently is this sacred energy absent exactly at the moment when it is wanted! That single word "machine," applied, in the very climax of the poem, to his "perfect woman nobly planned," is a touch of the dead hand that almost makes us think of a woman at Madame Tussaud's.

So much for Wordsworth's habitual method of treating his subjects. A few words must be said on the nature of those subjects. His practice is to write poems on the simplest incidents of everyday experience. He teases his little boy of five years to tell him whether he likes best to be "on Kilve's smooth shore by the green sea, or here at Liswyn farm." The child says carelessly that he would rather be at

Kilve than where he is, but does not know why.
Five times does the father press the boy to "tell him
why." At last the little fellow, happening to glance
up at the vane on the house-top, and hoping to silence
the old fidget, says that there was no weathercock at
Kilve and that was "the reason why." On this
incident we have fifteen stanzas, the fifteenth being as
follows:

> O dearest, dearest Boy! my heart
>   For better lore would seldom yearn,
> Could I but teach the hundredth part
>   Of what from thee I learn.

I suppose a true Wordsworthian would find no end
of lessons in all this; to the practical mind it seems
to illustrate no truth more profound than that, if you
tease a child with twaddle, he will say anything that
comes uppermost to stay the infliction. The poet sees
old Simon Lee at work on the root of an old tree, and
helps him to get over a difficulty. The man thanks
him. The incident suggests nearly a hundred lines,
the whole history of Simon being sketched, and the
sorrow of bleak age shown stealing, as is usual with
melancholy Wordsworth, over the brightness of youth
and the power of manhood. It is an eminently
characteristic and quietly beautiful piece, the last two
of its double stanzas being these:

> "You're overtasked, good Simon Lee,
>   Give me your tool," to him I said;
> And at the word right gladly he
>   Received my proffered aid.

> I struck, and with a single blow
>   The tangled root I severed,
> At which the poor old man so long
>   And vainly had endeavoured.
>
> The tears into his eyes were brought,
>   And thanks and praises seemed to run
> So fast out of his heart, I thought
>   They never would have done.
> —I've heard of hearts unkind, kind deeds
>   With coldness still returning;
> Alas! the gratitude of men
>   Hath oftener left me mourning.

Such incidents occur to every one. The village pastor could fill volumes with them. Wordsworth dwells longer upon them than other people, and his persistent practice of poetical composition and undisputed genius enabled him to detail them with a more felicitous simplicity than commonplace people could attain; but he rarely gives them a diamond point of thought, or fuses them in the fire of his imaginative glance. His reflections are those which occur naturally to every humane man. It can hardly be doubted that he carried too far the principle of trusting for his subjects to the trivialities of everyday experience. The routine pacing of the sunbeam in serene weather along the dial-plate will not ordinarily yield signs and wonders, either of religion or of poetry.

A large proportion of Wordsworth's existence was passed in what may be described as a state of refined spiritual dreaminess, bordering on lethargy. A friend rebukes him for sitting on a grey stone and musing half a day. He writes a poem by way of answer, and urges that "we can feed this mind of ours in a wise passiveness." But the passive mood was with him too frequent, and the thoughts that loomed on him through the haze, as he "dreamed his time away," were apt to be only half true.

> One impulse from a vernal wood
> May teach you more of man,
> Of moral evil and of good,
> Than all the sages can.

If so, the sages teach precious little. He made more of the teaching of nature than was fit; man learns from man.

> Books! 'tis a dull and endless strife;
> Come, hear the woodland linnet,
> How sweet his music! on my life
> There's more of wisdom in it.

No, there is not. Milton had a very different notion of books. Wordsworth's highest excellence, as well as his deepest defects, have connection with this passive habit of mind. In his musing moods he occasionally strikes chords that vibrate to no hand so finely as to his.

> If thou be one whose heart the holy forms
> Of young imagination have kept pure,
> Stranger! henceforth be warned; and know that pride,
> Howe'er disguised in its own majesty,
> Is littleness; that he who feels contempt
> For any living thing, hath faculties
> Which he has never used; that thought with him
> Is in its infancy. The man whose eye
> Is ever on himself doth look on one,
> The least of Nature's works, one who might move
> The wise man to that scorn which Wisdom holds
> Unlawful, ever. O be wiser, thou!

> Instructed that true knowledge leads to love,
> True dignity abides with him alone
> Who, in the silent hour of inward thought,
> Can still suspect, and still revere himself,
> In lowliness of heart.

Even in these noble lines there is a trace of unreality. It is not true that we ought to feel contempt for no living thing. Wordsworth himself elsewhere expresses a just and manly contempt for the sordid worldling who had given away his heart. The following is better,—shows Wordsworth, in fact, to my thinking, at his best:

>   There lives
> A Judge . . . .
> . . . .
> In whose all-seeing eye a noble aim
> Faithfully kept is as a noble deed
> In whose pure sight all virtue doth succeed.

Nothing in religious poetry could be more majestically noble than that. I do not remember meeting the same thought in any other author. It is one of those thoughts which, when memorably expressed, form the best boon a poet bestows upon his race, and are in very truth words of God to stay the soul in trouble. But this, as I said before, is what Mr. Arnold thinks the weak vein in the poet; and he does not include the sonnet in which these lines occur amongst his selections. I entirely agree with Mr. Arnold that Wordsworth was a true and even a great poet; fundamentally healthy and wise; with a passion for nature that made him a force among his countrymen: but I differ with him sharply when he lifts Wordsworth above the head of Hugo and of Schiller, and of all those poets that appeared in Britain between the death of Milton and the birth of Queen Victoria. Of two of these last I shall more particularly, though briefly, speak; and first of Robert Burns.

No man presents poetical genius or inspiration as a *glow* more peremptorily than Burns. Imagination is his natural mood,—his intellect works by vision,—his soul is an eye. And the peculiar poetic mania of seeing all things alive was eminently his. This is the greatest imaginative gift, and distinguishes the *maker;* but the gift of penetrating sympathy, whereby the poet gets into the heart of everything that lives, or that he dowers with life, belonged also in the rarest perfection to Burns. Compared with his, the poetical genius of Wordsworth is lax, is slow.

Take a piece which, though characteristic of Burns, is unmistakably one of his minor efforts,—*The Twa Dogs.* He had noticed his own sheep-dog, or "collie," gambolling with a gentleman's Newfoundland, and it occurred to him that a conversation between the two might furnish the "something serious" which, his publisher told him, would be a desirable feature in his first volume. He sees the dogs in manner as they lived, and he makes us see them. The "locked, letter'd braw brass collar" of the one, the glossy black coat, white breast, curling tail, and honest face of the other, mark them out in all the distinctness of canine rank and canine individuality. Burns gets at once into their hearts and enjoys their sport.

> Nae doubt but they were fain o' ither,
> An' unco pack an thick thegither;
> Wi' social nose whyles snuff'd an' snowkit
> Whyles mice an' moudieworts * they howkit;
> Whyles scour'd awa' in lang excursion,
> And worry'd ither in diversion.

That is as vivid as painting, and painting could not give the movement of the dogs. Tired at length of play, they sit down and talk of mankind. Their remarks are redolent of satire, and the raciest pith and sense, lit up here and there by vignette pictures of peasant life, not to be surpassed in graphic felicity and genial warmth. But observe how thoroughly he enters into the hearts of the dogs!—how he understands the sentiments of dog-land, and writes like a very dog! Consider this, on a functionary whose character must be a subject of interest in every kennel.

> Our whipper-in, wee, blastit wonner,
> Poor worthless elf, it eats a dinner,
> Better than ony tenant man.

If a dog could speak, would he not say just that about the whipper-in? The collie, for his part, describes the life of the poor, assuring his friend that, though hard, it has its alleviations. There are the high-tides of Hallow-mass and New Year's Day, when the frost-winds are barred out, and the "ingle" burns bright.

> The cantie auld folks crackin' crouse,
> The young anes rantin' through the house,—
> My heart has been sae fain to see them,
> That I for joy hae barkit wi' them.

---

* Moles.

The Ettrick Shepherd said that he had seen this description verified a hundred times to the letter. It is true to the kind heart of Burns that he should have embraced the old within the circle of household joyfulness. Age in Wordsworth is despondent, heavy-laden, apathetic; not in Burns. And the loyal dependent of man is accepted into the human circle, and heightens the merriment by his genial bark. Very precious in its moral quality is the regard that Burns has for the lower creatures. Often it is simply the tenderness that shrinks from the idea of their pain, his unaffected dislike of the huntsman's art evincing extraordinary fineness and gentleness of nature in a peasant. But often, also, it is a feeling of mingled justice and mercy with reference to the services they render man, and of sympathetic appreciation of their companionship. His *New Year Morning Salutation* of the old farmer to his old mare has a poetry in it as much deeper than the poetry of feudal knighthood, as the poetry of industry and home is deeper than the poetry of strife.

> Though now thou's dowie, stiff, an' crazy,
> An' thy auld hide's as white's a daisy,
> I've seen thee dappl't, sleek, and glaizie,
>   A bonnie grey.

With manly pride and beautiful tenderness, he recalls the day when the dappled mare bore home his bride, and recounts her triumphs on the road and in the furrow. And now, when they both are old, his trusty servant will find that she has a friend.

> We've worn to crazy years thegither;
> We'll toyte about wi' ane anither;
> Wi' tentie care I'll flit thy tether,
>   To some hain'd* rig.

Mr. Arnold fully acknowledges the necessity, to the appreciation of Burns, of having some acquaintance with Scotch; and it is thoroughly genial in him to say that the language of Burns deserves study from cultivated Englishmen as the language of Chaucer deserves it: such a phrase as "we'll *toyte* about wi' ane anither" is untranslatable—the marvellous onomatopoetic accuracy of the word which describes the tottering motion of an old man and an old horse belongs to the original inseparably. "Tottering" is too hard—expresses too much of creaky brokenness— the "toyting" has something in it of the pleasant feebleness of second childhood in a sunny field. And how delicate is the "tentie care!"

Of *The Jolly Beggars* Mr. Arnold speaks in terms of admiration that may well satisfy the most enthusiastic reader of Burns. It is in his eyes a "puissant and splendid production," "a superb poetic success," displaying "a breadth, truth, and power which make the famous scene in Auerbach's Cellar, of Goethe's *Faust*, seem artificial and tame beside it, and which are only matched by Shakespeare and Aristophanes." For badness and for goodness the piece is entirely true to Burns—here he stands, the whole man, as we have Wordsworth in *Peter Bell* and *Michael*. The coarse-

---

* Saved; kept in reserve.

ness which mars Burns, the coarseness which was a broadly-marked, undeniable characteristic of the Scotland mirrored in his poetry, is here at its worst. It is not so bad as the coarseness of Chaucer; it is never dwelt on, as the subject and interest of the description, as in tales which could be mentioned of Chaucer's; it is put in, with flying, forceful touch, because it is *there*, a part of the visioned fact into which the eye of the poet is glaring, necessary if we must have utter veracity, however alien to ideal beauty: but it is lamentable, nevertheless.

If the stains on Burns's genius, however, are conspicuous in this poem, they do not quench its general blaze of power and brilliance. It displays in its utmost intensity and comprehensiveness that sympathy with mankind, which was his master-passion, and that creative gift of imagination by which he gave form and life. The gambolling of dogs and the fortunes of old mares interested him, but the merrymakings of his fellow-men had for him an irresistible and supreme fascination. Accordingly he dived, one night, with a brace of trusty companions, into a public-house in Mauchline of the lowest description, the resort of strolling tinkers, fiddlers, and other vagrants. What he witnessed forms the subject-matter of this poem; and he has made out of it perhaps the most exultant demonstration of the strength of life, and of the power of laughter to rise victorious over hardship and penury, to be found in any literature. Not one circumstance of the squalor and looped and windowed raggedness of these waifs and strays of human kind is disguised, and yet they are uproariously happy. There is no didacticism in the poem, yet it is a deep chapter in the philosophy of life. It shows nature's *reserve* power—her capacity, when she seems driven to extremity, to make life still tolerable.

We should note, as significant in many ways, that the poor vagrants have not a word to say against their social superiors. Of the democratic exasperation and teeth-gnashing, of which we have had so much since the French Revolution, there is not a forecast. Nor, though we have throughout a humourous contempt for the respectabilities, is there any suggestion of sympathy with mean thieving or swindling. " Braw John Highlandman," though he holds the Lowland laws in scorn, " is faithful to his clan." The tinker is proud of his trade, the fiddler pays for his cheer " at kirns and weddings " with music. The battered old soldier, *minus* an arm and a leg, is a hero every inch, one with whom Homer would have hobnobbed. He tells you where he got his wounds,—one, for example, " in a trench, when welcoming the French." That epithet " welcoming " is perfection. All the nobleness of chivalry is in it,—the frank valour of the soldier who bears no grudge against a noble foe,—and the reckless joy of battle. Then, with what brilliant lyrical touches—lyrical in their brevity and brightness, epic in their decisive selection of the right points—does old Wooden-leg glance along the wars of Great Britain in his time! The song is worthy of any war-poet from Tyrtæus to Beranger, and yet it is not in the least out of keeping with the character of the begging soldier.

> My 'prenticeship I past where my leader breath'd his last,
>   When the bloody die was cast on the heights of Abram;
> I serv'd out my trade when the gallant game was play'd
>   And the Moro low was laid at the sound of the drum.
>
> I lastly was with Curtis, among the floating batteries,
>   And there I left for witness an arm and a limb;
> Yet let my country need me, with Elliot to head me,
>   I'd clatter on my stumps at the sound of a drum.

That belongs to the perennial in poetry. Out of the dingy atmosphere of a tavern revel the old soldier rises into the changeless blue of universal human sympathy.

Mr. Arnold is severe upon Scottish life. "Burns's world of Scotch drink, Scotch religion, and Scotch manners, is often a harsh, a sordid, a repulsive world." Not "sordid," Mr. Arnold—peremptorily not sordid. A world of hard labour, of stern thrift, not of sordidness; the old farmer has had a hard life of it, but he can spare a "hain'd rig" for his old mare yet, though she will never do him another stroke of work. A rude coarse world in many of its aspects, but without any of those pestilential taints that kill or paralyse the soul; a world in which the peasant can respect his pastor, though he never fancies him a priest or hesitates to hold his own against him in argument; in which the farmer's cottage is his castle; in which there is severe, but not stunting or depressing labour, hard fare, but not the pinch of hunger; and the heath-clad or grass-clad breast of mother earth to rest on, the flashing sea to look at, the unpolluted air to breathe, the wheeling plover-flight to watch in the sky and the birch and hawthorn, to make love under, by the river side. Certain it is that Scottish national feeling did not bar the old soldier of Burns from taking the world-historical and British view of events. Every conflict he celebrates is *English*. I take leave to add that the *imperial* patriotism of Burns, Campbell, Scott, might rebuke that provincial patriotism which makes it so difficult to find in a poem by an English writer one word of cordial reference either to Ireland or to Scotland. Tennyson has an open heart for all English interests and parties, but at these, with freezing precision, he draws the line. In celebrating the deliverance by the Highlanders of the besieged remnant in Lucknow Residency, he makes his verse meaningless by speaking of the "pibroch of Europe," rather than name the land of Carlyle, Scott, and Burns.

Nor is it too daring to hold that Burns's love for Scotland did not pervert but ennoble his patriotism in general. It is because he wrote *Bruce's Address to his Soldiers before the Battle of Bannockburn* that he could sing with right enthusiasm of the Heights of Abram and the Storm of the Moro, of Wolfe at Quebec and Elliot at Gibraltar. Mr. Arnold would have had a still deeper and truer appreciation of Burns, if he had been as able as Carlyle to understand and sympathise with his Scottish feeling. No one understanding the part played by religion in the history of Scotland could think that Burns, for all his wild words of satire and his fiery scorn for hypocrisy, was an ironical free-thinker of the knowing modern type—" whistle o'er the lave o't "—as Mr. Arnold suggests : nor, if he had known what a thing is Scotch pride, in struggle with the *res angusta domi*, could he have imagined that it was from the outworks, and not from the central fastness and heart's heart of Burns, that *A man's a man for a' that* proceeded. In his boyhood, under his father's roof, Burns had known the struggle with straitened circumstances, and with all the strength of his soul had longed for the freedom and enlargement of an " honest independence." Throughout his life he had yearned for this, striven for it, keeping only apart from it, as holier than it, the sacred and thrilling joy of his poetry. And now, at thirty-six, when he knows that in the battle of life he has been what the world calls beaten—that he has lived and will die a poor man—he stands forth and sings this solemn psalm, instinct with the imperishable life of universal truth.

>Is there, for honest poverty,
> That hangs his head and a' that,
>The coward slave we pass him by,
> We dare be poor for a' that.
>For a' that, and a' that,
> Our toils obscure and a' that;
>The rank is but the guinea's stamp,
> The man's the gowd for a' that.

But in Burns, no more than in his old soldier, is there any of the *sæva indignatio* that tore the heart of Swift—any furious grudge against society—any pessimistic bitterness or despair of mankind.

> Then let us pray that come it may—
>   As come it will for a' that—
> That sense and worth, o'er a' the earth,
>   May bear the gree and a' that;
> For a' that, and a' that,
>   It's comin' yet for a' that,
> That man to man, the warld o'er,
>   Shall brithers be for a' that.

It was like Burns to speak slightingly of this mighty lyric when sending it to the unsouled clay of George Thomson. "It was little," says Lockhart, "in Burns's character to let his feelings on certain subjects escape."

In no respect do the poems of Wordsworth more strongly contrast with those of Burns than in what I would call, with strict meaning, historical value. The first book of Homer's *Iliad* makes the life of old heroic Greece visible to us. We see it and know it in a sense in which no mere statistical information could place it before us. In this sense Burns is the Scottish historian of his day and generation. His Tam o'Shanter, his Duncan Gray, his Doctor Hornbook, his lads and lasses frolicking at Halloween, his peasant opening the Bible and reverently reading it to his household in the evening, are as true to the Ayrshire of his time as the weeping Achilles and his divine mother, the mourning Priam and his dead Hector, are to that old Homeric world; and the same ring and shout of human laughter makes ancient and modern kin, when the preternatural portent of Halloween turns out to be "grumphy, asteer that night," and when Ajax, clearing from mouth and nostril the mud into which he had flopped, complains that he had been tripped up in the race by Pallas, and the surrounding Achaians "laugh sweetly" at the notion. Now Wordsworth's poems, as compared with those of Keats and Shelley, are racy of the soil. There is a good deal of Cumberland in them. But, compared with those of Burns, they are outside Cumberland life. They render its misty melancholy, but of its mirth they give hardly the faintest echo. Only once—in *The Waggoner*—do we hear much of dancing. The humour of the people, the movement of their life, their sports, their passionate loving, all which we must suppose them to have had, are absent. There is in fact nothing in English poetry that will take rank with the vital and vivid presentation of Scottish life and manners in the poems of Burns. The world has enjoyed it, not because it is Scotch, but because it is human.

Such pieces as the address to the *Daisy* and the address to the *Mouse* are too familiar to require more than mention. Their tenderness, their pathos, their aptness of allusion to human destinies, are universally felt. In the *Daisy* there are some lines so delicately fanciful that they form an enchanting variation on the strong vehemence of the poet's general mood. His plough had gone harshly over the "crimson-tipped flower." Burns touches on the circumstance.

> Alas! it's no thy neebor sweet,
> The bonnie lark, companion meet,
> Bending thee 'mang the dewy weet,
>   Wi' speckled breast,
> When upward-springing, blithe, to greet
>   The purpling East.

If Burns had never written another verse but that,

we should have known that he had a poetic nature. There is something feminine in it,—so there is in all gently fanciful poetry: doubtless the melody and magic of poetry have something to do with the blending together of the finest elements distinctive of man and the finest elements distinctive of woman,—breeze and stream co-operating in the modulated ripple. Between Milton and Burns you will not meet with a stanza like this. To Dryden, to Pope, to Cowper even, it would have seemed silly. It is hardly imaginative, but it is fancy's finest gold.

More imaginative, more earnest, is the address to the *Mouse*. The daisy's fate does not really stir the depths of any man's heart. Its woes are of the fancy. But a mouse feels as well as a man, and no one knew that better than Burns. He looks down with intensest sympathy on the sleek, soft, glittering-eyed little wonder, whose " wee bit housie" he has laid in ruins. " Oh, what a panic's in thy breastie!" The strong man's heart beats *in* the tiny, panting breast.

I can conceive nothing more finely perfect than the lines to the mouse; but if I were asked which of his poems conveys to me the most forcible impression of his power, not in its tenderness, but in its strength, I should name the lines to an unmentionable phenomenon —a creeping thing detested by saint and sinner—seen on a lady's bonnet in church. If you want to have Burns in the very tempest of his strength—in his vehemence, his fervent heat—the Thor knuckles white as his hammer smites the rock—read this unique and tremendous poem. We have seen that he could get into the hearts of dogs and mice; but now he goes lower in creation, and, in all the rapture of poetic vision, enters the soul of this crawling beast. As a moralist, as a satirist, as a humourist, Burns here culminates. There is the grandest world-irony in the lines,—a laugh deep, sardonic, shaking the man's whole frame. If Bottom and Dogberry and Malvolio had presented themselves in one incomparable moment to the mind of Shakespeare, he would have felt as Burns felt while watching the entomological specimen on the lady's bonnet. The impudence that protects the complacent creature, as it "strunts rarely o'er gauze and lace "— the semi-starvation that is the lightly borne penalty of beggarly pride, "dining sparely" in its exalted station—these come out in the first stanza. Then, with that inquisitiveness of prying imagination which led him into Poosy Nancy's tavern when the revel was in full scream, the poet dives into the Tartarean deeps of entomological existence. Returning to the upper air, he once more concentrates his attention on the devious, yet mounting, course of the specimen in view. For a moment it disappears under the ribbons.

> Now haud you there, ye're out o' sight,
> Below the fatt'rils snug and tight!

Not likely! The aspiring creature, proudly re-emergent, mounts and mounts, until it beams forth on

> The very tapmost, tow'ring height
> O' Miss's bonnet.

Two verses of admirably arch and pungent humour

follow, and then, in two more, about "winks and finger-ends" that are taking notice, and the beneficent gift of seeing ourselves as others see us, this masterpiece ends.

> O Jenny, dinna toss your head,
> Or set your beauties all abread;
> Ye little ken what cursed speed
>   The blastie's makin'.
> Thae winks and finger-ends, I dread,
>   Are notice takin'.
>
> O wad some Power the giftie gie us
> To see oursels as ithers see us!
> It wad frae mony a blunder free us,
>   An' foolish notion;
> What airs in dress and gait wad lae' us,
>   And e'en devotion!

Consider the range of poetic faculty between the rugged strength of these verses and the delicate beauty and tenderness of the following:

> The hoary cliffs are crown'd wi' flowers,
> White o'er the linns the burnie pours,
> And rising weets wi' misty showers
>   The birks of Aberfeldy;
>
> Let fortune's gifts at random flee,
> They ne'er shall draw a wish frae me,
> Supremely blest wi' love an' thee,
>   In the birks of Aberfeldy.

Lyrical poetry is the essential poetry, the poetry of life in its highest moments, the poetry of spring and of passion. Its distinctive note is love; and it will not be disputed that in the songs and lyrical ballads of Burns is to be found as noble an expression of love as exists in language. His love-lyrics have the play and colour of the fountain and the heat of the furnace. Mr. Arnold signalises the nice perfection of *Tam Glen;* but surely it is only the light touch and sportive mood of Burns that we have in *Tam Glen.* For anything to equal the best love-songs of Burns, we must step beyond the English language, and listen to Clärchen's song in *Egmont*, or Amalia's in *The Robbers.* The genius of English, stately, proud, and cold, is not so favourable to lyric poetry as the German of Goethe and Schiller, or the Scotch of Burns. If Burns is one of the greatest love-poets of the world, Wordsworth can hardly be called a love-poet at all. Of youth-and-maiden rapture there is, in his poems, almost no *sympathetic* expression.

We have, indeed, the stateliness of his verse to make some amends. I would grant that, in style, he has the advantage of Burns. Style is a high quality, and, if other things are equal, the poet whose work has most style is the better poet. But style is, perhaps, irreconcilable with the wild and witching sweetness of the Doric lyre. Style seems also to involve some element which, if not irreconcilable with superlative genius, is yet not quite congenial to it. The greatest poets of all, though they can occasionally be stylists, are by preference and on the whole humourists. Dante, Milton, Schiller, are stylists, not humourists; Homer, Shakespeare, Goethe, are humourists rather than stylists. We praise the stylists, and *ought* to read them. We cannot help reading the humourists.

It seems almost a shame, however, to pit Wordsworth against a poet whom he so deeply valued, so generously recognised. He is always at his best in writing about Burns, and never has the greatness of Burns been more correctly defined than in the following monumental stanza:

> Through busiest street and loneliest glen
>   Are felt the flashes of his pen;
> He rules 'mid winter's snows, and when
>   Bees fill their hives;
> Deep in the general heart of men
>   His power survives.

No poet is more expressly the poet of a class—a refined, a superior class, if you will, but a strictly limited one—a class confined hitherto, Mr. Arnold tells us, to England—than Wordsworth. No poet in all the starry throng has struck more decisively those perennial chords in the human heart to which *all* hearts vibrate than Burns.

And Byron?—Can we, unless blinded by early associations or by that insular prejudice which was personified and has been canonised in Dr. Johnson, maintain against Europe that the author of *Childe Harold* and *Don Juan* was an inferior poet to the author of *The Excursion?* I am prepared to endorse a very dark indictment against Byron, both as a man and as a poet. If we exempt the vices of cruelty and dishonesty, I see not what could have been more immoral than his life; and I cannot, after most carefully considering the point, doubt that, as an artist, he, who had been gifted by nature so bounteously, who was in possession of so many of the true spells of poetic art, deliberately stained and defiled his work in order that it might be bought, anointing it with honey of hell in order that the base sweetness might attract the flies of Beelzebub. I admit also that, apart from the artistically illegitimate attractions of licentiousness in his poems, we find in them occasionally an utter prosiness which it is hard to explain. Byron's dead bits are palpably, offensively dead, and they are apt to occur in his fine work. The "there let him lay," at the end of one of the stanzas of the address to the ocean at the end of *Childe Harold*, is unsurpassable both in vulgarity and in feebleness.

> A king sat on the rocky brow
>   That looks o'er sea-born Salamis;
> And ships, by thousands, lay below,
>   And men in nations;—all were his!
> He counted them at break of day—
> And when the sun set where were they?

That is, to my thinking, as noble poetry, of the lyrical-descriptive kind, as can be conceived. The words that succeed—

> And where are they?

are sheer fatuity. The first question calls up a crowd of ideas, all sublime; the second clashes with the first, or blends with it, and both become nonsense. Once more, I do not make much of the philosophy or the politics of Byron. The profundities and audacities of speculation in *Cain* are in fact the commonplaces, the mere chips and sweepings, of the schools of theological and philosophical controversy. All that vapouring against kings and priests—that swaggering defiance of the conventional ordinances of society—depended on mere ignorance as to the part really played by kings and priests in human history, and was put to flight by the first dawning rays of Carlyle's genial sagacity and historical instinct.

Enough; I am tempted by no enthusiasm to overrate the power of Byron; but it seems to me almost incredible that Mr. Arnold should set Wordsworth above him. Goethe, at the time when Byron attained his reputation, was greater as a critic than as a poet, and he deliberately pronounced Byron's genius incommensurable. Scott accounted for his own abandonment of poetry in three words, "Byron beat me." For Shelley Byron was "the Pythian of his age," and Wilson, who himself had seemed at one moment to be no unlikely candidate for the poetical crown, was satisfied with the honour of strewing flowers in Byron's path. We mark the noble poet, expelled from England, lighting up Europe with the splendour of his genius, which runs like liquid fire along the course of the Rhine, and glitters among the Alpine summits. He had an eye that could pierce to nature's most exquisite loveliness, but it was seldom his mood to watch the glancing of the silver streamlet, like "the shy chamois' eye," or to mark the delicate fluttering of daffodils. He loved to look on nature in her moments of sublimity and of terror, and at such moments he flung the life of his creative imagination into the glory and the gloom. He is the fellow of the mountains in their Titan mirth, and laughs with them amid the rattling thunderbolts and the hissing rain.

> The sky is changed!—and such a change! Oh night,
>   And storm, and darkness, ye are wondrous strong,
> Yet lovely in your strength, as is the light
>   Of a dark eye in woman! Far along,
> From peak to peak, the rattling crags among,
>   Leaps the live thunder! Not from one lone cloud,
> But every mountain now hath found a tongue,
>   And Jura answers, through her misty shroud,
>   Back to the joyous Alps, who call to her aloud.
> * * * * *
> And this is in the night:—most glorious night!
>   Thou wert not made for slumber! let me be
> A sharer in thy fierce and far delight,—
>   A portion of the tempest and of thee!
> How the lit lake shines, a phosphoric sea,
>   And the big rain comes dancing to the earth!
> And now again 'tis black,—and now, the glee
>   Of the loud hills shakes with its mountain-mirth,
>   As if they did rejoice o'er a young earthquake's birth.

Has Wordsworth written anything like that? Can we wonder that Europe thrilled to touches like these, while it remained indifferent to poetical admonitions addressed to robins for killing butterflies? Here is a personification of battle—a vision of the thing alive—executed while we can still trace the 'prentice hand in Byron's manner.

> Death rides upon the sulphury Siroc,
> Red Battle stamps his foot, and nations feel the shock.
> * * * * *
> Lo! where the Giant on the mountain stands,
>   His blood-red tresses deep'ning in the sun,
> With death-shot glowing in his fiery hands,
>   And eye that scorcheth all it glares upon;

> Restless it rolls, now fixed, and now anon
> Flashing afar,—and at his iron feet
> Destruction cowers, to mark what deeds are done.

Why should I refer to a host of such passages as that on the eve of Waterloo, that on the dying gladiator, or to what, though faulty here and there, is a magnificent poem, *The Isles of Greece?* A generation or two ago, these were recognised, and when the present reaction from the past over-praise of Byron shall have spent its force, they will again be recognised as supreme as magnificent.

But critics have not given due consideration to that part of Byron's performance in which he had begun to divest himself of his affectations, to fling aside the stage dress of misanthropy and self-condolence which had so impressed the shilling gallery, and to let his native shrewdness and genuine sympathy have full play. Those cantos of *Don Juan* which lead up to and describe the siege of Ismail show Byron at his best; and their quality is high indeed. In no poetry in the world—not in Shakespeare's or Homer's—do we feel ourselves more decisively to be among living men, among great human interests, and in the hand of a poet who understands both the one and the other. The portrait of Suwarrow is unrivalled in recent English verse. In the best characters in his novels, Scott is as graphic and as true; but Scott never sufficiently emancipated himself from the sense of what was due to style and stateliness in poetry to dare to put such work into his Marmion, his Fitzjames, his Bruce, as

Byron puts into his Suwarrow. Byron's humour here stands him in good stead,—no touch indeed save that of a humourist could have realised such a personality as Suwarrow's; and yet the grotesque does not in the least—when the delineation of the leader is viewed in connection with the description of the siege as a whole—compromise the sublime. But Byron apprehends more than the personality of Suwarrow. He apprehends, with a practical discernment as shrewd as that of Frederick of Prussia, the principles on which Suwarrow conducts the whole business, the inexorable necessity of putting the first before the second—the dreary details of drill before the pomp and circumstance of battle—and the electrical effect of an original mind in breathing new energy into masses of men. It is not too much to say that, in the cantos to which I now refer, the principle may be found of all those books in which Mr. Carlyle, with so vast an influence upon historical literature, has illustrated "the sway of your great men o'er little."

> There was not now a luggage-boy but sought
> Danger and spoil with ardour much increased,
> And why? because a little, odd, old man,
> Stript to his shirt, was come to lead the van.

Suwarrow did not call upon the army to rush at once to the charge; he bethought him of something else first.

> It is an actual fact, that he, Commander-
>   In-chief, in proper person deign'd to drill
> The awkward squad, and could afford to squander
>   His time, a corporal's duty to fulfil.

He could invent, however, as well as drill, and abandon
routine at the proper time.

> Also he dress'd up, for the nonce, fascines
>   Like men with turbans, scimitars, and dirks,
> And made them charge with bayonets these machines,
>   By way of lesson against actual Turks;
> And when well practised in these mimic scenes,
>   He judged them proper to assail the works;
> At which your wise men sneered in phrases witty:
> He made no answer; but he took the city.

Lord Macaulay is much too sweeping in his conclusion that Byron had no dramatic power. The Corsair, Lara, Manfred character, is artificial and shallow, and without question reflects the superficial affectations which Byron found so telling upon " folly and green minds." But Don Juan has not the smallest resemblance to the stalking, moon-apostrophising Manfred; Lambro is not in the least like Cain; and if Suwarrow shows us anything of Byron, it is his sterling sense and command of the science of ruling men. "John Johnson," who accompanied Juan to the Russian camp, is dismissed by Macaulay as "a most signal failure." The portrait is sketchy and slight, but this expression is extravagantly over-charged. Few as are the touches by which Johnson is realised for us, he is a living man, with a marked and thoroughly English character.

> Seldom he altered feature, hue or muscle,
> And could be very busy without bustle.

His meeting with Suwarrow—the brief, terse, soldierly dialogue that passes between them—the frank yet quite unsentimental pleading of the rough but kind fellow for the women—are managed with dramatic propriety. Suwarrow himself is as dramatically conceived and executed as Dalgetty.

And then the breadth, the occasional sublimity, of the purely descriptive passages!—

> Hark! through the silence of the cold, dull night,
>   The hum of armies gathering rank on rank!
> Lo! dusky masses steal in dubious sight
>   Along the leaguer'd wall and bristling bank
> Of the armed river, while with straggling light
>   The stars peep through the vapours dim and dank,
> Which curl in curious wreaths:—how soon the smoke
> Of hell shall pall them in a deeper cloak!
>
> * * * * *
>
> The night was dark, and the thick mist allowed
>   Naught to be seen save the artillery's flame,
> Which arched the horizon like a fiery cloud,
>   And in the Danube's waters shone the same—
> A mirror'd hell! the volleying roar and loud
>   Long booming of each peal on peal, o'ercame
> The ear far more than thunder; for heaven's flashes
> Spare, or smite rarely—man's make millions ashes.

It is infinitely to be regretted that *Don Juan*, besides being unequal, besides having a great deal in it which, whether as wit, as wisdom, or as humour, is wretchedly poor stuff, should be brought down to the level of *Tom Jones*, or lower, by its moral taint; but when we consider its vast range, its world-like variety, its diction and imagery, strong as iron, yet fantastically free as the tendrils, the wreaths, the festooned briers and roses of a forest lane in June, can we think otherwise than with surprise that Mr. Arnold should claim for the poetry of Wordsworth a higher place than for the poetry of Byron ?

In the present volume I try to give some account of the genius and productions of Mrs. Browning and the Brontë sisters. Mrs. Browning was a poet in the simple, yet intense, meaning of the ancient word —a *maker*, an imaginative life-giver and artist. Casting the mind's eye over what she did and what she was, I am strongly moved to claim for her precedence of Wordsworth in the procession of English poets. In no poet whatever was the lyrical glow more authentically fervid and genuine. In another respect she is exemplary and classic. The motivation of her work is perfect. To the great movements of thought and feeling, as they work themselves into action in the world of her time, she gives intense and melodious expression. We may figure her as hovering in her singing robes, a herald of victory, over the van of the spiritual armies that fought the good fight of advancing civilisation in two hemispheres, to strike down rebellion and slavery in the West, and despotism in Italy. Had she done as much for men as she did for women—had man's work, passion, character been delineated on a scale, and with a truth and power, correspondent to those with which, in the world of her art, she embodied woman's—I scarce know what place among the throned ones would have been too high for her. Woman, as Mrs. Browning shows her, is once more the entrancing object that men have loved without measure and without end,—loved as they have been loved in return, totally, passionately, with self-oblivious pride,—

> Such pride as from impetuous love may spring,
> That will not be refused its offering,—

as Shelley worthily sings. But Mrs. Browning is not so great in the delineation of men as in that of women. With all deductions, I reckon her one of the greatest poets of her time. I have, I think, been able to prove in the following pages that, in her treatment of the theme handled by Milton in *Paradise Lost*, she has succeeded in bringing out the human tenderness of the subject, and imparting a realisable personality to Adam and Eve, better than the Puritan poet.

Of Charlotte Brontë and her sisters I have written, if with erring appreciation, at least with honest affection. One's heart is drawn towards the three un-mothered girls who attracted the eyes of all Europe to the sequestered parsonage among the Yorkshire moors. What, after all, can we say of genius, but that it is inscrutable, heaven-descended, wonder-working? From a headland you look over a wide district, all wrapped in somnolent haze, beneath which nothing is distinctly visible. Suddenly, through a rift in a cloud, a sunbeam glances from the blue and touches one spot. There, in piercing brilliance, shine out tower and tree and meadow. Then the cloud closes, the ray is withdrawn, and once more the impartial haze drops its shroud upon the landscape. The genius of the Brontë sisters was that single ray, descending upon Yorkshire.

So intense was the clearness of it, so fine and sweet its beauty, that all England—all Europe—looked towards the remote moorland hill in the West Riding, with its parsonage and its graves. To that illuminated spot, while the ray still falls on it, I invite my readers to turn for a little time.

ELIZABETH BARRETT BROWNING.

CHAPTER I.

HER EARLIEST VERSES.

ELIZABETH BARRETT BARRETT, now better known as Mrs. Browning, seems almost literally to have lisped in numbers. Those for whom it was a sacred obligation to guard her fame and enforce her wishes manifested the utmost displeasure when Mr. Herne Shepherd, that inevitable literary treasure-digger, reissued the verses published by her in her seventeenth year. It is perhaps not surprising that, from the vantage-ground of "higher things" to which they have risen, poets should look with disdainful irritation on their "dead selves," and ask for them the boon of oblivion. But this is a weakness.

> How proud we are
> In daring to look down upon ourselves!

says Mrs. Browning in her mature time, intending to signify that such pride is not strong, but weak; not great, but mean. No fact in a man's history can do him injustice, and the nobly proud man wants only justice. Nor is the labour of friends, in guarding one's reputation from one's dead self, other than labour thrown away. The world inexorably forgets everything that is not preserved by its intrinsic merit, and inexorably refuses to forget all that really takes its ear. The few lines in which, through some felicity of inspiration, or some happy chance of association or local colour, a boy Cowley, Pope, or Byron, has struck a deathless note, are as safe as the strains of their ripest genius; but all the publishers in England could not perpetuate a tenth of what they wrote in boyhood.

None of Mrs. Browning's earliest verses will, I think, form part of the world's current coin of poetry, but they are pleasant and instructive as biographical records of a poet's youth. They set before us her bright presence as she moved about her father's parsonage, an ardent, affectionate girl, not without her meditative hours, her melancholy moments, but happy because full of love and truth and admiration. A long poem on *Mind*, not much superior on the whole to College prize-poetry, is interesting as a stammering prophecy of that intensely spiritual enthusiasm which was to glow like purifying fire in all her works. The spirituality of her poems attests their high quality; for spirituality is the characteristic of all supreme art. It is because of its spirituality that the sculpture of Greece is radiantly pure. It treats the body with a sense of beauty so elevating that, as we look, we think not of bodily things. The "marble burns, and becomes transparent with very spirit." A thoroughly base painter, on the other hand, as Mr. Ruskin, from whom these words are quoted, again observes, " puts a scent of common flesh about his marble Christ." To say that poetry is sensuous—that it suggests the body rather than the soul, matter rather than spirit, flesh rather than immortality—is to say that it is bad poetry. In Mrs. Browning's, from first to last, the spirituality burns with the intensity of flame.

Another lovely characteristic of Mrs. Browning that comes out in these early poems is the strength of her domestic affections. She finds in her father her " best Mæcenas." She writes with tender joy of her studies and readings with her brother. She is already on the side of progress and freedom, and is the gentlest comforter of the exiled widow, who dies heart-broken when her patriot husband is executed. I quote a passage from *Mind*. We may note with interest that the poetry freshens and brightens from commonplace exactly when the girl-poet turns from her books to her personal experiences.

> If human faults to Plato's page belong,
> Not even with Plato willingly go wrong.
> But though the judging page declare it well
> To love Truth better than the lips which tell;
> Yet 'twere an error, with injustice class'd,
> T'adore the former, and neglect the last.
> Oh! beats there, Heaven! a heart of human frame,
> Whose pulses throb not at some kindling name?
> Some sound which brings high musings in its track,
> Or calls perchance the days of childhood back,
> In its dear echo,—when, without a sigh,
> Swift hoop, and bounding ball, were first laid by,
> To clasp in joy, from schoolroom tyrant free
> The classic volume on the little knee,
> And con sweet sounds of dearest minstrelsy,

Or words of sterner lore; the young brow fraught
With a calm brightness which might mimic thought,
Learnt on the boyish hand—as, all the while,
A half-heaved sigh, or aye th' unconscious smile
Would tell how, o'er that page, the soul was glowing,
In an internal transport, past the knowing!
How feelings, erst unfelt, did then appear,
Give forth a voice, and murmur, "We are here!"
As lute-strings, which a strong hand plays upon;
Or Memnon's statue singing 'neath the sun.

The negative qualities of these earliest pieces are as good as their positive. They are an effluence, not strong, but sweet, of tenderness and of beautiful enthusiasm, and they are illustriously void of asperity, of conventional satire, of conceit, of any kind of flippancy. They show that, if Mrs. Browning did not in her girlish years write poetry, she looked poetry, felt poetry, lived poetry, *was* a radiant incarnation of music and beauty moving about the Hereford parsonage within sight of the Malvern Hills.

CHAPTER II.

THE SERAPHIM, AND DRAMA OF EXILE.

THE first poems by which Mrs. Browning chose to be permanently represented have as their subject that tale of sin and redemption which occupied the mature genius and veteran skill of Milton. Speaking somewhat largely, we may say that the *Drama of Exile* corresponds, in subject, to Milton's *Paradise Lost*, and *The Seraphim* to his *Paradise Regained*. In the *Drama of Exile*, indeed, the victory of Christ is touched upon, just as Satan's defeat is referred to in *Paradise Lost*, but it is in the second of Mrs. Browning's poems that the triumph of the Saviour is expressly delineated, as Milton reserved for *Paradise Regained* the specific conflict between Christ and Satan. We may, therefore, compare broadly the treatment of the entire theme by two great poets, the one a man, the other a woman; the one a Puritan, the other the daughter of a clergyman of the Church of England.

As works of literary art, the performances of Mrs. Browning cannot enter into rivalry with those of

Milton. In constructive power, in sustained strength and severe beauty of language, in majestic harmony and subtle modulation of music, organ, harp, and flute, *Paradise Lost* and *Paradise Regained* surpass *A Drama of Exile* and *The Seraphim*. The language is the weakest part of these poems. It exhibits Mrs. Browning's mannerism without those qualities by which her mannerism was subsequently softened and chastened into a deeper melodiousness. The diction is rugged; the imagery often borders on the grotesque; we are always conscious of more or less extravagance, always of more or less obscurity. The very first verse in the *Drama of Exile* has an oddity of rhyme which Milton would never have let pass. Lucifer, addressing his hosts, whom he calls up to deform and destroy the world which he has conquered for them, speaks thus :

> Rejoice in the clefts of Gehenna,
> My exiled, my host!
> Earth has exiles as hopeless as when a
> Heaven's empire was lost.

On the other hand, Mrs. Browning is in some respects—and these important—more successful in the treatment of the subject than Milton. She throws a finer tenderness into her portraiture of Adam and Eve, especially of the latter. Charlotte Brontë expressed in terms of scornful brilliancy the dissatisfaction with which women generally look upon Milton's account of Eve. It is a picture of the first woman by a man who holds uncompromisingly that woman's supreme happiness is to contribute to and sympathise with the happiness of her lord and master. In doing justice to Eve, Mrs. Browning does justice also to Adam, breathing passionate life into the statuesque propriety of Milton's first man.

Mrs. Browning has the superiority also in the conception formed and the view presented of redemption. All who have carefully considered *Paradise Lost* and *Paradise Regained* as the parts of one great poem on sin and salvation, must have been struck by the fact that Milton has almost ignored the death of Christ. In *Paradise Lost* he was not required to say much of it, but he almost wholly omits it also from *Paradise Regained*. The four books of that marvellously learned and very beautiful poem are taken up with an account of Christ's temptation in the wilderness. The triumph of Christ over Satan is viewed by Milton as essentially a triumph in argument. At the end of the argument and of the four books containing it, do we not experience, when we first read the poem, a sense of utter incompleteness? Additional books seem to be wanted for the treatment of the rest of Christ's life and of His death. The universal judgment of Christendom has attached more consequence, in the general scheme of redemption, to the death on Calvary, than to the temptation in the wilderness, and the body of Catholic theology corresponds to this Christian sentiment. It is well known that Milton in the latter portion of his life held Arian opinions; and the only way in which I can account for the virtual omission of the crucifixion from *Paradise Regained* is by supposing that, when he wrote the poem, he had ceased to accept the Catholic view of Christ's death as a propitiatory sacrifice. Be this, however, as it may, Mrs. Browning, in *The Seraphim*, presents to us the victory of Christ over evil as consummated on the cross. Both in that poem and in the *Drama of Exile*, she seeks to penetrate into the spiritual meanings of the death of Christ, into the mystery of sorrow shared by Divinity, into love that, through death, conquers death and hell. If the feeling of Christendom, sanctioned by the opinion of such men as Lessing, Goethe, and Hegel, is right in apprehending atonement as distinctive of Christianity, then Mrs. Browning must be allowed to be more comprehensive than Milton in her treatment of their common theme.

The *Drama of Exile* opens with a fiercely exultant chant poured forth by Lucifer, who has completed the ruin of the human pair, and stands on the outer side of the gate of Eden, near the flaming sword. He and his angels have fallen from heaven on account of their sin, and his belief is that the Almighty Himself cannot save any created being that once has sinned. He has defaced God's image in the person of Adam; "unkinged is the king of the garden:" and he now calls upon his "locusts" to come up and feed in "the green of the world."

> Come up! we have conquered by evil.
> Good reigns not alone,
> *I* prevail now! and, angel or devil,
> Inherit a throne!

Suddenly Gabriel appears, and a conversation between him and Lucifer ensues. It is but partially successful. The words used by Lucifer, in defiance of God and expression of trust in his own resolution, sound feebly after those of Milton's Satan. Lucifer affects an air of jaunty scornfulness and irony which recalls the mockery, though not the envenomed malignity, of Goethe's Mephistopheles. Gabriel is courteous even to Lucifer, and noble in all tones of thought. The fiend, believing sin to be, in the nature of things, unpardonable, suggests that he and his demons could stand with a sword between man and Eden as well as Gabriel and his angels. Gabriel replies:

> Thou speakest in the shadow of thy change.
> If thou hadst gazed upon the face of God
> This morning for a moment, thou hadst known
> That only pity fitly can chastise,
> While hate avenges.

Lucifer rejoins that no pity has been shown to *him*.

> When I fell back, down,—staring up as I fell,—
> The lightnings holding open my scathed lids,
> And that thought of the infinite of God,
> Hurled after to precipitate descent;
> When countless angel faces still and stern
> Pressed out upon me from the level heavens
> Adown the abysmal spaces, and I fell
> Trampled down by your stillness, and struck blind,
> By the sight within your eyes,—'twas then I knew
> How ye could pity, my kind angel-hood!

Gabriel does not deem it inconsistent with loyalty to Heaven to express sympathy with the fallen spirit.

> Yet, thou discrowned one, by the truth in me
> Which God keeps in me, I would give away

All—save that truth and His love keeping it,—
To lead thee home again into the light,
And hear thy voice chant with the morning stars,
When their rays tremble round them with much song
Sung in more gladness!

To the dialogue between Lucifer and Gabriel succeeds a chorus of Eden spirits, bewailing the expulsion of the human pair. Some of the verses have a pathetic beauty.

Hearken, oh hearken, ye shall hearken surely,
  For years and years,
The noise beside you, dripping coldly, purely,
  Of spirits' tears!
The yearning to a beautiful denied you,
  Shall strain your powers;
Ideal sweetnesses shall overglide you,
  Resumed from ours!
In all your music, our pathetic minor
  Your ears shall cross;
And all good gifts shall mind you of diviner,
  With sense of loss!

On the whole, however, there is more of fancy than of true imagination in this song of the river-spirits, bird-spirits, and flower-spirits of Eden, and it is with a sense of relief that, at its close, we find ourselves listening neither to angels nor to nightingales, but to Adam and Eve. They have been fleeing before the glare of the flaming sword, and Eve now sinks down weary, able only to look into Adam's face. She calls upon him to strike her dead, in order that, the curse having spent itself on her, he may be restored to happiness.

O Adam, Adam! by that name of Eve—
Thine Eve, thy life—which suits me little now,

Seeing that I confess myself thy death
And thine undoer, as the snake was mine,—
I do adjure thee, put me straight away,
Together with my name.

Adam answers:
My beloved,
Mine Eve and life—I have no other name
For thee or for the sun than what ye are,
My utter life and light! If we have fallen,
It is that we have sinned,—we: God is just:
And, since His curse doth comprehend us both
It must be that His balance holds the weights
Of first and last sin on a level. What!
Shall I who had not virtue to stand straight
Among the hills of Eden, here assume
To mend the justice of the perfect God,
By piling up a curse upon His curse,
Against thee—thee—
    Eve.   For so, perchance, thy God
Might take thee into grace for scorning me;
Thy wrath against the sinner giving proof
Of inward abrogation of the sin!
And so the blessed angels might come down
And walk with thee as erst.

The self-sacrificing nobleness of Eve calls forth all the chivalry of Adam's nature, and he tells her that he is the greater transgressor of the two.

If God,—
Who gave the right and joyaunce of the world
Both unto thee and me,—gave thee to me,
The best gift last, the last sin was the worst,
Which sinned against more complement of gifts
And grace of giving. God! I render back
Strong benediction and perpetual praise
From mortal feeble lips (as incense-smoke,
Out of a little censer, may fill heaven),
That Thou, in striking my benumbed hands
And forcing them to drop all other boons

> Of beauty, and dominion, and delight,—
> Hast left this well-beloved Eve—this life
> Within life—this best gift between their palms,
> In gracious compensation!

Milton does not make Adam say anything so nobly beautiful as that. Eve replies.

> *Eve.* Is it thy voice?
> Or some saluting angel's—calling home
> My feet into the garden?
> *Adam.* O my God!
> I, standing here between the glory and dark—
> The glory of Thy wrath projected forth
> From Eden's wall, the dark of our distress
> Which settles a step off in that drear world—
> Lift up to Thee the hands from whence hath fallen
> Only creation's sceptre—thanking Thee
> That rather Thou hast cast me out with her,
> Than left me lorn of her in Paradise,
> With angel looks and angel songs around
> To show the absence of her eyes and voice.

The sense of this is as deep and true as the poetry is beautiful. It is not possible for us to conceive how, in this world at least, human beings could be much to each other, and human affection have exercise and expansion, if there were no want, no sorrow, no toil, no necessity of mutual ministering. Physical evil is in our planet a condition of moral progress, and it was in the first pangs of sorrow and suffering that the exiles from Eden would know how dear they were to each other.

Hitherto the poet has shown us chiefly the compensations and redeeming features of the state into which Adam and Eve have fallen; but the tragedy now begins to deepen. By imagery too gigantesque and vague—the signs of the zodiac being introduced into the machinery of the poem—the anguish of the creatures of the earth, on account of the sin that has been brought into it, is shadowed forth.

> That phantasm, there,
> Presents a lion—albeit twenty times
> As large as any lion—with a roar
> Set soundless in his vibratory jaws,
> And a strange horror stirring in his mane!
> And, there, a pendulous shadow seems to weigh—
> Good against ill, perchance; and, there, a crab
> Puts coldly out its gradual shadow-claws,
> Like a slow blot that spreads—till all the ground,
> Crawled over by it, seems to crawl itself.

The Spirit of the Earth, that once sang only of joy and peace, now mourns perpetually.

> I feel your steps, O wandering sinners, strike
>   A sense of death to me, and undug graves!
> The heart of earth, once calm, is trembling like
>   The ragged foam along the ocean waves:
> The restless earthquakes rock against each other;
> The elements moan round me—" Mother, mother,"
>   And I wail!

The feeling with which Lucifer regards the exiles from Eden is that of scorn, modified by a sense of their advantage over him in being able to pray to God and to hope for pardon. This is the peculiarity of Mrs. Browning's Lucifer as distinguished from Milton's devil, and from Goethe's. I am not sure that Mrs. Browning has kept the character in perfect consistency with itself. Lucifer at first appears to be exultant, confident, resolute in his sin, and proud of it.

> The red sign
> Burnt on my forehead, which you taunt me with,
> Is God's sign that it bows not unto God,
> The potter's mark upon his work, to show
> It rings well to the striker.

This is not the speech we should expect from one who appreciates the infinite advantage over him possessed by the human pair in that they are admitted to converse with God. "Your prayers," says Lucifer, "tread high as angels." They are not doomed, as he says that he is, to hate, and tempt, and destroy. His hatred of them "glares without, because it burns within," with the searching fires of remorse.

> I, angel, in antagonism
> To God and His reflex beatitudes,
> Moan ever in the central universe
> With the great woe of striving against Love—
> And gasp for space amid the Infinite.

The Satan of *Paradise Lost* would never have said that; but I shall not assert the same so decisively of the Satan of *Paradise Regained*, for the fiend of Milton's second poem is much softened down. Mrs. Browning is careful to make it appear that Lucifer does not repent. He is "self-elect to Kingship of resistant agony toward the good;" and, therefore, her delineation may be formally consistent with itself. But such a conception of the character embraces elements of essential impossibility and contradictoriness. A spirit that felt it to be anguish to contend against love would be at heart a good spirit.

Bowed and bent almost to despair by the cruelty of the creatures that in Eden had been their obedient servants, Adam and Eve now cry to God, the latter placing her hope in the promise.

> O my Seed,
> Through the tempestuous years that rain so thick
> Betwixt my ghostly vision and thy face,
> Let me have token; for my soul is bruised
> Before the serpent's head is.

In answer to this appeal, "a vision of Christ appears in the midst of the zodiac, which pales before the heavenly light." The vision rebukes the spirits of the earth for the "cruel and unmitigated blame" they have cast upon their masters.

> This regent and sublime Humanity,
> Though fallen, exceeds you! This shall film your sun,
> Shall hunt your lightning to its lair of cloud,
> Turn back your rivers, footpath all your seas,
> Lay flat your forests, master with a look
> Your lion at his fasting. . . .
>   Over you
> Receive man's sceptre,—therefore be content
> To minister with voluntary grace
> And melancholy pardon every rite
> And function in you, to the human hand.

He bids Adam be the spokesman of blessing to Eve.

> Speak, Adam. Bless the woman, man;
> It is thine office.

Adam's blessing is in itself a beautiful and touching poem, full of wise meaning. I abridge it very considerably.

> Raise the majesties
> Of thy disconsolate brows, O well-beloved,
> And front with level eyelids the To come,
> And all the dark o' the world. Rise, woman, rise

To thy peculiar and best altitudes
Of doing good and of enduring ill,—
Of comforting for ill, and teaching good,
And reconciling all that ill and good
Unto the patience of a constant hope,—
Rise with thy daughters! If sin came by thee,
And by sin death, the ransom-righteousness,
The heavenly life, and compensative rest
Shall come by means of thee. Be satisfied;
Something thou hast to bear through womanhood,
Peculiar suffering answering to the sin,—
Some pang paid down for each new human life,
Some weariness in guarding such a life,
Some coldness from the guarded, some mistrust,
And pressures of an alien tyranny
With its dynastic reasons of larger bones
And stronger sinews. But, go to! thy love
Shall chant itself its own beatitudes,
After its own life-working. A child's kiss,
Set on thy sighing lips, shall make thee glad;
A poor man, served by thee, shall make thee rich;
A sick man, helped by thee, shall make thee strong;
Thou shalt be served thyself by every sense
Of service which thou renderest. . . .
Thy hand which plucked the apple, I clasp close,—
I bless thee in the name of Paradise,
And by the memory of Edenic joys
Forfeit and lost. . . . .
I bless thee to the desert and the thorns,
To the elemental change and turbulence,
And to the roar of the estranged beasts,
And to the solemn dignities of grief,—
To each one of these ends—and to their END
Of death and the hereafter.

The rest of the poem is taken up with prophetic adumbration of the victory of Christ. Lucifer learns that he shall be finally baffled, because the sorrow in which he thought it impossible that God could share has been partaken of by the Divine Man, and Christ has become " an exile from His heaven, to lead these exiles homeward."

I cannot do justice to these poems without quoting one or two additional passages illustrative of their imaginative and intellectual power, and the strength, blended with splendour, of their language. In a passage as thoughtful as it is beautiful, words are put into the mouth of Christ, describing the influence of His life and death upon the human family. The poet writes as one who believes the prophecy she records. At this time Mrs. Browning's mind was thoroughly imbued with what would be called evangelical theology. The prophecy has, in great part, still to be fulfilled, but in its fulfilment is the best hope of the world. Christ speaks:

> At last,
> I, wrapping round Me your humanity,
> Which, being sustained, shall never break nor burn
> Beneath the fire of Godhead, will tread earth,
> And ransom you and it, and set strong peace
> Betwixt you and its creatures. With My pangs
> I will confront your sins; and since those sins
> Have sunken to all Nature's heart from yours,
> The tears of My clean soul shall follow them,
> And set a holy passion to work clear
> Absolute consecration. In My brow
> Of kingly whiteness shall be crowned anew
> Your discrowned human nature. Look on Me!
> As I shall be uplifted on a cross
> In darkness of eclipse and anguish dread,
> So shall I lift up in My pierced hands,
> Not into dark, but light—not unto death,
> But life,—beyond the reach of guilt and grief,
> The whole creation. Henceforth in My name

> Take courage, O thou woman—man, take hope!
> Your grave shall be as smooth as Eden's sward,
> Beneath the steps of your prospective thoughts,
> And, one step past it, a new Eden-gate
> Shall open on a hinge of harmony,
> And let you through to mercy. Ye shall fall
> No more, within that Eden, nor pass out
> Any more from it. In which hope, move on,
> First sinners and first mourners. Live and love,—
> Doing both nobly, because lowlily!
> Live and work, strongly,—because patiently!
> And, for the deed of death, trust it to God
> That it be well done, unrepented of,
> And not to loss. And thence, with constant prayers
> Fasten your souls so high, that constantly
> The smile of your heroic cheer may float
> Above all floods of earthly agonies,
> Purification being the joy of pain!

It is written that the last enemy that shall be overcome is Death. With sublime audacity the young poet-woman imaginatively realises the taming and slaying of the pale horse on which rides Death. Christ " shall quell him with a breath, and shall lead him where He will, with a whisper in the ear, full of fear, and a hand upon the mane, grand and still." What woman has ever lived except Mrs. Browning that could have imagined and achieved the following passage? It contains some fantastic lines, but the imagination of a great poet throbs audibly in it as a whole.

> Through the flats of Hades, where the souls assemble,
> He will guide the Death-steed calm between their ranks,
> While, like beaten dogs, they a little moan and tremble
> To see the darkness curdle from the horse's glittering flanks.
> Through the flats of Hades, where the dreary shade is,—

Up the steep of heaven, will the Tamer guide the steed,—
Up the spheric circles—circle above circle,
We who count the ages shall count the tolling tread—
Every hoof-fall striking a blinder, blanker sparkle
From the stony orbs, which shall show as they were dead,
All the way the Death-steed with tolling hoofs shall travel,
Ashen grey the planets shall be motionless as stones,
Loosely shall the systems eject their parts coeval,—
Stagnant in the spaces, shall float the pallid moons;
Suns that touch their apogees, reeling from their level,
Shall run back on their axles in wild, low, broken tunes;
Up against the arches of the crystal ceiling
From the horse's nostrils shall steam the blurting breath;
Up between the angels pale with silent feeling,
Will the Tamer calmly lead the horse of Death;
Cleaving all that silence, cleaving all that glory,
Will the Tamer lead him straightway to the Throne:
"Look out, O Jehovah, to this I bring before Thee
With a hand nail-piercèd,—I, who am Thy Son."
Then the Eye Divinest, from the Deepest, flaming
On the mystic courser, shall look out in fire!
Blind the beast shall stagger where It overcame him,—
Meek as lamb at pasture—bloodless in desire—
Down the beast shall shiver,—slain amid the taming,—
And, by Life essential, the phantasm Death expire.

Hitherto our quotations have been from the *Drama of Exile*. The next is from *The Seraphim*. That poem describes the emotions with which Zerah and Ador, two of the heavenly host, contemplate the work of Christ upon earth, and in particular the death upon Calvary. One or two descriptive touches, rendering the appearance of the crowd, are terrible in their graphic vividness.

With the living's pride
They stare at those who die,—who hang
In their sight and die. They bear the streak

>   Of the crosses' shadow, black not wide,
>   To fall on their heads, as it swerves aside
>   When the victims' pang
>   Makes the crosses creak.

The thieves, penitent and impenitent, who were crucified with Christ, are depicted.

>   *Zerah.*   One
>   Is as a man who has sinned, and still
>   Doth wear the wicked will,
>   The hard malign life-energy,
>   Tossed outward, in the parting soul's disdain,
>   On brow and lip that cannot change again.
>   *Ador.*   And one—
>   *Zerah.*   Has also sinned.
>   And yet (O marvel!) doth the Spirit-wind
>   Blow white those waters?—Death upon his face
>   Is rather shine than shade,
>   A tender shine by looks beloved made.
>   He seemeth dying in a quiet place,
>   And less by iron wounds in hands and feet,
>   Than heart-broke by new joy too sudden and sweet.

Could anything be more tender in its loveliness than the line, "He seemeth dying in a quiet place"?

While the seraphs look upon the crucifixion, they muse on the fact that, much as they and their angel kindred may love God, they cannot love Him so well as redeemed mankind.

>   *Ador.*   Do we love not?
>   *Zerah.*   Yea,
>   But not as man shall! Not with life for death,
>   New-throbbing through the startled being! Not
>   With strange astonished smiles, that ever may
>   Gush passionate like tears and fill their place!
>   Nor yet with speechless memories of what

> Earth's winters were, enverduring the green
>   Of every heavenly palm,
>   Whose windless, shadeless calm
> Moves only at the breath of the Unseen.
> Oh, not with this blood on us—and this face,—
> Still, haply, pale with sorrow that it bore
> In our behalf, and tender evermore
> With nature all our own, upon us gazing!—
> Nor yet with these forgiving hands upraising
> Their unreproachful wounds, alone to bless.
> . . . . Love Him more, O man!
>   Than sinless seraphs can.

The description of the moment when Christ dies, and the earth is shrouded in darkness, is one of the most sublime passages that has been written since the death of Milton.

> *Zerah.* The pathos hath the day undone:
>   The death-look of His eyes
>   Hath overcome the sun,
>   And made it sicken in its narrow skies.
> *Ador.*   Is it to death?   He dieth.
> *Zerah.*   Through the dark
> He still, He only, is discernible—
> The naked hands and feet, transfixed stark,
> The countenance of patient anguish white,
> Do make themselves a light
> More dreadful than the glooms which round them dwell,
> And therein do they shine.

The epilogue, in which the poet gently comments on her own daring song, is full of grace and pathos.

>   Ah! what am I
>   To counterfeit, with faculty earth-darkened,
>   Seraphic brows of light
>   And seraph language never used nor hearkened?

> Ah me! What word that seraphs say could come
> From mouth so used to sighs—so soon to lie
> Sighless, because then breathless in the tomb?
> * * * * * *
> Forgive me, that mine earthly heart should dare
> Shape images of unincarnate spirits,
> And lay upon their burning lips a thought
> Cold with the weeping which mine earth inherits!
> And though ye find in such hoarse music, wrought
> To copy yours, a cadence all the while
> Of sin and sorrow—only pitying smile!—
> Ye know to pity, well.
> I, too, may haply smile another day
> At the far recollection of this lay,
> When God may call me in your midst to dwell,
> To hear your most sweet music's miracle
> And see your wondrous faces. May it be!
> For His remembered sake, the Slain on rood,
> Who rolled His earthly garment red in blood
> (Treading the wine-press) that the weak, like me,
> Before His heavenly throne should walk in white.

Such are the astonishing poems in which Elizabeth Barrett Barrett, now above thirty, announced that another great poet had arisen in England, a poet of almost excessive fervour and intensity, whose imagination would quail before nothing in heaven, earth, or hell, and who possessed, at the same time, the deepest tenderness that could dwell in a woman's heart. Putting aside Dante and Milton, I know nothing in religious poetry at all comparable, for imaginative power, with the *Drama of Exile* and *The Seraphim*. That they are imperishable is, I should say, probable; but the probability is clouded with a doubt from the fact that they are conspicuously defective in one quality of great and deathless poetry, to

The Defect of these Poems. 25

wit, simplicity. Able as she was to use "the mother tongue of noble passion," the woman singer could not perfectly trust to simple language. It would, perhaps, be more correct to say that her imagination was too vehement, too impetuous, to be restrained by judgment, and that, like a strong, wild horse of the desert, when first mounted, it took the bit in its teeth and ran away with the rider. At all events, the imagery of these poems, especially of the first, is so vaguely gorgeous and erudite,—the invention so elaborate and complex, —that many readers will be permanently repelled by them. "The sense reels," I wrote formerly, and a new reading has not altered my opinion, "under the bewildering pageantry of earth spirits, and bird spirits, and river spirits, of zodiacs, and stars, and chorussing angels; the mind is perplexed with gnomons, and apogees, and vibrations, and infinites. One stares on all this as one might on the foam, glorious in its shivered snow and wavering irises, which roars and raves round a coral reef. The vessel draws near the reef, and many an eye looks into the foam; but its beauty fascinates only for a moment, and the sail fills, and the island is left for ever. Never, perhaps, is it known that in the heart of that island, hidden by the torn fringes of tinted foam, there was soft green grass, and a quiet, crystal fountain, and cottages smiling in the light of flowers, and all the home affections."

I beg to express the earnest hope that my readers, if they have not yet studied these memorable poems, will not permit themselves to be repelled by the demands they make upon the attention and the thinking faculty. They bear throughout the impress of an original mind and a sovereign imagination, and the deep beating of a woman's heart makes rare, sweet melody in them from first to last. Amid the stormy grandeurs of their imagery, this deep music comes in with enhanced effect, as the penetrating tenderness of "Home, Sweet Home" might come in amid the melodious crash and clamour of orchestral thunderings.

CHAPTER III.

A VISION OF POETS, AND THE POET'S VOW.

IN *A Vision of Poets* and *The Poet's Vow*, the influence of Tennyson is traceable. If *A Dream of Fair Women* and *The Palace of Art* had never been written, the likelihood is that neither would have seen the light. And yet it is not easy to point out the effect produced by Tennyson, for the poems are in different measures from his, and the mode of treatment in the respective works is diverse. The influence is felt—first, in cadences that recall Tennysonian tones; secondly, in the construction of one, at least, of the poems; and, thirdly, in their reasonings and conclusions. *A Vision of Poets* opens thus:

> A poet could not sleep aright,
> For his soul kept up too much light
> Under his eyelids for the night.
>
> And thus he rose disquieted
> With sweet rhymes ringing through his head,
> And in the forest wandered.

In Tennyson's *Dream of Fair Women*, the poet falls asleep and straightway wanders in "an old wood." The resemblance here is so close that, although Mrs.

Browning, in the subsequent arrangement of her machinery, does not follow Tennyson, the recollection of it clings to the reader. I cannot say that, in the invention and delineation of the visions which the hero of Mrs. Browning's poems sees in the forest, she is so felicitous as Tennyson. Again she lacks simplicity. Her poem is too long, also, and she detracts from the effect of stanzas of great power and splendour by addition of others that are of far inferior excellence. Nevertheless, there is in the piece the vitality of genius. Several of the word-portraits of "God's prophets of the Beautiful" are true to the life and rich in suggestive meaning.

> Here, Homer, with the broad suspense
> Of thunderous brows, and lips intense
> Of garrulous god-innocence.

The "broad suspense of thunderous brows" has, to my thinking, more sound than sense; but the "garrulous god-innocence"—the child-like, joyous consciousness that gods and heroes are inexpressibly interesting, and worthy of being talked about and sung about without end—must strike every one who at all knows the Homeric poems as singularly happy and accurate.

> There Shakespeare! on whose forehead climb
> The crowns of the world. Oh, eyes sublime
> With tears and laughter for all time!

Turning again to the ancients, she throws a few words on the page, and likeness after likeness starts up.

> Hesiod old,
> Who, somewhat blind and deaf and cold,
> Cared most for gods and bulls. And bold,

> Electric Pindar, quick as fear,
> With race-dust on his cheeks, and clear
> Slant startled eyes that seem to hear
>
> The chariot rounding the last goal,
> To hurtle past it in its soul.
> And Sappho, with that gloriole
>
> Of ebon hair on calmed brows—
> O, poet-woman! none foregoes
> The leap, attaining the repose!

She throws Spenser into a group with Ariosto, and adds a stanza which hardly does justice to Dante.

> And Spenser drooped his dreaming head
> (With languid sleep-smile you had said
> From his own verse engendered)
>
> On Ariosto's, till they ran
> Their curls in one.—The Italian
> Shot nimbler heat of bolder man
>
> From his fine lids. And Dante stern
> And sweet, whose spirit was an urn
> For wine and milk, poured out in turn.

We have sketches of Alfieri, Berni, Tasso, Racine, Corneille, Petrarch, Camoens, Calderon, De Vega, Goethe, Schiller, Chaucer, and many more. I can make room only for Milton, Burns, and Shelley.

> Here Milton's eyes strike piercing-dim:
> The shapes of suns and stars did swim
> Like clouds from them, and granted him
>
> God for sole vision. . . .
>
> And Burns, with pungent passionings
> Set in his eyes. Deep lyric springs
> Are of the fire-mount's issuings.
>
> And Shelley, in his white ideal,
> All statue blind.

There is immense ability crowded into these brief limnings. The pungent passionings of Burns's eyes—the volcanic fire of soul from which gushed forth his songs—these are the descriptive strokes of one who had looked into the very heart of the man. Scott saw Burns once, but he never forgot his eyes, which burned, says Sir Walter, like gig-lamps. The lines on Shelley are as wonderful as any in the poem. "The words contain," I said once, "the key to Shelley's biography. It was precisely the dazzling radiance of Shelley's ideal which struck him stone-blind to the actual world."

As we proceed in our examination of Mrs. Browning's poems, we find them becoming more human in subject and more simple in treatment. Lucifer and Gabriel and the Seraphim give place to earth-born poets; but even the poets form part of the pageantry of a vision. In *The Poet's Vow*, however, we have human personages, without any visionary or phantasmagoric aids or hindrances to the imagination. At the outset—in the second and third stanzas of the poem—there occurs a brief but beautiful description of evening.

> The rowers lift their oars to view
>   Each other in the sea,
> The landsmen watch the rocking boats
>   In a pleasant company,
> While up the hill go gladlier still
>   Dear friends by two and three.
>
> The peasant's wife hath looked without
>   Her cottage door and smiled,

> For there the peasant drops his spade
>   To clasp his youngest child
> Which hath no speech, but his hands can reach
>   And stroke his forehead mild.

This picture of Nature's hushed landscape at the fall of evening prepares us for the strikingly original conception of a man—a poet—whose very serenity attests the coldness of his heart.

> You would not think that brow could e'er
>   Ungentle moods express:
> Yet seemed it, in this troubled world,
>   Too calm for gentleness;
> When the very star, that shines from afar,
>   Shines trembling, ne'ertheless.

There was in his face none of that "softening light" which the presence of others, awakening sympathy in us, supplies. "None gazed within the poet's face; the poet gazed in none;" he had resolved to wean himself from all association with the base brotherhood of mankind, to be rid of the "weights and shows of sensual things," to hear no cry haunting the earth as with the appeal of Abel's blood. Earth, he says, with all her creatures, has been cursed in the curse of man; but he does not partake in the sin; and, in sympathy with Nature, he is sensible of "an holy wrath" that impels him to break the bondage knitting him to his kind. Accordingly he makes a vow, to this effect :—

> Hear me forswear man's sympathies,
>   His pleasant yea and no—
> His riot on the piteous earth
>   Whereon his thistles grow!
> His changing love—with stars above!
>   His pride—with graves below!

> Hear me forswear his roof by night,
>   His bread and salt by day,
> His talkings at the wood-fire hearth,
>   His greetings by the way,
> His answering looks, his systemed books,
>   All man, for aye and aye.

Alone with Nature, he expects that his purged heart, "rent" from its human debasements, will drink of Nature's wine of wonder and beauty, and that he will share with clouds and trees and waters the blessing of serenity which they had before earth was blasted by Adam's sin. The mystic affection of Nature encircling him will be better than that of child, friend, wife, or countryman.

> And ever, when I lift my brow
>   At evening to the sun,
> No voice of woman or of child
>   Recording "Day is done,"
> Your silence shall a love express
>   More deep than such an one!

Having determined irrevocably, he takes measures to give effect to his resolution. Sharing his silver and gold among his crowding friends, he finds his gifts accepted with bland complacency, and his hand taken, for the last time, "in a somewhat slacker hold." The crowd having passed away, he has to deal with two who remain, one of them his friend of friends among men, the other his more than friend among women. He proposes that his best friend shall wed Rosalind, his "plighted bride," that his ancestral lands shall serve her for dower, and that the pair shall neither

remember nor lament him. Rosalind looks upon him
silently, with unspeakable meaning in her face,

> Like a child that never knew but love,
> Whom words of wrath surprise.

The tears come when she attempts to speak, but at
last her words make way, and she gently remonstrates
against his gospel of heartless pride.

> I thought—but I am half a child,
> And very sage art thou—
> The teachings of the heaven and earth
> Should keep us soft and low.

She spurns, as every true woman would, his considerate offer of a livelihood. If Elaine cannot have Lancelot, the knight may keep his proffered money. Nor will Rosalind marry the respected friend to whom her lover graciously hands her over.

> I will not live Sir Roland's bride—
> That dower I will not hold!
> I tread below my feet that go,
> These parchments bought and sold.
> The tears I weep are mine to keep,
> And worthier than thy gold.

Sir Roland rebukes him in terms less touching, but more sublime.

> And thou, O distant, sinful heart,
> That climbest up so high,
> To wrap and blind thee with the snows
> That cause to dream and die—
> What blessing can from lips of man
> Approach thee with his sigh?
> Ay! what, from earth—create for man,
> And moaning in his moan?

> Ay! what from stars—revealed to man,
>   And man-named, one by one?
> Ay, more! what blessing can be given,
> Where the spirits seven do show in heaven
>   A MAN upon the throne?—
>
> A man on earth He wandered once,
>   All meek and undefiled:
> And those who loved Him, said "He wept"—
> None ever said He smiled,
> Yet there might have been a smile unseen,
> When He bowed His holy face, I ween,
>   To bless that happy child.

The poet persists in his purpose. If Rosalind and Sir Roland will not have his lands, the poor shall be endowed with them. For his part, he betakes him to the ruined hall of Courland, where bats cling to the ceilings and lizards run on the floors, to live in isolation from mankind.

Year after year passes on; but whether it is that Christians wend by to their prayers, or that bridal parties trip along in festive array, or that little children stand near the wall to see the green lizards, he has no word, no blessing, no sympathy for anything in human shape.

Rosalind, pining heart-broken, lies at last on her death-bed. She then tells the "loving nurse" to smooth her tresses when she is dead, to uplift her hands, laying them, palm to palm, to place her on a bier, and to put beneath her head a pillow formed of flowers like those which she used to gather when she and her poet-lover played as children in the woods. When "the corpse's smile" appeared on the face, the nurse was to place upon the breast a scroll, and "the youngest children dear" were to carry the dead Rosalind, not to the churchyard, but to the old hall of Courland.

> And up the bank where I used to sit
>   And dream what life would be,
> Along the brook, with its sunny look
>   Akin to living glee,
> O'er the windy hill, through the forest still,
>   Let them gently carry me.
>
> * * * * *
>
> And when withal they near the hall,
>   In silence let them lay
> My bier before the bolted door,
>   And leave it for a day:
> For I have vowed, though I am proud,
> To go there as a guest in shroud,
>   And not be turned away.

These instructions are obeyed. The poet, secure at midnight from human intrusion, unbolts his door, looks out beneath the stars, and sees their cold light on the face of the dead.

> It lay before him, human-like,
>   Yet so unlike a thing!
> More awful in its shrouded pomp
>   Than any crownèd king,
> All calm and cold, as it did hold
>   Some secret, glorying.
>
> A heavier weight than of its clay
>   Clung to his heart and knee,
> As if those folded palms could strike,
>   He staggered groaningly,
> And then o'erhung, without a groan,
> The meek close mouth that smiled alone,
>   Whose speech the scroll must be.

The words of the scroll are too many for quotation, except in part.

> I have prayed for thee with silent lips
>   In the anguish none could see;
> They whispered oft, " She sleepeth soft "—
>   But I only prayed for thee.
>
> Go to! I pray for thee no more—
>   The corpse's tongue is still.
> Its folded fingers point to heaven,
>   But point there stiff and chill.
> No farther wrong, no farther woe,
> Hath license from the sin below
>   Its tranquil heart to thrill.
>
> I charge thee, by the living's prayer,
>   And the dead's silentness,
> To wring from out thy soul a cry
>   Which God shall hear and bless!
> Lest heaven's own palm droop in my hand,
> And pale among the saints I stand,
>   A saint companionless.

The parallelism between the death of Rosalind and the journey of her corpse to the hall of Courland and the death of Elaine and the journey of her corpse to Camelot, as detailed in one of Tennyson's Idylls, can hardly escape notice. Mrs. Browning, however, was first in the field, unless, indeed, the journey of the dead Rosalind was suggested by the voyage of the Lady of Shalott, which may, I think, be fairly excluded from the list of probabilities. There can, at all events, be no dispute as to the originality of Mrs. Browning in relation to the part played by the corpse. The dead Lady of Shalott has no scroll on breast or in hand, and the scroll was laid by Mrs. Browning on the breast of her Rosalind before the letter was put into the dead hand of Elaine by Tennyson. Rosalind's scroll, moreover, serves a more important purpose than Elaine's letter. Elaine comes to take farewell of Lancelot. She makes no complaint, utters no reproach, asks Lancelot to join others in praying for her soul as "a knight peerless." The conception of an appeal made by the dead to the living, as a means of producing a complete change and transformation in the latter, belongs exclusively to Mrs. Browning. The appeal of the dead Rosalind proves irresistible. The poet bows his face on the corpse in a paroxysm of anguish and remorse.

> 'Twas a dread sight to see them so—
> For the senseless corpse rocked to and fro
> With the wail of his living mind.

His "long-subjected humanness" asserted itself with lion-like strength, "and fiercely rent its tenement in a mortal agony."

> I tell you, friends, had you heard his wail,
> 'Twould haunt you in court and mart,
> And in merry feast until you set
> Your cup down to depart—
> That weeping wild of a reckless child
> From a proud man's broken heart.

Meanwhile the "worshipped earth and sky," the stars and hills for which he had renounced human fellowship, "looked on all indifferently." Finding no solace in these, he turned to his dead Rosalind and died upon her breast:

> For when they came at dawn of day
> To lift the lady's corpse away,
> Her bier was holding twain.

Tennyson, describing the temptation treated of in *The Palace of Art*, says that "he that shuts love out, in turn shall be shut out from love, and on her threshold lie howling in outer darkness." The words are an expressive statement of Mrs. Browning's thesis in *A Poet's Vow*. But there is a difference in the way in which, in the respective poems, the temptation is yielded to. The "sinful soul" of Tennyson's allegory turns from the crowd—from the nation—from the general mass of mankind, but by no means relinquishes humanity. She takes refuge in art, in literature, in philosophy. She dwells with the great poetic makers of all time. Sculpture and painting fill the corridors of her palace with images, and light up its walls with pictures. She hates mankind, but adores the select few who have risen above the multitude, and the very essence of her sin is the pride on which she values herself as a sister of these. Mrs. Browning's poet forsakes man altogether, his "systemed books" as well as his popular follies, his poems and pictures as well as his senates and market-places, and seeks, in the companionship of Nature, a sympathy more pure, lofty, and serene than humanity, high or low, can yield. Her poem, therefore, is the ethical complement of Tennyson's, and *The Palace of Art* and *A Poet's Vow* form between them an exhaustive treatment, under poetic symbols, of the cardinal sin of isolation from human interests, duties, affections, joys, and griefs.

CHAPTER IV.

THE ROMAUNT OF MARGRET—ISOBEL'S CHILD —THE ROMANCE OF THE SWAN'S NEST— BERTHA IN THE LANE.

THE *Romaunt of Margret* is cast, to some extent, in the mould of the old ballads,—to about the same extent as Rossetti's *Sister Helen*,—but it lacks the simplicity of the deep-thoughted harpers and minstrels whose reliques were collected by Bishop Percy and Walter Scott. It is a mysterious, painful, uncanny poem, suggestive of ghosts and haunted river-sides, and telling, dimly and eerily, a tale of love and suicide. A " fair ladye " sits by a river that runs by a hill and through forest trees, dreaming pleasantly of her lover. The darkness of night deepens the black of her hair, " and the pale moonlight on her forehead white like a spirit's hand is laid." Her shadow lies on the river, steady and changeless while the river never rests:

> Most like a trusting heart
> Upon a passing faith,—
> Or as, upon the course of life,
> The steadfast doom of death.

We now begin to feel that the forest is the scene of some "enchantment drear." The lady's shadow collects itself into a wraith or double.

> It shaketh without wind,
>   It parteth from the tide,
> It standeth upright in the cleft moonlight—
>   It sitteth at her side.
>
> Look in its face, ladye,
>   And keep thee from thy swound!
> With a spirit bold thy pulses hold,
>   And hear its voice's sound!
>
> For so will sound thy voice,
>   When thy face is to the wall!
> And such will be thy face, ladye,
>   When the maidens work thy pall!

The lady and her ghostly double engage in talk, and though it is difficult to assign a precise meaning to the utterances of the wraith, they imply that, for some too darkly-hinted reason, the lady has lost the supreme and trustful love of her brother, her sister, and her father, and that her chosen knight is dead. The wraith, after telling her that those of her own blood have ceased to love her, speaks of the absent knight:—

> He *loved* but only thee!
>   *That* love is transient, too,
> The wild hawk's bill doth dabble still
>   I' the mouth that vowed thee true.
> Will he open his dull eyes,
>   When tears fall on his brow?
> Behold, the death-worm to his heart
>   Is a nearer thing than thou.

Accepting these intimations of her other self, the lady decides that life is intolerable.

> Her face was on the ground—
>   None saw the agony!
> But the men at sea did that night agree
>   They heard a drowning cry.
> And when the morning brake,
>   Fast rolled the river's tide,
> With the green trees waving overhead,
>   And a white corse laid beside.

The gloomy intent of the whole poem seems to be suggested in the last four lines.

> O failing human love!
>   O light by darkness known!
> O false, the while thou treadest earth,
>   O deaf, beneath the stone!

Whether the pride of the baron, her father, in whose court are a hundred knights, had parted the lovers, we are not distinctly told. As much may, however, be inferred; for while the brother and sister weep for the lady and kiss her corpse, the baron stands "alone yet proudly" in his hall. Pride and death have triumphed over love. The poem displays imaginative power, but the machinery, though perhaps in keeping with that of the old folk-lore ballads, is grotesque. It is an attempt to realise in poetic form the semi-delirious dreamings of an unhappy lady before committing suicide; and it may be doubted whether such a subject was worthy of Mrs. Browning.

In *Isobel's Child* our woman-poet is again at her strongest. For torrent-like fulness of meaning, for rich and solemn swell of musical harmony, for the compression that betokens maturity of power, for truth of imaginative colouring, this poem is perhaps superior to anything we have yet examined of her work. She wrote it before her marriage, yet it seems safe to say that the emotions of maternity were never expressed with such impassioned tenderness.

The weary nurse has gone to rest, tired by an eight-day watch, and now Isobel takes her babe on her own knee, rejoicing inexpressibly in the thought that the fever is waning, that the child is sleeping well in the shadow of her smile. Outside, the sun is darkened as if in strange eclipse, the forest and the clouds are rent or tossed with storm, but the external noises only deepen the silent joy of the mother's soul.

> So motionless she sate,
> The babe asleep upon her knees,
> You might have dreamed their souls had gone
> Away to things inanimate,
> In such to live, in such to moan;
> And that their bodies had ta'en back,
> In mystic change, all silences
> That cross the sky in cloudy rack,
> Or dwell beneath the reedy ground
> In waters safe from their own sound.
> Only she wore
> The deepening smile I named before,
> And *that* a deepening love expressed—
> And who at once can love and rest?

Her smile was joyful in proportion to the anxiety she had suffered in the eight-day watch, which, indeed, had been "an eight-day weeping." The picture of the mother and the child—say, rather the group chiselled by fine words as if in vivid marble—is a thing to be remembered.

> Motionless she sate,
> Her hair had fallen by its weight
> On each side of her smile, and lay
> Very blackly on the arm
> Where the baby nestled warm,—
> Pale as baby carved in stone
> Seen by glimpses of the moon
> Up a dark cathedral aisle !
> But, through the storm, no moonbeam fell
> Upon the child of Isobel—
> Perhaps you saw it by the ray
> Alone of her still smile.

We now learn that, during the eight days of watching, Isobel had prayed importunately that her child might live. She had been bold in her prayer.

> Oh, take not, Lord, my babe away—
> Oh, take not to Thy songful heaven,
> The pretty baby Thou hast given.
> * * * * *
> Think, God among the cherubim,
> How I shall shiver every day
> In Thy June sunshine, knowing where
> The grave-grass keeps it from his fair
> Still cheeks! and feel at every tread
> His little body which is dead
> And hidden in the turfy fold,
> Doth make the whole warm earth a-cold!
> O God, I am so young, so young—
> I am not used to tears at nights
> Instead of slumber—nor to prayer
> With sobbing lips and hands outwrung!
> * * * * *
> Dear Lord, who spreadest out above
> Thy loving, transpierced hands to meet
> All lifted hearts with blessing sweet,—

> Pierce not my heart, my tender heart,
> Thou madest tender! Thou who art
> So happy in Thy heaven alway,
> Take not mine only bliss away!

Her petition is granted. The child is manifestly recovering. But, with a touch of the supernatural, which is well managed in the poem, the baby begins to speak to Isobel and she listens.

> O mother, mother, loose thy prayer!
>   Christ's name hath made it strong!
> It bindeth me, it holdeth me
> With its most loving cruelty
> From floating my new soul along
>   The happy, heavenly air!
> It bindeth me, it holdeth me
> In all this dark, upon this dull
>   Low earth, by only weepers trod!—
> It bindeth me, it holdeth me!
> Mine angel looketh sorrowful
>   Upon the face of God.

The child prevails. The prayer is recalled. When the nurse, awakening in the morning sun, looks to the mother, she sees the babe dead on Isobel's arm. She could utter no cry, so calm was the mother's face.

> "Wake, nurse!" the lady said:
> "*We* are waking—he and I—
> I on earth, and he in sky!
> And thou must help me to o'erlay
> With garment white this little clay,
> Which needs no more our lullaby.
>
> I changed the cruel prayer I made,
> And bowed my meekened face, and prayed
> That God would do His will! and thus
> He did it, nurse! He parted *us*.
> And His sun shows victorious

> The dead calm face, and I am calm;
> And Heaven is hearkening a new psalm."

Resigned to wait until she shall meet her child in heaven, she addresses herself to her earthly duties, satisfied that God's will is more loving than hers.

The Romance of the Swan's Nest is a brilliant little poem, delicately light in its pictorial touch, pensively gay in its musical cadence. It opens with a vignette portrait of the heroine.

> Little Ellie sits alone
> 'Mid the beeches of a meadow,
> By a stream-side, on the grass,
> And the trees are showering down
> Doubles of their leaves in shadow,
> On her shining face and hair.
>
> She has thrown her bonnet by;
> And her feet she has been dipping
> In the shallow water's flow—
> Now she holds them nakedly
> In her hands, all sleek and dripping,
> While she rocketh to and fro.

As she rocks, she thinks of a swan's nest, with two precious eggs, which she has found among the reeds. A vision of the knight who is to be her lover rises before her. He will be a noble fellow, playing on the lute to the enchantment of ladies, smiting with the sword to the astonishment of men; and his steed is to be a red-roan steed of steeds, shod in silver and housed in blue. This paragon is to be sent by little Ellie "to put away all wrong," and to empty the quiver of the wicked. Three times he is to send his foot-page to Ellie for a word of comfort. She is to be coy and proud. The first time she will send him a white rose-bud; the second a glove; at the third time of asking, she will permit him to return and claim her hand. When he has come, and they are man and wife, she will show him the swan's nest among the reeds. Mrs. Browning shall tell the rest.

> Little Ellie, with her smile
> Not yet ended, rose up gaily,—
>   Tied the bonnet, donned the shoe—
>   And went homeward, round a mile,
> Just to see, as she did daily,
>   What more eggs were with the *two*.
>
>   Pushing through the elm-tree copse,
> Winding by the stream, light-hearted,
>   Where the osier pathway leads—
>   Past the boughs she stoops—and stops:
> Lo! the wild swan had deserted—
>   And a rat had gnawed the reeds.
>
>   Ellie went home sad and slow.
> If she found the lover ever,
>   With his red-roan steed of steeds,
>   Sooth I know not! but I know
> She could never show him—never,
>   That swan's nest among the reeds!

Bertha in the Lane calls for no special remark. The heroine dies of a broken heart, because her lover forsakes her for her younger sister. The tone of the poem is oppressively sad. In Bertha the poet depicts one of those weak, gentle, beautiful, ill-starred persons, who seem born to make way for happier and more potent natures. The following lines describe the

Bertha in the Lane.

character with psychological exactness and fine poetic imagery. It is Bertha who speaks, addressing the sister who has been preferred by the lover.

> I had died, dear, all the same—
> Life's long, joyous, jostling game
> Is too loud for my meek shame.
>
> We are so unlike each other,
>   Thou and I, that none could guess
> We were children of one mother,
>   But for mutual tenderness.
> Thou art rose-lined from the cold,
> And meant, verily, to hold
> Life's pure pleasures manifold.
>
> I am pale as crocus grows
>   Close beside a rose-tree's root!
> Whosoe'er would reach the rose,
>   Treads the crocus underfoot—
> *I*, like May-bloom on thorn-tree—
> *Thou*, like merry summer bee!
> Fit, that *I* be plucked for *thee*.

CHAPTER V.

HER PHILANTHROPIC POETRY. THE RUNAWAY SLAVE; THE CRY OF THE CHILDREN.

MRS. BROWNING, as is attested by every one of her works from which I have quoted, wrote not under the impulse of mere art-enthusiasm, but in the expression of emotions and convictions intensely her own. It was natural for such a poet that the great agitations of her time should draw responses from her heart, and that, when she sympathised with any movement for the bettering of mankind, and the vanquishing of wrong, she should make her voice heard in tones of thrilling melody above the clamours of the conflict.

In the poem entitled *The Runaway Slave at Pilgrim's Point*, she tells, in her own rapid, vehement, suggestive manner, a tale of infinite cruelty and wrong inflicted upon a woman slave. The piece is thrown into the form of a monologue, the injured slave being the narrator of her own sorrows. She finds in her black colour an inevitable and terrible curse, and wonders why, since the dark bird sings merrily in the wood, and the darkest night is passed

over by the sweetest stars, black human creatures
should seem so God-forsaken.

> Indeed we live beneath the sky,
>   That great smooth Hand of God stretched out
> On all His children fatherly
>   To save them from the dread and doubt
> Which would be, if, from this low place,
> All opened straight up to His face
>   Into the grand eternity.
>
> And still God's sunshine and His frost,
>   They make us hot, they make us cold,
> As if we were not black and lost:
>   And the beasts and birds, in wood and fold
> Do fear and take us for very men!
> Could the weep-poor-will or the cat of the glen
>   Look into my eyes and be bold?

But though the blue sky was above her head, "like God's great pity," yet, when she and the slave youth whom she loved prayed to God, no dew of blessing had descended on them.

> I look on the sky and the sea,
>   We were two to love, and two to pray,—
> Yes, two, O God, who cried to Thee,
>   Though nothing didst Thou say.
> Coldly Thou sat'st behind the sun!
> And now I cry who am but one,
>   How wilt Thou speak to-day?

They two were black. They "had no claim to love and bliss." The oppressors "wrung" her cold hand out of his.

> They dragged him—where? I crawled to touch
>   His blood's mark in the dust!

To the murder of her lover " a deeper wrong " was added.

> Mere grief's too good for such as I,
> So the white men brought the shame, ere long
> To strangle the sob of my agony.

She had a child. Its whiteness pained her. When she glanced on its face she saw a look that made her mad,—

> The *master's* look, that used to fall
> On my soul like his lash, or worse.

In her madness she was prompted to curse it; to save it from her curse, she strangled it. She wandered in the forest till her madness passed away, and then the pursuers came upon her.

> I am not mad: I am black.
> I see you staring in my face—
> I know you staring, shrinking back—
> Ye are born of the Washington-race:
> And this land is the free America:
> And this mark on my wrist (I prove what I say)
> Ropes tied me up here to the flogging-place.

She dies cursing the white men in her " broken heart's disdain," after calling the slaves to rise and end what she has begun. This is an appalling story, almost too haggard and hideous in its details for art, but not too strongly coloured for reality, and not, I think, open to legitimate objection as a contribution to the literature of slave emancipation. If the anger of the world is to be invoked against a wrong, especially when that wrong is so ancient and so firmly buttressed about by interests as was American slavery, its features must be portrayed in all their blackness.

I am not prepared to say that there is enough of intrinsic beauty, music, and power in this terrible poem to ensure its long outliving the baneful system which it did its part to overthrow; but there is nothing from Mrs. Browning's pen more inspired in its melody, or more glorious in its tragic beauty and pathos,—more instinct with what Mr. Ruskin calls the stuff of immortality,—than that to which I next call the reader's attention. I refer to the celebrated piece in which she lent her advocacy to the cause of the young creatures worn to an untimely death in English factories. The *Cry of the Children* is as sure to live as Hood's *Song of the Shirt* or *Bridge of Sighs*. It is composed in stanzas twelve lines long, each of them coming like a great wave of rhythmic sound, burdened with meaning and appeal, and breaking with a power that must shake the flintiest heart. In the first of them we feel that Mrs. Browning is in her highest mood, like that of Deborah when she called upon Israel, or that of the Delphic priestess when the temple rang with the clamorous earnestness of her message.

> Do ye hear the children weeping, O my brothers,
>   Ere the sorrow comes with years ?
> They are leaning their young heads against their mothers,—
>   And *that* cannot stop their tears.
> The young lambs are bleating in the meadows,
>   The young birds are chirping in the nest,
> The young fawns are playing with the shadows,
>   The young flowers are blowing towards the west—

> But the young, young children, O my brothers,
>   They are weeping bitterly!—
> They are weeping in the playtime of the others,
>   In the country of the free.

They look up "with their pale and sunken faces," and the anguish of hoary age "draws and presses down the cheeks of infancy." They have taken but few steps on the earth, yet they are already weary, and their "grave-rest" is far to seek. They sometimes, indeed, die when still children; but why, they ask, should they wish to live? When "little Alice" died, they looked into the pit in which she was laid, and saw no room in it for work. None would cry to her, as she slept in that bed, "Get up, little Alice! it is day." If they saw her, they would not know her, for she has been long enough away from work to let a smile grow upon her face. "It is good when it happens," say the children, "that we die before our time." In vain you call them into the fields to play.

> "For oh," say the children, "we are weary,
>   And we cannot run or leap—
> If we cared for any meadows, it were merely
>   To drop down in them and sleep.
> Our knees tremble sorely in the stooping—
>   We fall upon our faces trying to go;
> And, underneath our heavy eyelids drooping,
>   The reddest flower would look as pale as snow.
> For all day we drag our burden tiring
>   Through the coal-dark underground—
> Or, all day, we drive the wheels of iron
>   In the factories round and round.

> "For, all day the wheels are droning, turning—
>   Their wind comes in our faces—
> Till our hearts turn—our heads, with pulses burning,
>   And the walls turn in their places—
> Turns the sky in the high window blank and reeling—
>   Turns the long light that drops adown the wall—
> Turn the black flies that crawl along the ceiling—
>   All are turning, all the day, and we with all—
> And all day the iron wheels are droning;
>   And sometimes we could pray,
> 'O ye wheels' (breaking out in a mad moaning)
>   'Stop! be silent for to-day!'"

Vain, also, is it to tell the children to pray. The metallic motion and clang around them make their voices inaudible to the men who are near them, and how could God hear? Two words only they remember in the nature of prayer, and these—"Our Father"—they utter at midnight as a charm. Mrs. Browning informs us in a footnote that this was an historical fact. If God heard the words, He would surely, think the little ones, send them some assuagement of their anguish.

> "But no!" say the children, weeping faster,
>   "He is speechless as a stone;
> And they tell us of His image is the master
>   Who commands us to work on."
> "Go to!" say the children,—"up in heaven,
>   Dark, wheel-like, turning clouds are all we find.
> Do not mock us; grief has made us unbelieving—
>   We look up for God, but tears have made us blind."
> Do you hear the children weeping and disproving,
>   O my brothers, what ye preach?
> For God's possible is taught by His world's loving—
>   And the children doubt of each.

It is some consolation, after reading these terrible

lines, to know that, in this case also, Mrs. Browning's words were not thrown away, and that the imperious cry of England's relenting heart quelled and overcame that false and remorseless logic—false because inhuman — which would deliver over children to the taskmaster, secure that mere considerations of the taskmaster's interest would sufficiently protect them.

CHAPTER VI.

LYRIC PENCILLINGS.

WITH a sense of relief, however, we turn from these melancholy strains to such bright poetic pencillings as *A Child Asleep*, *The Sea-Mew*, and *To Flush, My Dog*. In all of these there is an undertone of pathos, but no more than suffices to give tone and modulation to their delicate mirthfulness. The sleeping child is a subject that has often been attempted both in sculpture and in painting. No hand has touched it with more tender felicity than Mrs. Browning's.

> How he sleepeth; having drunken
>   Weary childhood's mandragore!
> From his pretty eyes have sunken
>   Pleasures to make room for more—
> Sleeping near the wither'd nosegay which he pulled the day before.
>
> Nosegays! leave them for the waking:
>   Throw them earthward where they grew.
> Dim are such beside the breaking
>   Amaranths he looks unto—
> Folded eyes see brighter colours than the open ever do.
>
> Heaven-flowers, rayed by shadows golden
>   From the palms they sprang beneath,
> Now perhaps divinely holden,
>   Swing against him in a wreath—
> We may think so from the quickening of his bloom and of his breath.

The light and joyful spirit of the verses seems to be associated rather with fancy than with earnest imagination, but fancy attains to something of solemnity and sacredness when it takes such flights as we have in the two verses that follow.

> Softly, softly! make no noises!
>   Now he lieth dead and dumb—
> Now he hears the angels' voices
>   Folding silence in the room—
> Now he muses deep the meaning of the Heaven-words as they come.
>
> Speak not! He is consecrated—
>   Breathe no breath across his eyes.
> Lifted up and separated
>   On the hand of God he lies,
> In a sweetness beyond touching,—held in cloistral sanctities.

The Sea-Mew is one of the most perfect in form of Mrs. Browning's productions. It is a brief ballad-lyric narrating how the young sea-mew lay dreaming on the waves, "and throbbing to the throbbing sea," how he was carried to a garden, and how he died there. I quote three of the verses.

> We were not cruel, yet did sunder
> His white wing from the blue waves under,
>   And bound it, while his fearless eyes
>   Shone up to ours in calm surprise,
> As deeming us some ocean wonder!
>
> We bore our ocean bird unto
> A grassy place, where he might view
>   The flowers that curtsey to the bees,
>   The waving of the tall green trees,
> The falling of the silver dew.

> But flowers of earth were pale to him
> Who had seen the rainbow fishes swim;
> And when earth's dew around him lay,
> He thought of ocean's wingèd spray,
> And his eye waxèd sad and dim.

With the human touch the human agony passed upon him, and looking up to the waveless sky of blue he died.

Flush, a dog presented to Mrs. Browning by her friend, Miss Mitford, was her faithful attendant in the sick-room during a long illness. It belonged, Mrs. Browning tells us in a footnote, to a beautiful race of dogs, rendered famous by Miss Mitford in England and America. "The Flushes," she adds, "have their laurels as well as the Cæsars,—the chief difference (at least the very head and front of it) consisting, perhaps, in the bald head of the latter under the crown." The picture of her own Flush places the dog visibly before us.

> Like a lady's ringlets brown,
> Flow thy silken ears adown
>   Either side demurely
> Of thy silver-suited breast,
> Shining out from all the rest
>   Of thy body purely.

> Darkly brown thy body is,
> Till the sunshine striking this
>   Alchemise its dulness,
> When the sleek curls manifold
> Flash all over into gold
>   With a burnished fulness.

> Underneath my stroking hand,
> Startled eyes of hazel bland
>   Kindling, growing larger,
> Up thou leapest with a spring,
> Full of prank and curveting,
>   Leaping like a charger.
>
> Leap! thy broad tail waves a light;
> Leap! thy slender feet are bright,
>   Canopied in fringes.
> Leap—those tasselled ears of thine
> Flicker strangely, fair and fine,
>   Down their golden inches.

These are admirably graphic lines,—worthy of being set beside those in which Burns commemorates his "friend and comrade" Luath. But the climax of interest, beauty, and pathos is not reached until the poet describes the service rendered by Flush in her sick-room.

> Other dogs may be thy peers
> Haply in these drooping ears,
>   And this glossy fairness.
>
> But of *thee* it shall be said,
> This dog watched beside a bed
>   Day and night unweary,—
> Watched within a curtained room,
> Where no sunbeam brake the gloom
>   Round the sick and dreary.
>
> Other dogs in thymy dew
> Tracked the hares and followed through
>   Sunny moor or meadow—
> This dog only crept and crept
> Next a languid cheek that slept,
>   Sharing in the shadow.

> And this dog was satisfied
> If a pale thin hand would glide
> Down his dew-laps sloping,—
> Which he pushed his nose within,
> After,—platforming his chin
> On the palm left open.

Among the dogs of literature, Flush will have a place of honour till the English language is forgotten. In the long illness of the poet, which originated in the rupture of a blood-vessel in her lungs, and was brought to a dangerous crisis at Torquay by the drowning of her favourite brother, whose boat was upset before her eyes, Flush contributed more perhaps than Plato and Æschylus, whose works would be thrust beneath the pillow to escape the prying glance of her physician, to cheer her spirits and restore her health.

CHAPTER VII.

LADY GERALDINE'S COURTSHIP.

IF Mrs. Browning's intelligent readers were asked to name her most characteristic poem, they would probably fix upon *Lady Geraldine's Courtship.* The choice would lie between that and *The Duchess May.* The finest wine of her genius, the intensest elixir of her poetic sympathy, the very essence of her womanly pride, and not less of her womanly ecstasy of self-surrendering humility, as well as her most original imagery, puissant thought, and splendid language, are present in both poems. I should not, for my own part, undertake to say which of the two is the more characteristic; but I should pronounce it impossible for any one to have a right insight into these two without possessing a fairly accurate idea of the distinctive character of her genius.

Lady Geraldine's Courtship belongs to the same class of poems as *Locksley Hall.* It is a story of love, and its love-story is delineated in connection with certain social truths or doctrines which the poet intends to teach. Of these doctrines little is expressly said, but it is nevertheless from the bearing of the poems upon them that their chief significance is derived. *Lady Geraldine's Courtship* and *Locksley Hall* are profoundly democratic in spirit. They belong to the period when the atmosphere of our island was still tingling with the Reform Bill agitation; when the hope and aspiration of ardent spirits were stirred with visions of class reconciled to class; of high and low, rich and poor, warming towards each other in the glow of a common brotherhood; of all distinctions being effaced except those between honest men and knaves, between base men and honourable. "Cursed," says Tennyson in *Locksley Hall*, "be the social lies that warp us from the living truth;" "cursed be the gold that gilds the straitened forehead of the fool." Love, asserting its God-given power and right to make two hearts happy, and to make their love, united in marriage, a fountain of home-happiness for many, is in that poem baffled by worldly pride. In *Lady Geraldine's Courtship* the same doctrine of the right divine of love to set its foot on the neck of pride is poetically preached in Mrs. Browning's manner. Let us read, to begin with, her sketch of the personages who are the sole actors in the tale, no other persons being so much as named, although the shadowy presence of some others is indicated.

> There's a lady—an Earl's daughter,—she is proud and she is noble,
>   And she treads the crimson carpet, and she breathes the perfumed air,
> And a kingly blood sends glances up her princely eye to trouble,
>   And the shadow of a monarch's crown is softened in her hair.

She has halls among the woodlands, she has castles by the breakers,
   She has farms and she has manors, she can threaten and command,
And the palpitating engines snort in steam across her acres,
   As they mark upon the blasted heaven the measure of the land.

There are none of England's daughters who can show a prouder presence;
   Upon princely suitors praying she has looked in her disdain:
She was sprung of English nobles, I was born of English peasants;
   What was I that I should love her—save for competence to pain?

I was only a poor poet, made for singing at her casement,
   As the finches or the thrushes, while she thought of other things.
Oh, she walked so high above me, she appeared to my abasement,
   In her lovely silken murmur, like an angel clad in wings!

These words purport to be part of a letter addressed by the poet, Bertram, to his "friend and fellow-student." He proceeds with his description of the lady, and at last names her.

Many vassals bow before her as her carriage sweeps their doorways;
   She has blest their little children,—as a priest or queen were she!
Far too tender, or too cruel far, her smile upon the poor was,
   For I thought it was the same smile which she used to smile on *me*.

She has voters in the Commons, she has lovers in the palace—
   And of all the fair Court-ladies, few hath jewels half as fine:
Oft the prince has named her beauty 'twixt the red wine and the chalice:
   Oh, and what was *I* to love her? my beloved, my Geraldine!

Being a poet, however, he "could not choose but love her," since poets are born to love all things set above them, all things good and fair, and the Muses are nymphs of the mountain, not of the valley. As a well-reputed poet, he was admitted to rich men's tables, but even the courtesies he experienced made him feel the distance that separated him from his patrons. They talked of their moors, whispering now and then in insolently condescending terms of their plebeian guest.

Quite low-born! self-educated! somewhat gifted though by Nature,—
   And we make a point of asking him,—of being very kind :
You may speak, he does not hear you ; and, besides, he writes no satire,—
   All these serpents kept by charmers leave their natural sting behind.

The scorn of these worldlings he encountered with equal scorn, and might have repaid it in glance or word, if Lady Geraldine had not suddenly stepped into the circle and invited him to Wycombe Hall, her mansion in Sussex. This invitation he accepted. Results followed.

Oh, the blessed woods of Sussex, I can hear them still around me,
   With their leafy tide of greenery still rippling up the wind!
Oh, the cursed woods of Sussex! where the hunter's arrow found me,
   When a fair face and a tender voice had made me mad and blind!

The second of these lines is exceedingly fine; but, on the whole, they recall too vividly the change that passed on the moorland and the shore—" Oh, the dreary, dreary moorland! Oh, the barren, barren shore ! "—when Amy, in *Locksley Hall*, became unkind. The parallel is by no means exact, yet the suggestion of Tennyson's passage is inevitable.

A few stanzas further on, we meet with another Tennysonian parallel. Bertram describes Geraldine as he saw her when first her beauty compelled him to love.

Thus, her foot upon the new-mown grass—bareheaded—with the flowing
   Of the virginal white vesture gathered closely to her throat,
With the golden ringlets in her neck just quickened by her going,
   And appearing to breathe sun for air and doubting if to float,—
With a branch of dewy maple, which her right hand held above her,
   And which trembled a green shadow in betwixt her and the skies,—
As she turned her face in going, thus, she drew me on to love her,
   And to worship the divineness of the smile hid in her eyes.

The lines in Tennyson, of which these remind me, occur in *The Gardener's Daughter*.

He cried, "Look! look!" Before he ceased I turned,
And, ere a star can wink, beheld her there.
For up the porch there grew an Eastern rose,
That, flowering high, the last night's gale had caught,
And blown across the walk. One arm aloft—
Gowned in pure white, that fitted to the shape—
Holding the bush, to fix it back, she stood.
A single stream of all her soft brown hair
Pour'd on one side: the shadow of the flowers
Stole all the golden gloss, and, wavering
Lovingly lower, trembled on her waist—
Ah, happy shade—and still went wavering down,
But, ere it touched a foot that might have danced
The green sward into greener circles, dipt,
And mixed with shadows of the common ground!
But the full day dwelt on her brows, and sunn'd
Her violet eyes, and all her Hebe bloom,
And doubled his own warmth against her lips,
And on the bounteous wave of such a breast
As never pencil drew. Half light, half shade,
She stood, a sight to make an old man young.

Is it a mere trick of the associative faculty which connects these two passages—Mrs. Browning's and Tennyson's? I should not allege that Mrs. Browning was conscious of imitating; and the passages might be cited to illustrate the difference in the literary execution of the two poets: Tennyson minute, patient, copious in detail, laying on touch after touch with the calmness of a painter in his studio, Mrs. Browning giving comparatively few touches, and throwing these upon the canvas with impetuous, hurrying speed. Nevertheless, the decisive feature in both descriptions is the branch held in the hand of the lady; and I cannot help thinking that, whether Mrs. Browning knew it or not, the maple branch was held aloft by Geraldine, because the rose branch had been held aloft by Alice.

Lady Geraldine frequently favoured Bertram with her conversation, and their talk was apt to turn on high themes, such as the relation of "symbols" to their "essential meaning." They were evidently disposed to agree with the author of *Sartor Resartus*, that the truth embodied in symbols by the men of old has in our time outgrown, in various instances, the embodying sign. Bertram, a poet of Radical tendencies, thinks that we have too much symbol,—more of symbol than of substance. Geraldine admits that, wherever you go in these British Islands, you find names for things, shows for actions, money passing itself off for human worth; but she will not grant that all has, as yet, "run to symbol." Were that the case, the world would be a book not worth reading, which she would toss aside. Talk like this, more instructive than exhilarating, was diversified by lighter entertainment.

Sometimes on the hillside, while we sate down in the gowans,
  With the forest green behind us, and its shadow cast before,
And the river running under, and across it from the rowans
  A brown partridge whirring near us till we felt the air it bore,—

There, obedient to her praying, did I read aloud the poems
  Made to Tuscan flutes, or instruments more various of our own;
Read the pastoral parts of Spenser—or the subtle interflowings
  Found in Petrarch's sonnets—here's the book—the leaf is folded down!

Or at times a modern volume,—Wordsworth's solemn-thoughted idyl,
  Howitt's ballad-verse, or Tennyson's enchanted reverie,—
Or from Browning some "Pomegranate," which, if cut deep down the middle,
  Shows a heart within blood-tinctured, of a veined humanity!

He describes her talk, which was gravely gay and sportively earnest, the root striking deep into sense and meaning, as if "to justify the foliage and the waving flowers above." She was inclined to agree with Bertram that we people of the nineteenth century, with our science and our engines, think too much of ourselves, and fancy that we are more in advance of our fathers than may really be the case. Four noble stanzas occur here, noble at once in thought and imagination, on which a long essay might be written without exhausting their wealth of suggestion.

And her custom was to praise me when I said,—The age culls
  simples,
  With a broad clown's back turned broadly to the glory of the
    stars.
We are gods by our own reck'ning, and may well shut up the
  temples,
  And wield on, amid the incense-steam, the thunder of our cars.

For we throw out acclamations of self-thanking, self-admiring,
  With, at every mile run faster, "O the wondrous, wondrous age!"
Little thinking if we work our SOULS as nobly as our iron,
  Or if angels will commend us at the goal of pilgrimage.

Why, what *is* this patient entrance into Nature's deep resources,
  But the child's most gradual learning to walk upright without
    bane?
When we drive out, from the cloud of steam, majestical white
  horses,
  Are we greater than the first men who led black ones by the
    mane?
If we trod the deeps of ocean, if we struck the stars in rising,
  If we wrapped the globe intensely with one hot electric breath,
'Twere but power within our *tether*—no new spirit-power com-
  prising—
  And in life we were not greater men, nor bolder men in death.

A grand thought, and as true as it is grand! The scientific achievement of our time, magnificent as it has been in its own field, must, if it is to be of the highest value, be but a prelude to those spiritual searchings which alone are distinctive of mankind. In the cultivation of those physical sciences whose aim and end is to increase the convenience of life,—to supply the wants of the body and exercise the faculties of the brain,—we do nothing different in kind, though of course immensely different in degree, from what the chaffinch does in building its nest. Our "tether" is

longer than the chaffinch's, but if we know nothing
except what physical science reveals to us, we have no
"spirit-power," and are no nearer the Eternal and the
Divine. Mrs. Browning clearly agrees with Tennyson that physical science, be its contributions to our
bodily service what they may, cannot satisfy the spirit
of man; and the experience of our age, which, with
all its engines and all its luxuries, speaking across
oceans and piercing mountains, is infinitely sad,
appears to confirm this view of the case. Atheism
now loudly proclaims itself a doctrine of despair.
Shelley's dawn-dream of a happy earth, the "reality
of heaven," has been succeeded by the clamorous
anguish that announces our world as the reality of hell.

Bertram loved Geraldine, but did not permit himself
to believe that he did so with any "idiot hope" of ever
possessing her. The stag, however, vainly tries to go
on grazing with a great gun-wound in his throat. It
"reels with sudden moan." So did Bertram. What
brought matters to a crisis was that he happened,
being forced to it by circumstances, to overhear a
haughty nobleman make a proposal of marriage to the
lady. She receives the suitor with coldness, but, in
repelling him, says something which stings Bertram
to madness. He whom she marries shall, she declares,
be noble and rich, and she will "never blush to think
how he was born." In other words, interprets the
agitated Bertram, she will marry no plebeian, she can
respect only rank and wealth, and as I have neither
purse nor pedigree, she scorns to look at me. "Mad"

or "inspired" by this persuasion—he gives us leave
to choose which of these epithets we think most
appropriate to his state of mind, and I unhesitatingly
choose the former—he dashed into the lady's presence and made a few observations. In the course of
these, he "plucked up her social fictions" and " trod
them down with words of shaming." A sample of
what he said is included in the letter to his friend
and fellow-student.

" For myself I do not argue," said I, " though I love you, madam,
  But for better souls that nearer to the height of yours have
      trod—
And this age shows, to my thinking, still more infidels to Adam,
  Than directly, by profession, simple infidels to God.

" Learn more reverence, madam, not for rank or wealth—*that*
      needs no learning!
  That comes quickly—quick as sin does! ay, and culminates in
      sin ;
But for Adam's seed, MAN! Trust me, 'tis a clay above your
      scorning,
  With God's image stamped upon it, and God's kindly breath
      within.

" Have you any answer, madam? If my spirit were less earthy—
  If its instrument were gifted with a better silver string—
I would kneel down where I stand, and say—Behold me! I am
      worthy
  Of thy loving, for I love thee! I am worthy as a king.

" As it is your ermined pride, I swear, shall feel this stain upon
      her,
  That I, poor, weak, tost with passion, scorned by me and you
      again,
Love you, madam—dare to love you—to my grief and your dis-
      honour—
  To my endless desolation, and your impotent disdain!"

At last he stopped. She looked up, with wonder and tears in her eyes, and said only "Bertram!" Thereupon he fainted, and when he came to himself he was in his own room, and sought relief to his feelings by expressing them in the letter into which we have been looking. That finished, Mrs. Browning herself takes up the tale.

As Bertram leant backward in his chair, his lips still quivering with love and grief, he became aware of a vision of a lady, first standing silent between the purple lattice-curtains, then gradually approaching him. The form, the features, the eye, the brow, the lip were Geraldine's, but he could not believe that they were corporeal.

Said he—"Wake me by no gesture,—sound of breath or stir of gesture;
Let the blessed apparition melt not yet to its divine!
No approaching—hush! no breathing! or my heart must swoon to death in
The too utter life thou bringest—O thou dream of Geraldine!"

Ever, evermore the while in a slow silence she kept smiling—
But the tears ran over lightly from her eyes, and tenderly;
" Dost thou, Bertram, truly love me? Is no woman far above me
Found more worthy of thy poet-heart than such a one as *I?* "

*   *   *   *   *   *

Softened, quickened to adore her, on his knees he fell before her,
And she whispered low in triumph—"It shall be as I have sworn!
Very rich he is in virtues,—very noble,—noble, certes;
And I shall not blush in knowing that men call him lowly born."

These lovers were presumably married, and we are free to suppose that they lived happily ever after;

but, if they did, Bertram must have been a very true poet indeed, and Lady Geraldine an uncommonly sensible woman. The piece, however, is not to be tried by prosaic rules. It is poetry, and not prose. You do not expect the cloud-flocks of the West Wind, that look so beautiful on the blue fields of the sky, to yield you woollen coats and saddle of mutton. *Lady Geraldine's Courtship* is steeped in melody,—the language, the imagery, the sentiment, the thought, all instinct with music, floating and flowing and rippling along in an element of liquid harmony and modulated brilliance.

CHAPTER VIII.

THE RHYME OF THE DUCHESS MAY.

WHILE declining to adjudicate between masterpieces, I confess that the poem which most closely connects itself with Mrs. Browning in my own mind—the poem on which my imagination dwells most wonderingly, and to which my heart clings most fondly—is *The Rhyme of the Duchess May*. Its blemishes are mere motes in the sunlight of its general power. Its artistic unity and completeness are not less remarkable than its strong drawing and vivid local colour. In this, as in other instances, the critic of Mrs. Browning is called to discriminate between two things: the realistic basis, and the imaginative form. No poet deals more realistically with passion than Mrs. Browning,—she feels and gives its living throb with the penetrating vehemence, the fiery tenderness of Burns; but the imaginative drapery in which she clothes her conceptions is apt to be looseflowing and gorgeous as mist kindled by lightnings and rent by storms. In the *Duchess May* the passion of wifely devotion is shown in its intensest yet most real fervour, triumphing in death, triumphing over death; but the imaginative form and covering in which this central passion is wrapped may be held to be somewhat wildly romantic.

The poem opens with the description of a country churchyard, in which the bell tolls slowly for the dead. Six willow trees grow on its north side, their shadows, as they rock solemnly in the wind, slanting across the graves. On the south and the west runs a small river, and through the willow branches you see hills, whence the river comes out of the distance. The poet sits amid the stillness of the graves, broken only by the knelling of the death-bell and the low voices of tree and river, and reads the "ancient rhyme," the "tale of life and sin," which follows. The effect of the tolling of the bell is aimed at by iteration, in each triplet, of the words, "Toll slowly."

We are at once hurried into the main current of interest. The Castle of Linteged rises suddenly before us, built from nothing by the wand of the poetical magician.

Down the sun dropt large and red, on the towers of Linteged,—
  Toll slowly.
Lance and spear upon the height, bristling strange in fiery light,
  While the castle stood in shade.
There the castle stood up black, with the red sun at its back,—
  Toll slowly.
Like a sullen smouldering pyre, with a top that flickers fire,
  When the wind is on its track.

That crimson background, with the tower cut out black against it, gives tone to the whole picture about to be unfolded. Not the pencil of Tintoret, not the pen of Dante, ever struck a truer note of imaginative harmony.

The Duchess May was the ward of her uncle, the old Earl of Leigh, who betrothed her in her childhood, for the sake of her gold, to his son, Lord Leigh. On coming of age she disliked the young lord, haughtily defied both him and his father, and bestowed her hand upon Sir Guy of Linteged. After the marriage the bridal train, pursued by the Leighs, rode off at midnight, through storm and rain, for the Castle of Linteged.

And the bridegroom led the flight on his red-roan steed of might,—
    Toll slowly.
And the bride lay on his arm, still, as if she felt no harm,
    Smiling out into the night.

These lines suggest the contrast of passion which, in its essential unity, delineates and defines the personality of the lady: defiance of kindred, scorn of all terrors of midnight and storm, dauntless courage and inflexible pride, where love is to be fought for and vindicated—perfect rest, submission, confidence, halcyon repose, as of a sea-bird on its native wave, as of a child on the breast of its mother, in the encircling arms of love accepted and returned.

Sir Guy and his wife reach the castle in safety, and for three months the very elixir of happiness is theirs. Then Lord Leigh—the rejected suitor—advances with an overpowering force, and, after a fortnight's siege, the castle is about to fall into his hands. Sordid and implacable, he will wed his betrothed, whether she loves him or hates him, and though he must reach her across the corpse of her present husband. In this she is resolved, through life and death, to foil him. Attired in purple robes, her ducal coronet on her brow, she looks down upon him from the wall, smiting him with her scorn.

Meanwhile Sir Guy has been superintending operations in the east tower, the highest of all. He sees that there is no hope, and, bethinking him that he alone stands between his wife and followers and safety, determines to put an end to his life. The Duchess May, he is content to think, though loving him truly, will get over her distress, soothed and well-entreated by his victorious foes, and will make shift with Lord Leigh after all. Is she not a woman?

She will weep her woman's tears, she will pray her woman's
    prayers,—
            Toll slowly;
But her heart is young in pain, and her hopes will spring again
            By the suntime of her years.

He binds his men by oath not to strike a blow that night. He then demands of his two faithfullest knights that, as a last service, they will lead the good steed, ridden by him in that unforgotten night-journey, up the turret-stair to the top of the east tower. His purpose is to mount the horse, make it leap from the wall, and thus to die on his war-steed. But the Duchess May has a heart as strong and proud as his. She will show her husband what lightnings may lurk amid the softness of a woman's tears. As the knights are goading the horse up the stair, she comes from her chamber and inquires into their errand. They tell her that, in an hour, the breach will be complete, and that her lord, wild with despair, is about to leap from the castle-wall. For a moment the sweetness of love past and the bitterness of present anguish overcome her: she bows her head, and tear after tear is heard falling on the ground. The knights, good-hearted but not gentle with the gentleness of chivalry, rudely assay to comfort her.

Get thee in, thou soft ladye!—here is never a place for thee!
   Toll slowly.
Braid thy hair and clasp thy gown, that thy beauty in its moan
   May find grace with Leigh of Leigh.

But her tears have fallen. She is herself again. Love's pride has set its iron heel on love's tenderness.

She stood up in bitter case, with a pale yet steady face,
   Toll slowly,
Like a statue thunderstruck, which, though quivering, seemed to look
   Right against the thunder-place.

She takes from the knights the rein of the horse. He now needs no goading.

Soft he neighed to answer her, and then followed up the stair,
   For the love of her sweet look.
On the east tower, high'st of all—there where never a hoof did fall,—
   Toll slowly,
Out they swept, a vision steady,—noble steed and lovely lady,
   Calm as if in bower or stall.

The wife has said in her heart that, if her husband leaps from the castle-wall, she will leap also. He endeavours, with frantic earnestness, to urge the horse over alone, but she will not quit her hold, and entreats him to take her with him. The breach falls in as she pleads, and the crash of wall and window, the shouts of foemen and the shrieks of the dying, rise in one roar around the pair. Then love prevails. In vain does Sir Guy wrench her small hands twice and thrice in twain. She clings to him as in a swoon of agonised determination. At last, when the horse, rearing on the edge of the precipitous battlement, could no longer be stopped, " she upsprang, she rose upright," she took her seat beside her husband.

And her head was on his breast, where she smiled as one at rest,—
   Toll slowly.
" Ring," she cried, " O vesper bell, in the beechwood's old chapelle!—
   But the passing bell rings best."
They have caught out at the rein, which Sir Guy threw loose—in vain,—
   Toll slowly.
For the horse in stark despair, with his front hoofs poised in air,—
   On the last verge rears amain.
Now he hangs the rocks between—and his nostrils curdle in,—
   Toll slowly,
Now he shivers head and hoof—and the flakes of foam fall off;
   And his face grows fierce and thin!
And a look of human woe from his staring eyes did go,—
   Toll slowly;
And a sharp cry uttered he, in a foretold agony
   Of the headlong death below.
And, " Ring, ring, thou passing bell," still she cried, "i' the old chapelle."
   Toll slowly.
Then back-toppling, crashing back,—a dead-weight flung out to wrack,—
   Horse and riders overfell.

No sterner realism than we have in this description is possible. The horse is frightfully, yet literally, true to life. Mrs. Browning once more proves that it is on the rugged crags of reality that imagination preens her wings for flight into the ideal. The human passion described is also, doubt it not, true to fact: Mrs. Browning's heart sympathetically thrilled with it, as she lit that smile on the face of the bride, sinking into the abyss of death in her husband's arms: with all her gentleness, Mrs. Browning could have smiled that smile, and leaped from that wall! Woman's love can make of the chariot of death a car of victory; amid the flames of the funeral pyre it can find the softest bed.

The Duchess May is one of the most admirably drawn figures that ever came from the pencil of art. Every line is so definite, yet so delicate in its curvature; every tint so clear and warm, yet so soft in its blending, so fine in its gradation. Her external attributes—her haughtiness, her beauty, her queenliness of mien and manner,—are touched in with the airy vividness of Scott: her inmost heart is laid bare,—her womanly tenderness, unfathomable as the blue wells of the sky, her womanly pride, her womanly ecstasy of self-sacrifice,—with, I speak deliberately, the power of a Shakespeare. In some respects she reminds one of Scott's Die Vernon, in some of Charlotte Brontë's Shirley. Had the Duchess May been the heroine of a three-volume novel, Shirley might indeed have played her part indifferently well, though some additional brightening, and softening, and warming—some tones and touches from Dorothea Brooke, the loveliest of all George Eliot's female characters—would have been required even by Charlotte Brontë's glorious Yorkshire lass. In one word, the Duchess May must be ranked with the Juliets and Desdemonas, beyond any flight of Walter Scott or Charlotte Brontë, and perhaps not to be adequately portrayed in any novel or drama with a pleasant ending, but only where tragedy in sceptred pall sweeps by.

The wild ancient Rhyme having sung itself out, we return to the calm of the churchyard, and are reminded of a serenity enveloping and subduing all passion. The poet fixes her eye on a little grave beneath a willow tree, on which is engraved an inscription stating that it is the grave of a child of three years. She draws, with rapid, vivid, graphic touches,—suggesting rather than detailing,—a contrast between the passage of the child-soul to heaven, encompassed by star-wheels and angel wings, and the passionate dashing up of those frantic lovers against the thick-bossed shield of God's judgment.

Now, your will is all unwilled—now, your pulses are all stilled,—
    Toll slowly.
Now, ye lie as meek and mild (whereso laid) as Maud the child,
    Whose small grave was lately filled.
Beating heart and burning brow, ye are very patient now,—
    Toll slowly.
And the children might be bold to pluck the king-cups from your mould,
    Ere a month had let them grow.

And so the poem ends in rest. The Rhyme, with its passion and its change, comes between the stillness before and after, like a meteor between two calm celestial spaces, leaving us in silent wonder at its artistic symmetry, its flawless unity, gazing up into the heavenly blue which overarches its volcanic fires.

CHAPTER IX.

POEMS OF AFFECTION.

AMONG rough-and-ready tests of greatness there is none, I think, more practically useful and trustworthy than that of width of range. The poet who has but one tune—one mood of feeling—one line of thought—one kind of imagery—one type of character—even though excellent within his restricted field, will hardly be pronounced a supreme singer. The uniformity of Dante's temper—ever intense, ever austere—detracts from his greatness, and is perhaps the chief reason why, though unsurpassed in particular delineation or in sheer imaginative might, he is admittedly a less poet than Homer or Shakespeare. We have seen that Mrs. Browning embraces in her poetic range at least two well-marked and diverse moods of thought and sympathy. She is passionately addicted to romance, and loves the pageantry of fancy and imagination; yet her tenderness, her capacity of interpreting, in fine sympathetic music, the simplest joys of the heart and the home, is as notable as her delight in those visions of the imagination in which romance verges on extravagance. By the tenderness of her genius she infused into the tale of Adam and Eve, and their expulsion from the Garden, a human interest that penetrates the heart far more thrillingly than the stately strain of Milton; and, in her shorter poems, we perpetually come upon lines and stanzas imbued with that domestic sentiment, that home-bred feeling, at which some sneer, but of which others are justly proud, as a characteristic of English society. It is in the pure sincerity of her heart that she asks,—

> What music certes can you find
> As soft as voices which are kind?

In the simply beautiful verses on the coronation and the wedding of Queen Victoria, she thus lays her poetical charge upon the bridegroom:

And since, Prince Albert, men have called thy spirit high and rare,
And true to truth and brave for truth as some at Augsburg were,—
We charge thee by thy lofty thoughts, and by thy poet-mind
Which not by glory and degree takes measure of mankind,
Esteem that wedded hand less dear for sceptre than for ring,
And hold her uncrowned womanhood to be the royal thing.

The verses on Napoleon are fine throughout, breathing a noble spirit of patriotism, which refuses to find satisfaction in the vengeance taken by England on a fallen foe; but perhaps their finest stanza is that in which the poet, though sternly declining to pronounce a judgment generally favourable to Napoleon, yet discerns one thing that entitles him to honour.

I do not praise this man: the man was flawed
For Adam—much more, Christ!—his knee, unbent—
His hand, unclean—his aspiration, pent
Within a sword-sweep—pshaw!—but since he had
The genius to be loved, why, let him have
The justice to be honoured in his grave.

She does not say very much—not *too* much, at all events—about her years of childhood; but the glimpses we have of them are always bright and always tender.

> Nine green years had scarcely brought me
>   To my childhood's haunted spring:
>   I had life like flowers and bees
>   In betwixt the country trees;
>   And the sun the pleasure taught me
>   Which he teacheth everything.
>
> If the rain fell, there was sorrow;—
>   Little head leant on the pane,
>   Little finger drawing down it
>   The long trailing drops upon it,—
>   And the " Rain, rain, come to-morrow,"
>   Said for charm against the rain.

Is not that a life-like picture,—touched in with the delicate accuracy of those wonderful old Dutchmen, the Mierises, Dows, Maases, and yet with something in it that reminds us of the sentiment of Edouard Frere? Still lovelier is the following:

> I hear the birthday's noisy bliss,
>   My sisters' woodland glee,—
>   My father's praise I did not miss,
>   When stooping down he cared to kiss
>   The poet at his knee.

I cannot remember any passage in which she has

spoken of her childhood except in terms of deep though pensive joyfulness; and the opening lines in *A Rhapsody of Life's Progress* may be looked upon as an authentic summing-up of its general impressions.

> We are born into life—it is sweet, it is strange!
> We lie still on the knee of a mild mystery,
>   Which smiles with a change!
> But we doubt not of changes, we know not of spaces,
> The heavens seem as near as our own mother's face is,
> And we think we could touch all the stars that we see.

Nor need we doubt that the affections formed in that early time retained their hold on her heart during life, and that it is her own feeling towards old friends that she expresses in this impassioned stanza from *Confessions*.

> The least touch of their hands in the morning, I keep day and night;
> Their least step on the stair still throbs through me, if ever so light;
> Their least gift, which they left to my childhood in long ago years,
> Is now turned from a toy to a relic, and gazed at through tears.

The *Lines on Mrs. Hemans*, those on *L. E. L.'s Last Question*, and those on *Cowper's Grave*, may be referred to as further illustrating Mrs. Browning's tenderness; but of these minor pieces, in none, perhaps, does she attain to so sweet a harmony of beauty and music as in that entitled *The Sleep*. In this poem—and the remark may be applied to these smaller pieces generally—the mannerism, which undeniably characterises her larger poems, falls almost wholly away, and she speaks in that common language which, if

only the poet can use it, lays a mightier spell upon the
heart than the most ingenious and surprising artifice.
The poem to which she prefixes those infinitely beautiful words of the psalm, "He giveth His beloved,
sleep," may be regarded as a hymn or paraphrase,
founded on the Scriptural expression. All my previous quotations from Mrs. Browning have been
fragmentary, and, therefore, necessarily inadequate, if
not unjust; for fragments cannot convey a just idea
of the unity of the wholes from which they are taken.
For this, if for no other reason, I shall quote the
poem entire.

>Of all the thoughts of God that are
>Borne inward unto souls afar,
> Along the Psalmist's music deep,
>Now tell me if that any is,
>For gift or grace, surpassing this—
> " He giveth His beloved, sleep " ?
>
>What would we give to our beloved?
>The hero's heart, to be unmoved,
> The poet's star-tuned harp, to sweep,
>The patriot's voice, to teach and rouse,
>The monarch's crown, to light the brows ?—
> " He giveth *His* beloved, sleep."
>
>What do we give to our beloved?
>A little faith all undisproved,
> A little dust to overweep,
>And bitter memories to make
>The whole earth blasted for our sake.
> " He giveth *His* beloved, sleep."
>
>" Sleep soft, beloved ! " we sometimes say,
>But have no tune to charm away
> Sad dreams that through the eyelids creep ;

But never doleful dream again
Shall break the happy slumber when
  ' He giveth *His* beloved, sleep."

O earth, so full of dreary noises!
O men, with wailing in your voices!
  O delvèd gold, the wailers heap!
O strife, O curse, that o'er it fall!
God strikes a silence through you all,
  And " giveth His beloved, sleep."

His dews drop mutely on the hill,
His cloud above it saileth still,
  Though on its slope men sow and reap.
More softly than the dew is shed,
Or cloud is floated overhead,
  " He giveth His beloved, sleep."

Yea, men may wonder when they scan
A living, thinking, feeling man
  Confirmed in such a rest to keep,
But angels say—and through the word
I think their happy smile is *heard*—
  " He giveth His beloved, sleep."

For me, my heart that erst did go
Most like a tired child at a show,
  That sees through tears the jugglers leap,—
Would now its wearied vision close,
Would childlike on His love repose,
  Who " giveth His beloved, sleep."

And, friends, dear friends,—when it shall be
That this low breath is gone from me,
  And round my bier ye come to weep,
Let one, most loving of you all,
Say, " Not a tear must o'er her fall—
  He giveth His beloved, sleep."

CHAPTER X.

HER LOVE SONNETS.

WE saw from a couple of lines in *Lady Geraldine's Courtship*, that the poetical genius of Robert Browning had made a deep impression upon Elizabeth Barrett Barrett. Whether those lines, which must have been gratifying in no ordinary degree to a young man, gave occasion to the acquaintance that sprang up between the two poets I cannot tell; but all the world knows that the mysteriously named *Portuguese Sonnets*, which appear at the end of the second volume of Mrs. Browning's Poems (edition of 1853), have for their subject the wooing and being wooed of those distinguished persons. The interest of the sonnets is enhanced by the circumstance that Miss Barrett passed a considerable number of years in a sickroom, and that the courtship was carried on during her period of convalescence. They are characterised by a profound sincerity, which may possibly have interfered with their literary elaboration, and their perfection as works of art; for the singer, conscious that she was not only dramatically, but actually in love, may have been afraid to give her imagination wing in the expression of her rapture.

In the first, the lover is represented as entering the shadowed room of the invalid while she muses tearfully on the darkness that has been cast by her malady across her life. She is aware that "a mystic shape" moves behind her, and draws her backward by the hair. The idea is, of course, taken from the famous passage in the Iliad, in which Athene takes Achilles gently, yet overpoweringly, by his yellow hair. The sonnet ends with these three lines:

> And a voice said in mastery, while I strove,
> "Guess now who holds thee?" "Death!" I said.
>   But, there
> The silver answer rang, "Not Death, but Love."

She is far from sure, however, that Love, not Death, will bear her from that chamber. In the next sonnet she tells her proposed deliverer that God may have said "Nay" to the deliverance, and that "Nay is worse from God than from all others." In the third she sinks to a lower vein, and reflects that her lover, exalted by his reputation, is in a higher social position than she.

> Thou, bethink thee, art
> A guest for queens to social pageantries,
> With gages from a hundred brighter eyes
> Than tears even can make mine, to ply thy part
> Of chief musician. What hast *thou* to do
> With looking from the lattice-lights at me,
> A poor, tired, wandering singer?

Continuing in this mood, she tells him, in plain terms, that she cannot smile upon him. "Stand further off, then. Go!" She reiterates the command in another sonnet; but confesses that she will never again be as she was before; never will she lift her hand so serenely in the sunshine as when she had not yet felt the touch of his palm upon it. Her determination, of course, does not prove irrevocable. We learn, in the seventh of the series, that, since she heard "the footsteps" of her lover's "soul" steal between her and death, she has been "caught up into love and taught the whole of life in a new rhythm." The "cup of dole" which God had given her has become sweet.

> The names of country, heaven, are changed away
> For where thou art or shalt be, there or here;
> And this—this lute and song—loved yesterday,
> (The singing angels know) are only dear,
> Because thy name moves right in what they say.

Clearly there is some hope for a lover whose lady says this. In the ninth she recurs to her unworthiness. She will not soil his purple with her dust. She cannot deny, however, that she loves him. This is a confession of some importance, and we are not surprised to find that she dwells on it a little. In the tenth sonnet she plucks up heart considerably, reflecting that her love qualifies her unworthiness; and a noble poem, with true love beating like a melodious pulse in every line, is the result.

> Yet, love, mere love, is beautiful indeed
> And worthy of acceptation. Fire is bright,
> Let temple burn, or flax—an equal light
> Leaps in the flame from cedar-plank or weed.
> And love is fire: and when I say at need

> *I love thee*—mark!—*I love thee!*—in thy sight
> I stand transfigured, glorified aright,
> With conscience of the new rays that proceed
> Out of my face toward thine. There's nothing low
> In love, when love the lowest: meanest creatures
> Who love God, God accepts while loving so.
> And what I *feel*, across the inferior features
> Of what I *am*, doth flash itself, and show
> How that great work of Love enhances Nature's.

These lines will recall to many the parallel passage in *In Memoriam*, in which Tennyson, while confessing his inability to meet his Arthur on a level of intellectual equality, asserts the greatness of his love.

> I loved thee, spirit, and love, nor can
> The soul of Shakespeare love thee more.

There is no reason, however, to doubt that emotional power is normally, though perhaps not invariably, proportioned to intellectual power, and that only a Shakespeare could either think or love like Shakespeare. The lady continues to betray something of coyness. "I stand unwon, however wooed." She loves, but renounces. She may as well tell him, nevertheless, on what grounds, if he must love her, she chooses to be loved. A delicately beautiful sonnet carries this love-message.

> If thou must love me, let it be for naught
> Except for love's sake only. Do not say,
> "I love her for her smile—her look—her way
> Of speaking gently—for a trick of thought
> That falls in well with mine, and certes brought
> A sense of pleasant ease on such a day"—
> For these things in themselves, Beloved, may

> Be changed, or change for thee—and love so wrought
> May be unwrought so. Neither love me for
> Thine own dear pity's wiping my cheeks dry—
> Since one might well forget to weep who bore
> Thy comfort long, and lose thy love thereby.
> But love me for love's sake, that evermore
> Thou may'st love on through love's eternity.

In yet another she lingers hesitating, and will not abandon her attitude of loving renunciation. In the sixteenth, however, she gives way. The lover has overcome! He has prevailed against her fears, and may throw the purple of his kingliness around her!

> Beloved, I at last record
> Here ends my doubt! If *thou* invite me forth,
> I rise above abasement at the word.
> Make thy love larger to enlarge my worth.

An exultant sonnet follows, in which she lauds the poetry of her lover.

> My poet, thou canst touch on all the notes
> God set between His After and Before,
> And strike up and strike off the general roar
> Of the rushing worlds, a melody that floats
> In a serene air purely.

She asks him how he will have her "for most use," since God has devoted her to the service of waiting on him.

> A hope, to sing by gladly? or a fine,
> Sad memory, with thy songs to interfuse?
> A shade, in which to sing, of palm or pine?
> A grave on which to rest from singing? Choose.

Are not these lines exquisitely appropriate to a

woman-poet addressing her accepted lover, who is also a poet? It is pleasant, all the same, to be reminded that in this ideal courtship there were some incidents of a sort met with on more ordinary occasions of the kind. The lady gave her lover a lock of hair, and commemorated the event in a sonnet, in which the undertone of sadness that may generally be heard in Mrs. Browning's poetry is clearly audible.

> I never gave a lock of hair away
> To a man, Dearest, except this to thee,
> Which now upon my fingers thoughtfully
> I ring out to the full brown length and say,
> "Take it." My day of youth went yesterday;
> My hair no longer bounds to my foot's glee,
> Nor plant I it from rose or myrtle-tree,
> As girls do, any more. It only may
> Now shade, on two pale cheeks, the marks of tears,
> Taught drooping from the head that hangs aside
> Through sorrow's trick. I thought the funeral shears
> Would take this first, but love is justified;
> Take it thou,—finding pure, from all those years,
> The kiss my mother left here when she died.

In return the poet-lover gives her a lock from his head. It is "purply black." She suggests that the shade of the poet's bay-crown lies on it, it is so dark, and places it on her heart, to be warm with her love until she grows cold in death. In the next she continues the expression of her love and pride, wondering how, although he was in the world a year ago, it had been possible that she was unconscious of his presence. "Atheists," she says, "are as dull, who cannot guess God's presence out of sight." The thought has probably occurred to many fond lovers

"How strange that we were both in the world so long without being aware of each other's existence!" but I do not remember seeing it elsewhere expressed in verse or prose. Having put love's chalice to her lips, she will now drink of it boldly. She tells her lover to repeat, again and again, that he loves her. She cares not though it may seem a "cuckoo-strain," for she will have the air filled with it as the vales are filled with the voice of the blithe bird of spring. You cannot have too many stars, or too many flowers, or too many assurances of love.

> Say thou dost love me, love me, love me—toll
> The silver iterance!—only minding, Dear,
> To love me also in silence, with thy soul.

The same strain of proud and exultant joy in love and the loved one is continued through several spirited and splendid sonnets. The sadness in them is but a dark background to the rainbow of their joy. She tells him in one of the noblest of the series, which I must quote entire, that her chamber had been peopled by visions before he came.

> I lived with visions for my company
> Instead of men and women, years ago,
> And found them gentle mates, nor thought to know
> A sweeter music than they played to me.
> But soon their trailing purple was not free
> Of this world's dust,—their lutes did silent grow,
> And I myself grew faint and blind below
> Their vanishing eyes. Then THOU did'st come—to *be*,
> Beloved, what they *seemed*. Their shining fronts,
> Their songs, their splendours—(better, yet the same,

> As river-water hallowed into fonts)
> Met in thee, and from out thee overcame
> My soul with satisfaction of all wants—
> Because God's gifts put man's best dreams to shame.

There are forty-three of these sonnets, and I had marked several others for extract; but my desire is to quote only enough to create in the reader an importunate wish for more. A very beautiful one describes the love-letters she had received, or, rather, chronicles a few of them in the order of ascending intensity of love. It would be too cruel to forbear quoting the thirty-eighth, which contains an account of three kisses which the lover had the bliss of bestowing upon the lady.

> First time he kissed me, he but only kissed
> The fingers of this hand wherewith I write,
> And ever since it grew more clean and white,
> Slow to world-greetings, quick with its "Oh, list,"
> When the angels speak. A ring of amethyst
> I could not wear here plainer to my sight,
> Than that first kiss. The second passed in height
> The first, and sought the forehead, and half missed,
> Half falling on the hair. O beyond meed!
> That was the chrism of love, which love's own crown,
> With sanctifying sweetness, did precede.
> The third upon my lips was folded down
> In perfect, purple state! since when, indeed,
> I have been proud and said, "My love, my own."

But the sonnet which of all the forty-three attests, to my thinking, most explicitly, that tenderness of domestic sympathy, that intense feeling of home joys, that loving remembrance of the friends of her childhood, which characterises Mrs. Browning, is the thirty-fifth: I quote part of it.

> If I leave all to thee, wilt thou exchange
> And *be* all to me? Shall I never miss
> Home-talk and blessing and the common kiss
> That comes to each in turn, nor count it strange,
> When I look up, to drop on a new range
> Of walls and floors—another home than this?
> Nay, wilt thou fill that place by me which is
> Filled by dead eyes too tender to know change?

So far as I know, there is not in the history of literature a parallel instance to the marriage of Elizabeth Barrett Barrett and Robert Browning. Poets both of undoubted genius, they were yet of markedly diverse genius. Their harmony may, on that account, have been only the more complete. In the works of Mr. Browning are to be found many references to Mrs. Browning, all couched in terms of ardent affection. More than once, indeed, when she is the subject of his verse, he seems to pass into a less rugged, a more tenderly melodious and chastened, mood of literary execution than that in which he usually works. We have nothing from his pen more delicate in its beauty than the *One Word More*, in which he dedicates to her his series of poems called *Men and Women*. Here are a few of the most quotable, not by any means the best, of the lines.

> Love, you saw me gather men and women,
> Live or dead or fashioned by my fancy,
> Enter each and all, and use their service,
> Speak from every mouth,—the speech, a poem.

> Hardly shall I tell my joys and sorrows,
> Hopes and fears, belief and disbelieving:
> I am mine and yours—the rest be all men's,
> Karshook, Cleon, Norbert, and the fifty.
> Let me speak this once in my true person,
> Not as Lippo, Roland, or Andrea,
> Though the fruit of speech be just this sentence—
> Pray you, look on these my men and women,
> Take and keep my fifty poems finished;
> Where my heart lies, let my brain lie also !
> Poor the speech; be how I speak, for all things.

Once he permits us to glance into the sacred privacy of his evening home. His "perfect wife" sits "reading by firelight," her "great brow" propped by "the spirit small hand"—a vignette picture that vividly reminds us of those of herself in her girlish verses, as she sat studying by the side of her favourite brother.

CHAPTER XI.

POEMS OF PATRIOTIC SYMPATHY.

WE saw how nobly Mrs. Browning responded to the highest sentiments, the most heroic endeavours, of her time, in connection with the movement for the abolition of slavery, and with the general philanthropic impulse and effort to alleviate the distress of factory operatives, of overworked children, and of all men and women into whose soul the iron of luxurious, indifferent, cruel civilisation had too deeply entered. *The Cry of the Children* is part of the inspired poetry of our age, a word of God in a very strict and solemn sense. Similar in spirit, though not so deeply imbued with immortal fire, is *A Song for the Ragged Schools of London*. It was written in Rome, and the locality lends colour to the poem.

> I am listening here in Rome,
>   And the Romans are confessing,
> " English children pass in bloom,
>   All God ever made for blessing.
>
> " *Angli angeli!* (resumed
>   From the mediæval story)
> Such rose angelhoods, emplumed
>   In such ringlets of pure glory!"

> Can we smooth down the bright hair,
>   O my sisters, calm, unthrilled in
> Our hearts' pulses ? Can we bear
>   The sweet looks of our own children,
>
> While those others, lean and small,
>   Scurf and mildew of the city,
> Spot our streets, convict us all,
>   Till we take them into pity ?

In this instance, too, Mrs. Browning's appeal has not been without effect. England has heard the cry of the children both in the factory and in the street; and if all has not yet been done that ought to be done, a great improvement has been effected upon the state of things as it was five-and-twenty years ago.

Her heart and brain were large enough not only for the cause of social and philanthropic reform, but for that of political advancement. She sympathised ardently with the Italians in their cherished hope of breaking the chains that bound them under many rulers, and of asserting their independence, unity, and freedom as a nation. When Napoleon III. crossed the Alps to strike the first decisive blow on behalf of Italy, she hailed him in an enthusiastic Ode, which one now reads with mixed feelings, dubious whether the poet, seeing the Emperor in the halo of his Italian policy, did not ascribe to him some merits and virtues that history will not concede. At all events, it has proved a true prophecy in recognising the expedition of the French Emperor as the beginning of a new era for Italy. In the first stanza the poet describes his elevation to the throne.

> Emperor, Emperor!
> From the centre to the shore
>   From the Seine back to the Rhine,
> Stood eight millions up and swore
>   By their manhood's right Divine
> So to elect and legislate,
>   This man should renew the line
> Broken in a strain of fate
> And leagued kings at Waterloo,
>   When the people's hands let go.

The eight millions shouted. Thinkers stood aside to let the nation decide. Some hated the new fact; some quailed; some cursed; some wept. The poet was silent.

> That day I did not hate,
>   Nor doubt, nor quail, nor curse.
> I, reverencing the people, did not bate
> My reverence of their deed and oracle,
> Nor vainly prate
>   Of better and of worse,
> Against the great conclusion of their will.

Liberals too often forget that it is a sin against freedom to drown in floods of flattery all acknowledgment of the faults and shortcomings whereby nations have contributed to their own undoing. No one could rejoice more heartily in the establishment of the French Republic than I do; but the enormous majorities by which the French people first called Napoleon III. to the Presidency, and then confirmed him on the throne, ought not to be swept from the historical memory. It is well that Mrs. Browning has put them on record.

Nevertheless, she did not feel herself called upon to celebrate or to sanction what had been done.

> O voice and verse
> Which God set in me to acclaim and sing
> Conviction, exaltation, aspiration,
> We gave no music to the patent thing,
> Nor spared a holy rhythm to throb and swim
> About the name of him
> Translated to the sphere of domination
>   By democratic passion.
> I was not used, at least,
>   Nor can be, now or then,
> To stroke the ermine beast
>   On any kind of throne,
>   (Though builded by a nation for its own),
> And swell the surging choir for kings of men—
>   " Emperor
>   Evermore."

Now, however, when he leaves "the purple throng of vulgar monarchs," and assays to help "the broken hearts of nations to be strong," she, a poet of the people, meets him on the Alpine snows, and finds him "great enough to praise." Reflecting on the hesitation, if not the express disapproval, with which English statesmen had regarded the Emperor's Italian enterprise, she addresses him thus :

> An English poet warns thee to maintain
> God's word, not England's: let His truth be true,
> And all men liars! with His truth respond
> To all men's lie.

The work was, indeed, but half done. Selfish and cruel principalities and powers stepped in to arrest the emancipation of Italy. But the poet expresses confidence that the imperfection of what has been done will one day be removed, and with this prophecy, long since fulfilled, she concludes her Ode:

> Courage, whoever circumvents!
> Courage, courage, whoever is base!
> The soul of a high intent, be it known,
> Can die no more than any soul
> Which God keeps by Him under the throne;
> And this, at whatever interim,
>   Shall live, and be consummated
> Into the being of deeds made whole.
> Courage, courage! Happy is he,
>   Of whom (himself among the dead
>   And silent), this word shall be said:—
>   That he might have had the world with him,
>   But chose to side with suffering men,
>   And had the world against him when
> He came to deliver Italy.
>   "Emperor
>   Evermore."

The two last words are repeated at the end of every stanza. Their effect will now strike some as ludicrous and some as melancholy. It remains true, however, that Napoleon III.'s Italian expedition was one of the soundest bits of work done in the recent political history of Europe.

If Napoleon III. was drawn aside by priests and women from his onward path as deliverer of Italy, it was not to Mrs. Browning that he could look for any sympathy in his weakness. The Jesuits and the Papacy have had few more fervent or more frank detesters than she. In common with a host of able men and women of her generation, she inherited, from the great Evangelical party of fifty or sixty years ago, not only its moral vehemence, but its cordial hatred of Popery. We find this in Carlyle, Macaulay, Stephen, Henry Rogers, Thackeray, Browning, and even in Tennyson, though in this last it has been kept under careful restraint. That habit of euphuistic reference to the Roman Church, that ecstasy of admiration for Dr. Newman, with which we are now so well acquainted, belong to a new generation, a generation delicate in its culture and refined in its feelings, but hardly, perhaps, dowered with the intellectual bone and sinew of the earlier race.

Mrs. Browning's poem, entitled *A View Across the Roman Campagna*, in which she addresses the Pope, or the Papacy, in language of keen imaginative scorn, would now be considered, in polite literary circles, very bad form. The lines, however, are fine, and there are some of us who would not yet be ashamed to confess sympathy with their spirit. The poet pictures to herself the Papacy as a great ship, tempest-tossed on the sea of the Campagna. In order that this idea may not seem to us too bold, and also that its expressiveness may be felt, we shall do well to read Mr. Ruskin's description of the plain of the Campagna. "Perhaps," says that prose-poet, "there is no more impressive scene on earth than the solitary extent of the Campagna of Rome under evening light. Let the reader imagine himself for a moment withdrawn from the sounds and motion of the living world, and sent forth alone into this wild and wasted plain. The earth yields and crumbles beneath his feet, tread he never so lightly, for its substance is white, hollow, and carious, like the dusty wreck of the bones of men. The long, knotted grass waves and tosses feebly in the evening wind, and the shadows of its motion shake feverishly along the banks of ruin that lift themselves to the sunlight. Hillocks of mouldering earth heave around him, as if the dead beneath were struggling in their sleep; scattered blocks of black stone four-square, remnants of mighty edifices, not one left upon another, lie upon them to keep them down. A dull purple poisonous haze stretches level against the desert, veiling its spectral wrecks of massy ruins, on whose rents the red light rests like dying fire on defiled altars. The blue ridge of the Alban Mount lifts itself against the solemn space of green, clear, quiet sky. Watch-towers of dark clouds stand steadfastly along the promontories of the Apennines. From the plain to the mountains, the shattered aqueducts, pier beyond pier, melt into the darkness, like shadowy and countless troops of funeral mourners, passing from a nation's grave."

Such is the sea on which floats the ship of Mrs. Browning's poem. It opens thus:

> Over the dumb Campagna-sea,
>   Out in the offing through mist and rain,
> Saint Peter's Church heaves silently
>   Like a mighty ship in pain,
>   Facing the tempest with struggle and strain.
>
> Motionless waifs of ruined towers,
>   Soundless breakers of desolate land:

> The sullen surf of the mist devours
>   That mountain-range upon either hand,
>   Eaten away from its outline grand.
>
> And over the dumb Campagna-sea
>   Where the ship of the Church heaves on to wreck,
> Alone and silent as God must be,
>   The Christ walks. Ay, but Peter's neck
>   Is stiff to turn on the foundering deck.
>
> Peter, Peter! If such be thy name,
>   Now leave the ship for another to steer,
> And proving thy faith evermore the same,
>   Come forth, tread out through the dark and drear,
>   Since He who walks on the sea is here.

But the modern Peter does not move. He is no longer rash, "as in old Galilee." He will not quit the good things of temporal power, and content himself with the homely fare of fishermen, even though Christ be of the party.

> Peter, Peter! He does not stir;
>   His nets are heavy with silver fish;
> He reckons his gains, and is keen to infer—
>   "The broil on the shore, if the Lord should wish;
>   But the sturgeon goes to the Cæsar's dish."

Many voices would now be raised in protest against the next verse, in which the Papacy is accused of having bent the knee to Mammon.

> Peter, Peter! thou fisher of men,
>   Fisher of fish wouldst thou live instead?
> Haggling for pence with the other Ten,
>   Cheating the market at so much a head,
>   Griping the bag of the traitor Dead.

Whether there is or is not justice in this charge, I

shall not decisively say. My own feeling is that it is exaggerated. Avarice does not seem to me to have been one of the eminent vices of the Papacy. The Church of Rome has not stooped to barter freedom for endowment.

The last verse is prophetic of woe to the Papacy; but the Church of Rome has outlived many grim prognostications.

> At the triple crow of the Gallic cock
>   Thou weep'st not, thou, though thine eyes be dazed:
> What bird comes next in the tempest-shock?—
>   Vultures! see,—as when Romulus gazed,—
>   To inaugurate Rome for a world amazed!

Mrs. Browning watched the course of the Italian war with an interest that may be imagined, and celebrated some of its heroic and touching incidents. One of these gave occasion to the piece entitled *Mother and Poet*, written at Turin after Gaeta was taken. I shall quote a few of the stanzas,—they tell their own tale. A patriot mother had sent her two sons to the war.

> At first, happy news came, in gay letters moiled
>   With my kisses,—of camp-life and glory, and how
> They both loved me; and, soon coming home to be spoiled,
>   In return would fan off every fly from my brow
>   With their green laurel-bough.
>
> Then was triumph at Turin: "Ancona was free!"
>   And some one came out of the cheers in the street,
> With a face pale as stone, to say something to me,
>   My Guido was dead! I fell down at his feet,
>   While they cheered in the street.

I bore it ; friends soothed me ; my grief looked sublime
  As the ransom of Italy. One boy remained
To be leant on and walked with, recalling the time
  When the first grew immortal, while both of us strained
    To the height he had gained.

And letters still came, shorter, sadder, more strong
  Writ now but in one hand, " I was not to faint,—
One loved me for two—would be with me ere long :
  And *Viva l'Italia!—he* died for, our saint,
    Who forbids our complaint."

My Nanni would add, " He was safe, and aware
  Of a presence that turned off the balls—was imprest
It was Guido himself who knew what I could bear,
  And how 'twas impossible, quite dispossessed,
    To live on for the rest."

On which, without pause, up the telegraph-line
  Swept smoothly the next news from Gaeta :—*Shot.*
Tell his mother. Ah, ah, "his," "their" mother,—not
  "mine,"
No voice says " *My* mother " again to me. What!
    You think Guido forgot ?

   *   *   *   *   *   *

Dead ! One of them shot by the sea in the east,
  And one of them shot in the west by the sea.
Both ! both my boys ! If in keeping the feast
  You want a great song for your Italy free,
    Let none look at *me.*

Speaking generally of Mrs. Browning's political poetry, I should pronounce it inferior, viewed as poetry, to most of her other work. Splendid as eloquence, it has not quite the poetic perfection of form. Its moral qualities are inestimable.

CHAPTER XII.

AURORA LEIGH.

THE most extensive of all Mrs. Browning's poems is *Aurora Leigh*, and its acceptance with readers of poetry has been attested by the sale of many editions. The poet, in dedicating it to her " dearest cousin and friend," John Kenyon, in 1856, describes it as "the most mature " of her works, and the one in which she has expressed her "highest convictions upon Life and Art." It is a tale in nine Books, and may, with some indefiniteness, yet reasonable accuracy, be pronounced a modern epic, of which the central figure is a woman, and whose theme is social amelioration. Not arms and the man, but social problems and the woman, are sung by Mrs. Browning, and whether she solves the problems or not, it must be admitted that she has produced a taking and beautiful poem. I have always felt that it had defects, some of them serious, but each new reading has heightened my conception of its power and splendour. The pitch of its intensity, sustained from beginning to end, is astonishing in a work not much shorter than *Paradise Lost*. There is no straining; nothing to hint that the poet worked with difficulty; and yet the richness of colour and strength of imaginative fire are such as we should look for in brief lyrical effusions rather than in a long narrative poem. In the rapidity and animation of the style—the quick succession of incident, the sense of motion everywhere—the book recalls the manner of Homer. It is instinct with music. We feel that the poet does not recite, she sings. In its rich and ringing melody, as well as in its warm imaginative glow, it is superior to George Eliot's *Spanish Gipsy*.

The first Book introduces us to the heroine. She is a poet, and speaks for herself. "I who have written much in prose and verse for others' uses will write now for mine." That Aurora Leigh is, to some extent, what Mrs. Browning was, cannot, I think, be doubtful; but I am convinced that we should err if we looked upon the resemblance between the two as very close. This heroine is not less a creation of her mind than the Duchess May or the Lady Geraldine, in both of whom, we may be sure, there are traces, and deep traces, of herself. Aurora is half-Italian by blood, and is not only born, but brought up till she is thirteen, in Italy; and the poet gives good heed to the fact that there is an Italian element in her character. Her father was an English gentleman of property, her mother a Florentine. The latter had died when Aurora was four years old. The mother's death suggests some priceless lines on mother's love, in which we seem to put our ear to Mrs. Browning's heart and hear its beating.

> I felt a mother-want about the world,
> And still went seeking, like a bleating lamb
> Left out at night, in shutting up the fold,—
> As restless as a nest-deserted bird
> Grown chill through something being away, though what
> It knows not. I, Aurora Leigh, was born
> To make my father sadder, and myself
> Not over-joyous, truly. Women know
> The way to rear up children (to be just),
> They know a simple, merry, tender knack
> Of tying sashes, fitting baby-shoes,
> And stringing pretty words that make no sense,
> And kissing full sense into empty words;
> Which things are corals to cut life upon,
> Although such trifles. . . . .
> . . . . Fathers love as well
> —Mine did, I know,—but still with heavier brains,
> And wills more consciously responsible,
> And not as wisely, since less foolishly;
> So mothers have God's licence to be missed.

Her father was an "austere Englishman," who, "after a dry lifetime spent at home in college-learning, law, and parish talk," fell suddenly in love with a girl whom he saw in an Italian church, and married her. When she died, he had her picture painted. The face, throat, and hands having been finished, her chambermaid, "in hate of the English-fashioned shroud," insisted that she should be clad in "the last brocade she dressed in at the Pitti." The effect was "very strange." The whiteness of the corpse-face, the red stiff silk of the dress, impressed the imagination of the child, and she would sit for hours upon the floor, staring at the picture. As she grew in years, and was taught by her father to read a variety of books, she associated whatever she read with the richly-dressed figure and dead-face, and it became to her the emblem of " the incoherences of change and death," mixed and merged in the fair "mystery of perpetual life." When this had continued for nine years, her father also died, and she was sent to England.

Coming from the Italian home of her childhood, Aurora Leigh thought England a poor affair.

> The train swept us on.
> Was this my father's England? The great Isle?
> The ground seemed cut up from the fellowship
> Of verdure, field from field, as man from man.

Her aunt received her without much show of affection.

> I think I see my father's sister stand
> Upon the hall-step of her country-house
> To give me welcome. She stood straight and calm,
> Her somewhat narrow forehead braided tight,
> As if for taming accidental thoughts
> From possible pulses; brown hair pricked with grey
> By frigid use of life (she was not old,
> Although my father's elder by a year);
> A nose drawn sharply, yet in delicate lines;
> A close, mild mouth, a little soured about
> The ends, through speaking unrequited loves,
> Or peradventure niggardly half-truths;
> Eyes of no colour,—once they might have smiled,
> But never, never have forgot themselves
> In smiling; cheeks, in which was yet a rose
> Of perished summers, like a rose in a book,
> Kept more for ruth than pleasure,—if past bloom,
> Past fading also.

There is a fleering, flippant tone in Aurora's description of her aunt, which betrays a coldness in the region of the heart constituting a very serious charge against the heroine. The half-contemptuous, knowing air of what follows is new in the poetry, as it was foreign to the character, of Mrs. Browning.

> The poor-club exercised her Christian gifts
> Of knitting stockings, stitching petticoats,
> Because we are of one flesh after all,
> And need one flannel (with a proper sense
> Of difference in the quality)—and still
> The book-club, guarded from your modern trick
> Of shaking dangerous questions from the crease,
> Preserved her intellectual. She had lived
> A sort of cage-bird life, born in a cage,
> Accounting that to leap from perch to perch
> Was act and joy enough for any bird.

At the first moment of seeing Aurora the aunt "seemed moved," kissed the girl, though with "cold lips," and suffered her to cling affectionately. But her demeanour suddenly changed. Having taken her niece into her own room, she revealed the true state of her feelings.

> With some strange spasm
> Of pain and passion, she wrung loose my hands
> Imperiously, and held me at arm's length,
> And with two grey-steel, naked-bladed eyes
> Searched through my face—ay, stabbed it through and
>   through,
> Through brows and cheeks and chin, as if to find
> A wicked murderer in my innocent face,
> If not here, there, perhaps. Then, drawing breath,
> She struggled for her ordinary calm,
> And missed it rather,—told me not to shrink,
> As if she had told me not to lie or swear.
> " She loved my father, and would love me too
> As long as I deserved it." Very kind.

Aurora explains her aunt's proceedings by saying that she had thought to find traces of her Italian mother in her face.

> My aunt
> Had loved my father truly as she could,
> And hated, with the gall of gentle souls,
> My Tuscan mother, who had fooled away
> A wise man from wise courses, a good man
> From obvious duties.

Whatever her prejudice against mother or child, the aunt failed in no duty to Aurora, giving proof, on the contrary, of sincere and considerate affection. She was not what a mother would have been; yet a kind-hearted girl would have felt towards her more like a daughter than Aurora felt. The sole excuse—doubtless an important excuse—for her bitterness, was her aunt's angry feeling towards her mother.

The girl was educated according to her aunt's views of what befitted an English lady.

> I learnt the Collects and the Catechism,
> The Creeds, from Athanasius back to Nice,
> The Articles, the Tracts *against* the times.

The italicised word is Mrs. Browning's pointed estimate of the Anglo-Catholic revival under Newman, Manning, and Pusey. Aurora learned classic French, German, a little algebra, a little geometry, a very little science, a good deal of genealogical history and geographical detail, much music, drawing, dancing, glass-spinning, bird-stuffing, flower-modelling in wax, "because she liked accomplishments in girls."

>   And last
> I learnt cross-stitch, because she did not like
> To see me wear the night with empty hands,
> A-doing nothing.

This education was torture to our heroine. "Certain of your feebler souls go out in such a process; many pine to a sick, inodorous light." She neither died nor pined into insipidity, but showed that she had a will, and managed to have a way, of her own. The situation was not without its assuagements. There was Romney Leigh, for example, her cousin, whom she "used as a sort of friend." He was a few years her senior, but still young—too young, indeed, to be, as he was, master of the estate of Leigh Hall, the sense of his responsibilities in relation to which made him precociously grave and earnest. He would cross the hills with gifts of grapes from his hot-houses, a book in his hand, which, when Aurora lifted the cover, was sure to be statistico-philanthropical. The aunt was indulgent in connection with the intercourse of the cousins.

> She almost loved him,—even allowed
> That sometimes he should seem to sigh my way;
> It made him easier to be pitiful,—
> And sighing was his gift. So, undisturbed
> At whiles she let him shut my music up,
> And push my needles down, and lead me out
> To see in that south angle of the house
> The figs grow black as if by a Tuscan rock,
> On some light pretext. She would turn her head
> At other moments, go to fetch a thing,
> And leave me breath enough to speak with him.

This was rather tenderly considerate in so austere a

lady. Might not Aurora have spared one kind word for an old maid who, whatever her faults, had the redeeming quality of knowing when she was in the way, and taking herself out of it? On the state of the girl's feelings towards Romney himself, we are not, at this stage of the narrative, favoured with definite information. One symptom is interesting: the skilful in love-lore will interpret it for themselves.

> Once, he stood so near
> He dropped a sudden hand upon my head,
> Bent down on woman's work, as soft as rain;
> But then I rose and shook it off as fire,
> The stranger's touch that took my father's place
> Yet dared seem soft.

At all events, Romney contributed to the enlivenment of Aurora's existence. She gradually found that life might be endurable even in chilly England, and under the auspices of an unsympathising aunt. She had a little room for herself, embosomed, like a finch's nest, in greenery. You could not put your head out at the window without getting "a dash of dawn-dew from the honeysuckle." Does not the reader feel its freshness? Beyond the elms you saw the low hills behind which "Cousin Romney's" chimneys sent up the blue smoke in fine wreaths.

> Far above, a jut of table-land,
> A promontory without water, stretched.
> You could not catch it if the day were thick,
> Or took it for a cloud; but otherwise
> The vigorous sun would catch it up at eve,
> And use it for an anvil till he had filled
> The shelves of heaven with burning thunderbolts,

> And proved he need not rest so early:—then
> When all his setting trouble was resolved
> In a trance of passive glory, you might see
> In apparition on the golden sky
> (Alas, my Giotto's background!) the sheep run
> Along the fine clear outline, small as mice
> That run along a witch's scarlet thread.

We may, I think, take it for granted that Mrs. Browning was here poetically painting directly from nature, and that she saw those minute sheep cut out in black against the sunset. It is due both to artists and poets to trust them, though the particular appearances which they chronicle may not have fallen within one's own observation. It is only under rare atmospheric conditions that the sheep on the headland could have been seen with Mrs. Browning's bodily eye; but the mind's eye sees them with vivid distinctness, and dwells on them with keen delight. That is enough.

Aurora is at her best in describing scenery, and she describes England better than Italy. She has a store of sonorous phrases, and of imposing, far-fetched imagery, at the service of Italian landscape; but, for all the loudness of her praise of Italian hills and skies, we feel that her heart is in England. She tries to be smart and satirical in depicting her father's country, but soon gets into a more genial mood.

> On English ground
> You understand the letter,—ere the fall,
> How Adam lived in a garden. All the fields
> Are tied up fast with hedges, nosegay-like;

> The hills are crumpled plains,—the plains, parterres,—
> The trees, round, woolly, ready to be clipped;
> And if you seek for any wilderness
> You find at best a park. A nature tamed
> And grown domestic like a barn-door fowl,
> Which does not awe you with its claws and beak,
> Nor tempt you to an eyrie too high up,
> But which, in cackling, sets you thinking of
> Your eggs to-morrow at breakfast, in the pause
> Of finer meditation. Rather say
> A sweet familiar nature, stealing in
> As a dog might, or child, to touch your hand
> Or pluck your gown, and humbly mind you so
> Of presence and affection.

This is, at best, cool and qualified commendation; but, a few pages on, she drops the flippant air, and writes with lyric ecstasy.

> I learnt to love that England. Very oft,
> Before the day was born, or otherwise
> Through secret windings of the afternoons,
> I threw my hunters off and plunged myself
> Among the deep hills, as a hunted stag
> Will take the waters, shivering with the fear
> And passion of the course. And when, at last
> Escaped—so many a green slope built on slope
> Betwixt me and the enemy's house behind—
> I dared to rest or wander—like a rest
> Made sweeter for the step upon the grass—
> And view the ground's most gentle dimplement
> (As if God's finger touched, but did not press
> In making England!), such an up and down
> Of verdure—nothing too much up or down,
> A ripple of land; such little hills, the sky
> Can stoop to tenderly, and the wheatfields climb;
> Such nooks of valleys, lined with orchises,
> Fed full of noises by invisible streams;

> And open pastures, where you scarcely tell
> White daisies from white dew, at intervals
> The mythic oaks and elm-trees standing out
> Self-poised upon their prodigy of shade—
> I thought my father's land was worthy, too,
> Of being my Shakespeare's.

Walking in such scenes with Cousin Romney and his friend the rising painter, Vincent Carrington, Aurora would be the gayest of the party, telling her cousin, when he sighed about the distresses of the poor, that howsoever the world might go ill, "the thrushes still sang in it." He bore with her "in melancholy patience, not unkind;" and thus encouraged, she sketched the bright side of things with a warmth of colour which, if it will not convince many that fever, cancer, madness, pestilence, or starvation are evils to be vanquished by songs and smiles, must have been charming to Romney, and is charming to us.

> I flattered all the beauteous country round,
> As poets use, the skies, the clouds, the fields,
> The happy violets hiding from the roads,
> The primroses run down to, carrying gold,—
> The tangled hedgerows, where the cows push out
> Impatient horns and tolerant churning mouths
> 'Twixt dripping ash-boughs,—hedges all alive
> With birds, and gnats, and large white butterflies,
> Which look as if the May-flower had caught life
> And palpitated forth upon the wind,—
> Hills, vales, woods, netted in a silver mist,
> Farms, granges, doubled up among the hills,
> And cattle grazing in the watered vales,
> And cottage-chimneys smoking from the woods,
> And cottage-gardens smelling everywhere,
> Confused with smell of orchards.

These descriptions of English landscape have not the minute elaboration of Tennyson, nor the vague sympathy, partly mystical, partly pantheistic, with nature, of Wordsworth, but they evince an unaffected heartiness, a buoyancy of loving joy, which neither Tennyson nor Wordsworth can rival. Cowper was as honest in his affection for English landscape—and Cowper was a very masterly describer,—but the movement of his genius was slower, his fancy less brilliant, his imagination less powerful, his sense of melody and rhythm in words feebler, than Mrs. Browning's. In melodious word-painting of English lowland country, she is unrivalled.

One morning, Aurora, gambolling like a Dryad among trees and flowers, had just selected for herself an ivy-wreath to bind across her brow, when she was aware of "Cousin Romney." It was her birthday, and he had come presumably to congratulate her on the occasion. He had something more to say, however, and he edged towards his purpose by telling Aurora that he had found, beside the stream, a book of hers—a book of poems. He had, he said, not read a word of it, but he nevertheless took the liberty to advise her to forswear poetical composition. They chatted lightly on this subject for a few moments, when he suddenly said, "Aurora!" There must have been something significant in the tone, for girls are not usually startled when their cousins call them by their names; and yet, says our heroine, "there I stopped short, breath and all." Romney thereupon kindly but long-windedly proposed that his cousin should give up poetry and take to world-regeneration instead, with him for guide, philosopher, and husband. His allusion to her poetry, which, remember, he had not been curious enough to read (Aurora, if at all like other girls and boys that write verses, would have pardoned him a good deal of boldness in doing *that*), is not felicitous.

> The chances are that, being a woman, young
> And pure, with such a pair of large, calm eyes,
> You write as well, and ill, upon the whole,
> As other women. If as well, what then?
> If even a little better still, what then?

In the second book or canto of a poem-novel, the hero may be expected to be almost impossibly maladroit; but I hope, for the honour of mankind, that no actual human being has ever been capable of anything so stupid as this. Romney proceeds to demonstrate to Aurora that women have no serious chance of doing good except by helping men to do it, explaining to his cousin her constitutional incapacity to attain high excellence with a glibness which might have fitted him to become an efficient lecturer against woman's rights. Hear him on woman's bondage to personal feeling.

> You generalise,
> Oh, nothing! not even grief! Your quick-breathed hearts,
> So sympathetic to the personal pang,
> Close on each separate knife-stroke, yielding up
> A whole life at each wound, incapable
> Of deepening, widening a large lap of life
> To hold the world-full woe. The human race
> To you means such a child, or such a man,

> You saw one morning waiting in the cold,
> Beside that gate, perhaps. You gather up
> A few such cases, and, when strong, sometimes
> Will write of factories and of slaves, as if
> Your father were a negro, and your son
> A spinner in the mills.

He goes on, in a long-winded manner, to infer that, when the woes of communities have to be dealt with, women are necessarily weak. The world—the general body of mankind—remains uncomprehended by them, and must remain uninfluenced. Women may be doting mothers, good wives, but they cannot save nations, or write true poems. Pausing in his harangue, he lets his cousin speak five words, and then starts again, entreating her, since she is fit for better things, such as marrying him, not "to play at art, as children play at swords." With delicate facetiousness, he puts himself in the position of a critic reviewing Aurora's poems.

> Oh, excellent!
> What grace! what facile terms! what fluent sweeps!
> What delicate discernment—almost thought!
> The book does honour to the sex, we hold.
> Among our female authors we make room
> For this fair writer, and congratulate
> The country that produces in these times
> Such women, competent to—spell.

It is a grave objection to the poem that these words are put into the mouth of a proposing lover. Such violation of probability exceeds the utmost licence permissible to art. Romney Leigh is not, in my opinion, a happily conceived figure. The character is such as, outside the circles of amiable and interesting lunacy, can hardly be supposed to exist. It is at best a type of nineteenth-century enthusiasm, not of permanent human nature. But I am not sure that anything in the delineation of Romney violates probability quite so harshly—and his career trenches on probability at several points—as his prefacing an offer of his hand to Aurora with a ponderous argument that her sex is incapable and herself a goose. With a sense of relief, we find at last that she cuts short his oration.

> " Stop there ! "
> I answered—burning through his thread of talk
> With a quick flame of emotion.

She tells him that she does not want praise, that she would rather dance on the tight-rope to amuse children at fairs, than write verse for men in a frivolous spirit. He breaks in again to ask her to choose nobler work in marrying him, and expatiates on the miseries that call for alleviation. She reminds him sharply that he has been demonstrating to her that women are unfit for the work of social improvement, and would like to know how, if she is too weak to stand alone, she can bear him leaning on her shoulder. This makes him speak rather more civilly.

> " Aurora, dear,
> And dearly honoured "—he pressed in at once
> With eager utterance—" you translate me ill.
> I do not contradict my thought of you,
> Which is most reverent, with another thought
> Found less so. If your sex is weak for art
> (And I who said so, did but honour you,
> By using truth in courtship), it is strong
> For life and duty."

The apology will not stand examination. He had pronounced women incapable of generalisation in any form, and he was logically bound to affirm that her strength for life and duty could be manifested only in so far as she strengthened him for undertakings to which men alone are competent. This Aurora perceives; and replies to his offer of his hand, that he loves " not a woman, but a cause ;" his wife was to be a helpmate,—not an end in herself.

> " Your cause is noble, your ends excellent,
> But I, being most unworthy of these and that,
> Do otherwise conceive of love. Farewell."

He continues to plead. Making more amends for his disparagement of her sex, he informs her, rather to our surprise, that he holds " the woman to be nobler than the man." Women can love better than men can, and love " generates the likeness of itself through all heroic duties." Still, the nobleness of woman is to find scope only through her love for man, and Aurora will not accept this condition of being useful. She has her duty, she tells him, as well as he, a duty which she can perform, though unmarried. As a poet, she works in the ideal; and life, she insists, would become vile and despicable unless men were taught by poets to aspire to the ideal. He may scorn her art, but she loves it, and will cling to it. Presently their aunt appears, and bids Aurora ask Romney to finish the talk indoors. He answers for her that his cousin has dismissed him, and abruptly takes leave. To her aunt, looking for explanation, Aurora says bitterly that he had come to take her "into service as a wife," and that she had refused him. An important conversation between aunt and niece ensues, and we are favoured with information which throws light upon the character of the former and upon the prospects of the latter.

The aunt explains that, if not from the point of view of romantic eighteen, yet from that of sober and judicious fifty-five, there were powerful arguments in favour of Romney's proposal. Were she, the aunt, to die, Aurora would be destitute.

> Without a right to crop
> A single blade of grass beneath these trees,
> Or cast a lamb's small shadow on the lawn,
> Unfed, unfolded.

Her father's Italian marriage had cost his daughter her inheritance. By a clause in the entail excluding offspring by a foreign wife, the estates passed to Romney Leigh. But Vane Leigh, Romney's father, aware of this, had written to Aurora's father, so soon as he heard that a daughter was born to him, asking the child in marriage for his son. This letter may be supposed to have set the father's mind at rest, and there the matter had been left; but now, if the girl in her wilfulness turned from Romney, she would not only bring poverty on herself, but defeat the family plans. What, asked the aunt, would she be at?

> You must have
> A pattern lover sighing on his knee:
> You do not count enough a noble heart,

> Above book-patterns, which this very morn
> Unclosed itself, in two dear father's names,
> To embrace your orphaned life! fie, fie! But stay,
> I write a word, and counteract this sin.

Aurora entreats her, with passionate earnestness, to do nothing of the kind. Her soul at least, she says, is not a pauper; she can live her soul's life without alms, and if she must die in making the attempt, she is not afraid to die. What could a prosaic old lady say to a poetical young niece in this frame of mind? It turns out that the aunt knows the time of day with remarkable accuracy.

> She seized my hands with both hers, strained them fast,
> And drew her probing and unscrupulous eyes
> Right through me, body and heart. "Yet, foolish Sweet,
> You love this man. I have watched you when he came,
> And when he went, and when we've talked of him:
> I am not old for nothing; I can tell
> The weather-signs of love—you love this man."

Who would have thought that the venerable maiden had so much wit in her! A burning blush upon Aurora's cheek and brow witnesses to the correctness of her observation; but the girl loudly accuses the blush of treason and falsehood.

> I attest
> The conscious skies, and all their daily suns,
> I think I loved him not, nor then, nor since,
> Nor ever. Do we love the schoolmaster,
> Being busy in the woods? much less, being poor,
> The overseer of the parish? Do we keep
> Our love to pay our debts with?

She then becomes so violent that her aunt drops her hands and ceases to smile.

> "We'll leave Italian manners, if you please.
> I think you had an English father, child,
> And ought to find it possible to speak
> A quiet 'yes' or 'no' like English girls,
> Without convulsions. In another month
> We'll take another answer . . . no, or yes."
> With that, she left me in the garden walk.

When a month had gone by, all was changed. The aunt had died suddenly, leaving Aurora her furniture and three hundred pounds. Romney vainly tries to convince his cousin that her legacy was thirty thousand pounds, which sum he had intended to present to his aunt, with a view to its being left to Aurora. They part. She betakes herself to London, trusting to her pen for a livelihood, and soon makes her way, if not to fortune, at least to fame. We are favoured with samples of the criticism published upon her writings.

> My critic Hammond flatters prettily,
> And wants another volume like the last.
> My critic Belfair wants another book
> Entirely different, which will sell (and live ?)
> A striking book, yet not a startling book,
> The public blames originalities,
> (You must not pump spring-water unawares
> Upon a gracious public, full of nerves—)
> Good things, not subtle, new yet orthodox,
> As easy reading as the dog-eared page
> That's fingered by said public, fifty years,
> Since first taught spelling by its grandmother,
> And yet a revelation in some sort !
> That's hard, my critic Belfair !

The criticism of Belfair is one which in substance has been probably made oftener than any other on the works both of Mrs. Browning and Mr. Browning.

It is indeed difficult—more difficult in the present day than it ever was before, on account of the enormous amount of passably good literature—to be original without being extravagant, to attract by sheer weight or worth of matter, presented with classic quietness of style, instead of by some "trick of singularity." But it remains a truth of universal application that mannerism, obscurity, eccentricity are notes, at best, of genius of the second order, and that simplicity and clearness are notes of genius of the first.

Seven years had come and gone. The life in the country, which had at times been irksome when Aurora's aunt pressed on her with her rules and restrictions, had begun to grow dear to memory, with mellow radiance in the lights and softness in the shadows. Any friend who could recall to her mind little matters of that time was welcome.

> A hedgehog in the path, or a lame bird
> In those green country walks, in that good time,
> When certainly I was so miserable,
> I seem to have missed a blessing ever since.

She worked in a chamber up three flights of stairs, and found the smoky sunsets and weltering fogs of London not unpropitious to poetical composition.

> I worked the short days out,—and watched the sun
> On lurid morns or monstrous afternoons,
> Like some Druidic idol's fiery brass,
> With fixed unflickering outline of dead heat,
> In which the blood of wretches pent inside
> Seemed oozing forth to incarnadine the air,—

> Push out through fog with his dilated disc,
> And startle the slant roofs and chimney-pots
> With splashes of fierce colour.

She " worked with patience, which is almost power." Being poor, she was " constrained, for life, to work with one hand for the booksellers," while working with the other for herself and art. She wrote for cyclopædias, magazines, reviews, weekly papers.

> I wrote tales beside,
> Carved many an article on cherry-stones
> To suit light readers,—something in the lines
> Revealing, it was said, the mallet-hand,
> But that, I'll never vouch for. What you do
> For bread, will taste of common grain, not grapes,
> Although you have a vineyard in Champagne.

She became known, and great folks asked her to their entertainments, to do service in capacity of lioness.

One day an extremely aristocratic person found her way up the three pairs of stairs, and announced herself as Lady Waldemar. She is described as typical of high-born English dames, gentle because so proud, too high above the common world to be put out by anything in it, with low voice and gracious and conciliating manner. We are privileged to listen to a protracted conversation between her and Aurora. Her ladyship announces that she is in love with Romney Leigh. Her first husband had died while she was still young, and she might marry a marquis when she chose, but Romney Leigh's name was good, his means were excellent, and in fact she was as mad with love

as he was with philanthropy. Then follows a passage
which I should be very sorry to consider a successful
imitation of the talk of English ladies in the rank of
Lady Waldemar. A critic is bound to show his author
at the worst, or nearly at the worst, as well as at what
he deems the best, and therefore I shall quote the
lines. Lady Waldemar speaks.

> Of a truth, Miss Leigh,
> I have not, without struggle, come to this.
> I took a master in the German tongue,
> I gamed a little, went to Paris twice;
> But, after all, this love! You eat of love,
> And do as vile a thing as if you ate
> Of garlic—which, whatever else you eat,
> Tastes uniformly acrid, till your peach
> Reminds you of your onion. Am I coarse?
> Well, love's coarse, nature's coarse—ah, there's the rub!
> We fair, fine ladies, who park out our lives
> From common sheep-paths, cannot help the crows
> From flying over—we're as natural still
> As Blowsalinda. Drape us perfectly
> In Lyons velvet,—we are not, for that,
> Lay-figures, look you! we have hearts within,
> Warm, live, improvident, indecent hearts,
> As ready for distracted ends and acts
> As any distressed sempstress of them all
> That Romney groans and toils for. We catch love
> And other fevers in the vulgar way.
> Love will not be outwitted by our wit,
> Nor outrun by our equipages:—mine
> Persisted, spite of efforts. All my cards
> Turned up but Romney Leigh; my German stopped
> At germane Wertherism; my Paris rounds
> Returned me from the Champs Elysées just
> A ghost, and sighing like Dido's. I came home
> Uncured—convicted rather to myself
> Of being in love—in love! That's coarse, you'll say.
> I'm talking garlic.

No Englishwoman who had any pretensions to the name of lady could express herself in terms like these.

Lady Waldemar proceeds to inform Aurora that Romney Leigh was about to inaugurate a new era by marrying Marian Erle, a needlewoman, and thus reconciling class to class. To this match Lady Waldemar vehemently objected, and her purpose in visiting Aurora was, she signified, to enlist her assistance in dissuading Romney, or the needlewoman, from the perpetration of such an absurdity. Our heroine refuses to interfere, and lets Lady Waldemar know her determination to this effect with considerable sharpness. Her ladyship makes her inferences, and, in retiring, lets fly this Parthian shaft at Aurora:

> Farewell, then. Write your books in peace,
> As far as may be for some secret stir
> Now obvious to me,—for, most obviously,
> In coming hither I mistook the way.

That is to say, Lady Waldemar formed the opinion arrived at by Aurora's aunt respecting the state of that young lady's feelings towards her cousin. Miss Leigh's conduct after Lady Waldemar had gone was, to say the least, not inconsistent with this view. Two hours afterwards she has penetrated to St. Margaret's-court, the hideous den, or rookery, in which Romney's affianced bride was to be found. There are dismal places in London, inhabited by a miserable and half-savage population; but Mrs. Browning's description of St. Margaret's-court is exaggerated beyond all bounds of credibility, and reads like a caricature of Dickens. I shall quote part of the passage, but without marking the division into lines. Edgar Poe, a critic of fine discrimination, proposes, as a sound test of the poetical quality of verse, to print it in the form of prose, and to take note whether it is melodious or is not.

"Within St. Margaret's-court I stood alone, close-veiled. A sick child, from an ague-fit, whose wasted right hand gambled 'gainst his left with an old brass button in a blot of sun, jeered weakly at me as I passed across the uneven pavement; while a woman, rouged upon the angular cheek-bones, kerchief torn, thin dangling locks, and flat, lascivious mouth, cursed at a window both ways, in and out, by turns some bed-rid creature and myself,—' Lie still there, mother! liker the dead dog you'll be to-morrow. What, we pick our way, fine madam, with those damnable small feet! We cover up our face from doing good, as if it were our purse! What brings you here, my lady? Is't to find my gentleman who visits his tame pigeon in the eaves? Our cholera catch you with its cramps and spasms, and tumble up your good clothes, veil and all, and turn your whiteness dead-blue.' I looked up; I think I could have walked through hell that day, and never flinched. 'The dear Christ comfort you,' I said, 'you must have been most miserable to be so cruel'—and I emptied out my purse upon the stones: when, as I had cast the last charm in the cauldron, the whole court went boiling, bubbling up, from all its doors and windows, with a hideous wail of laughs and roar of oaths, and blows perhaps. I passed too quickly for distinguishing, and pushed a little side-door hanging on a hinge, and plunged into the dark, and groped and climbed the long, steep, narrow stair 'twixt broken rail and mildewed wall that let the plaster drop to startle me in the blackness. Still, up, up! So high lived Romney's bride."

I think my readers will agree with me that, if we had not seen this in the form of poetry, we might have had some difficulty in distinguishing it from prose.

Marian Erle—the needlewoman of St. Margaret's-court, whom Romney Leigh intended to marry for the benefit of mankind—was not beautiful. You could not say whether her complexion was white or brown —it changed like a mist, "according to being shone on more or less." Her hair had the same peculiarity of dubious tint. It

> Ran its opulence of curls
> In doubt 'twixt dark and bright, nor left you clear
> To name the colour.

A small head, cheeks rather too thin, but dimpled, milky little teeth, and an infantile smile, complete the description of Romney's choice. That any good in the way of social reconcilement or the elevation of the masses could result from such a marriage is a thesis so obviously absurd that argument on the subject were thrown away. Romney's scheme can be accounted for only on one supposition—that his extreme softness of heart had resulted in, or had always been accompanied by, softness of head.

The character of Marian Erle is conceived on a principle so frequently exemplified by Dickens that it may be called the principle of the Dickens ideal. The conditions of birth and up-bringing are depicted as all but impossibly bad, and the human flower comes up amid squalor, hardship, and neglect, radiantly pure as a lily in paradise. Oliver Twist, born in a workhouse, reared under the auspices of Noah Claypole, Fagin, and the Dodger, proves to be a pattern of indestructible goodness. Marian Erle, the child of a father and a mother who reached the utmost limits of depravity, grew up with the qualities of an angel. Such an occurrence is not impossible. There are Oliver Twists and Marian Erles in the world. But ignorance, poverty, paternal and maternal wickedness and neglect, would be less malignant evils than they are if such characters, resisting evil as asbestos resists fire, were not very uncommon ; and it is generally felt that, in poems and novels, these immaculate personages are mere lay-figures, like the shepherds and shepherdesses of the stage, in whose delineation no very shrewd or searching knowledge of human nature is displayed.

Marian Erle was born upon " the ledge of Malvern Hill to eastward, in a hut, built up at night to evade the landlord's eye, of mud and turf." Her father did random jobs which steadier workmen despised, looked after swine on commons, picked hops, assisted Welsh horse-dealers

> When a drove
> Of startled horses plunged into the mist
> Below the mountain-road, and sowed the wind
> With wandering neighings.

He drank, slept, cursed his wife when there was no money to buy drink; and the woman " beat her baby in revenge for her own broken heart." The little girl picked up some knowledge at a Sunday-school, and felt vaguely that there was " some grand blind love " in the heavens when the sun dazzled her eyes. One day her mother, who had just been badly beaten, tried to introduce her to a life of infamy. Shrieking with horror, she started away and bounded down the hillside.

> They yelled at her,
> As famished hounds at a hare. She heard them yell,
> She felt her name hiss after her from the hills,
> Like shot from guns. On, on. And now she had cast
> The voices off with the uplands. On. Mad fear
> Was running in her feet and killing the ground;
> The white roads curled as if she burnt them up,
> The green fields melted, wayside trees fell back
> To make room for her. Then her head grew vexed,
> Trees, fields, turned on her, and ran after her;
> She heard the quick pants of the hills behind.
> The keen air pricked her neck. She had lost her feet,
> Could run no more, yet, somehow, went as fast—
> The horizon, red 'twixt steeples in the east,
> So sucked her forward, forward, while her heart
> Kept swelling, swelling, till it swelled so big
> It seemed to fill her body; then it burst,
> And overflowed the world and swamped the light,
> " And now I am dead and safe," thought Marian Erle—
> She had dropped, she had fainted.

Marian never saw her mother again. Picked out of a ditch by a passing waggoner, she was carried to a hospital in London. That was exactly the kind of place in which she was likely to fall under the notice of Romney Leigh. It would not have been easy for him to go lower in the social scale in order to find a bride who, as his wife, might represent the common people standing on a level of perfect equality with the ladies and gentlemen of England. The marriage was to be celebrated in the aristocratic chapel of St. James's. Romney Leigh invited a brilliant circle of peers, peeresses, and leaders in society to witness the ceremony, not forgetting to ask Marian's fellow-inmates of St. Margaret's-court to grace the wedding, and feast thereafter on Hampstead-heath. Under these circumstances, the party assembled in the church was of a very unusual kind.

> Of course the people came in uncompelled,
> Lame, blind, and worse—sick, sorrowful, and worse,
> The humours of the peccant social wound
> All pressed out, poured out upon Pimlico,
> Exasperating the unaccustomed air
> With hideous interfusion : you'd suppose
> A finished generation, dead of plague,
> Swept outward from their graves into the sun,
> The moil of death upon them. What a sight!
> A holiday of miserable men
> Is sadder than a burial-day of kings.
> They clogged the streets, they oozed into the church
> In a dark, slow stream, like blood. To see that sight,
> The noble ladies stood up in their pews,
> Some pale from fear, a few as red for hate,
> Some simply curious, some just insolent.

And some in wondering scorn, " What next ? What next ? "
These crushed their delicate rose-lips from the smile
That misbecame them in a holy place,
With broidered hems of perfumed handkerchiefs ;
Those passed the salts with confidence of eyes
And simultaneous shiver of moiré silk ;
While all the aisles, alive and black with heads,
Crawled slowly toward the altar from the street,
As bruised snakes crawl and hiss out of a hole
With shuddering involutions, swaying slow
From right to left, and then from left to right,
In pants and pauses. What an ugly crest
Of faces rose upon you everywhere
From that crammed mass ! You did not usually
See faces like them in the open day :
They hide in cellars, not to make you mad
As Romney Leigh is.—Faces ! O my God,
We call those, faces ? Men's and women's, ay,
And children's ; babies, hanging like a rag
Forgotten on their mother's neck—poor mouths,
Wiped clean of mother's milk by mother's blow,
Before they are taught her cursing.

It is not without rather severe disappointment that on examining *Aurora Leigh* with more care and closeness than I had brought to the task for many years, I have found the poem so much more faulty than previous readings led me to expect. The metaphoric richness, the wealth of picturesque phrase and coloured word, the animation, and even, on the whole, the melody, of *Aurora Leigh* are beyond praise. But it lacks modulation, variety, repose. There are, indeed, passages in which the thoughts and images fairly float themselves away in the sphere-dance of harmony ; wonderful passages, in which it is again demonstrated that true melody in language is but the rhythmic cadence natural to a mood of imaginative thought, sufficiently elevated, calm, and mighty. But over wide spaces of the poem the ear finds no delight. The crowding, the vehemence, the feverish haste and impatience, which so frequently characterise Mr. Kingsley's novels, can hardly fail to be recalled by many passages. The heroine invariably talks like one of Mr. Kingsley's characters. There is a lack of tenderer strains to refresh and relieve the ear; the atmosphere wants calm, the landscape wants perspective.

But it is with the poorness of the human element throughout the poem that I have, in the last reading, been most painfully impressed. I am indeed not so sure as I once was that Romney Leigh could not have existed. He had a bee in his bonnet, but genius may be combined with almost lunatic unpracticality. But Marian Erle is a fancy portrait, and Lady Waldemar is an impossibility. The only personages in the poem whose existences are thoroughly realised are Aurora and the aunt. Agreeable or disagreeable, Aurora has poetic vitality. Mrs. Browning made use, without question, of her own experiences, in delineating the successful authoress; and though we cannot impute to Aurora the high qualities of Mrs. Browning, or to Mrs. Browning the flightiness and flippancy and tone of conventional satire of her heroine, there are unmistakable traits of reality in the girl. The aunt, too, is a typical English lady of a certain class, and might, with more patient finish and more tender and intelligent sympathy, have been a lovely figure. But Marian Erle has no life that we can call her own. She is, and does, what the poet-novelist wants, neither more nor less, exactly as a woman of wood, in an artist's studio, wears black or white, red or green, a widow's cap or a huntress's feather, according to the painter's design and grouping. Lady Waldemar is not only an extravagant caricature of aristocratic coarseness in speech, but superficial and incorrect as a study of human nature. It was most unlikely that she should have fallen in love with such a man as Romney Leigh, yet a woman's freakishness may account for that; but has a clever, unprincipled, strong-willed, intriguing woman no cunning? Could Lady Waldemar have been so childishly maladroit and indelicate, as to let both Aurora and Marian into the secret of her love? In real life such an one as Lady Waldemar would be the last person in the world to wear her heart upon her sleeve.

If the individuals described in the poem yield so little satisfaction, the classes described make no amends. Mrs. Browning fails both with the aristocracy and with the poor. We have seen her account of the reception met with by Aurora when she visited Marian Erle in St. Margaret's-court, and her description of the crowd of poor people assembled in the chapel of St. James's to see Romney Leigh wed his plebeian bride. That Aurora should have been insulted in entering a house in St. Margaret's-court is of course possible; but I think that all who have engaged in visiting the poor in their own dwellings will admit that such an occurrence is in a high degree improbable. It cannot be said of the English poor that they are slow to recognise the wish to do them good, or to reciprocate kindly feeling. The hideous badness, the rabid ill-temper, attributed to the crowd that went from St. Giles's to see Marian Erle married to Romney Leigh, prove that Mrs. Browning had no real knowledge of the London poor. Romney Leigh, a gentleman of birth and wealth, spending his money for the benefit of the destitute and miserable, and proposing to show his sense of the brotherhood of humanity by marrying a needlewoman, would have been the darling of the multitude. They would have thought him a fool, but would have loved him for all that. Instead of coming to the wedding in foul rags, they would have come in the best things they could buy, beg, or borrow. They and their babies would have been well washed at least; their faces would have been as red as cherries or strawberries with satisfaction and jollity; their temper would have been in a state of radiant goodness, not only on account of the delightful wedding and the expected feast, but from that appreciation of the humour of the whole affair which a London crowd would assuredly have displayed. Had such a celebration as the marriage of Romney Leigh and Marian Erle ever taken place, the appearance of the crowd would most certainly have suggested to no one that " you had stirred up hell to heave its lowest dreg fiends uppermost." The absence of the element of humour in Mrs. Browning's mental composition is painfully conspicuous in these delineations, and is indeed fatal to their success.

So much for the class represented in this marriage on the side of Marian Erle. Now for the class represented by Romney Leigh. Aurora was placed by the bridegroom beside the altar-stair, "where he and other noble gentlemen and high-born ladies waited for the bride." Noble gentleman and high-born ladies, the friends of Romney Leigh, ought to have been favourable representatives of the English aristocracy. Some of them, however, had been asked to be present by Lady Waldemar, and the reader can make what allowance he pleases for their talk on that account. Let us take a sample of it.

> It was early : there was time
> For greeting and the morning's compliment ;
> And gradually a ripple of women's talk
> Arose and fell, and tossed about a spray
> Of English *s*'s, soft as a silent hush,
> And, notwithstanding, quite as audible
> As louder phrases thrown out by the men.
> —" Yes, really, if we've need to wait in church,
> We've need to talk there."—" She ? 'Tis Lady Ayr,
> In blue—not purple ! that's the dowager."
> —" She looks as young."—" She flirts as young, you mean.
> Why, if you had seen her upon Thursday night,
> You'd call Miss Norris modest."—" *You* again !
> I waltzed with you three hours back. Up at six,
> Up still at ten : scarce time to change one's shoes.
> I feel as white and sulky as a ghost,
> So pray don't speak to me, Lord Belcher."—" No,
> I'll look at you instead, and it's enough

> While you have that face." "In church, my lord! fie, fie!"
> "Adair, you stayed for the Division?"—"Lost
> By one." "The devil it is! I'm sorry for 't.
> And if I had not promised Mrs. Grove——"
> "You might have kept your word to Liverpool."
> "Constituents must remember, after all,
> We're mortal."—"We remind them of it."—"Hark,
> The bride comes! Here she comes, in a stream of milk!"
> "There! Dear, you are asleep still; don't you know
> The five Miss Granvilles? Always dressed in white
> To show they're ready to be married." "Lower!
> The aunt is at your elbow." "Lady Maud,
> Did Lady Waldemar tell you she had seen
> This girl of Leigh's?" "No, wait. 'Twas Mrs. Brookes
> Who told me Lady Waldemar told her—
> No, 'twasn't Mrs. Brookes."

Such tattle, whether uttered by aristocrats or by democrats, was surely not worthy of poetical record, and we may, I think, cherish the belief that it is impossibly vulgar and impossibly trivial.

With no better entertainment than such conversation, the ladies and gentlemen naturally grew impatient for the appearance of Marian Erle, and for the commencement of the ceremony. At length Romney stood forward, a letter in his hand, and, with face of appropriate ghostliness and ghastliness, announced that the girl had disappeared and that there would be no marriage. "I am very weak," he said, which was true. "I meant but only good," he added, which was also true, but little to the purpose.

> My friends, you are all dismissed. Go, eat and drink
> According to the programme,—and farewell.

So curt a dismissal was barely courteous, and the crowd, tired with waiting, did not receive it favour-

ably. The cry rose that the girl had had foul play.
One Amazon of logical mind thought that the thing
was too plain to be doubted.

> Disappear!
> Who ever disappears except a ghost?
> And who believes a story of a ghost?
> I ask you,—would a girl go off, instead
> Of staying to be married? A fine tale!
> A wicked man, I say, a wicked man!
> For my part I would rather starve on gin
> Than make my dinner on his beef and beer.

To this woman the crowd gave assent. A rush
was made upon Romney. Clamour of battle and
noise as of fifty Donnybrooks arose in the church.
Fine ladies shrieked or swooned, or "madly fled"
and fell, "trod screeching underneath the feet of
those who fled and screeched." Hearing the wild
cries of the mob, inciting itself to pull down Romney
and kill him, Aurora rushes into the middle of the
fray, to save him, or rather would have done so,
had she not been caught back by some one. The
rest goes without saying. She fainted; the police
succeeded in quelling the tumult; and the sublime
scheme for the union of class with class went the
way of all soap-bubbles. Romney, who was only too
good—so good as to be good for nothing, says the
shrewd Spanish proverb—modestly accused himself of
having been the ruin of his banished bride.

> The poor child!
> Poor Marian! 'twas a luckless day for her,
> When first she chanced on my philanthropy.

Where all is improbable to the verge of pantomime,

it seems idle to specify any one improbability; but it is difficult to imagine anything more unlikely to happen than that Marian Erle should have left Romney in the lurch on the eve of her marriage. She always speaks of him with ardent enthusiasm; his step on the stair is music to her ear; she has no term to suit him but angel; and yet a few glozing words from Lady Waldemar suffice to persuade her to leave the country without bidding him good-bye. Marian Erle would not only have been devoid of feminine ambition, pride, hope, and passion, but would have been more stupidly blind to Lady Waldemar's motives than any daughter of Eve, not a born idiot, could be, if she had permitted the fine lady to cheat her so easily out of a husband. Of course the pretext was that Romney would be unhappy with Marian and supremely happy with Lady Waldemar; but she would be a strange woman who could be persuaded by a rival that the man who had chosen her must be wretched in spite of her wifely devotion to him, and that she could never be happy as his wife. It is important to observe also that, in arguing Marian into the desertion, Lady Waldemar gives no proof of that inexpressible adroitness of logic and rhetoric, by which Shakespeare enables us to understand how his bad people carry out their plots. And even if we grant that Lady Waldemar might have prevailed upon Marian Erle to decline the match, is it credible that her ladyship would have timed the explosion for the wedding-day, thus giving the utmost publicity to the affair? Would she, last of all, have allowed Marian to inform Romney of her departure in a letter in which Lady Waldemar was said to have come nine times to see her, and was unmistakably referred to as an "over-generous friend," who had promised to care for Marian and keep her happy? Having condescended to steep the incidents and characters of a sensation novel in the empyrean colours of her genius, Mrs. Browning does not manage her plot with the ingenuity of a tenth-rate novelist.

Aurora now addresses herself with fresh earnestness to literature, but she is haunted more than ever by the thought of Romney. She has come round to her lover's opinion, which also was Goethe's, that women work for the individual or for the family, not for the race, an opinion which, as we saw, she formerly renounced and resented.

> There it is;
> We women are too apt to look to one,
> Which proves a certain impotence in art.
> We strain our natures at doing something great,
> Far less because it's something great to do,
> Than, haply, that we so commend ourselves
> As being not small, and more appreciable
> To some one friend.

She determines that she will work as a true artist. She will "have no traffic with the personal thought in Art's pure temple." She will aim, as men aim, at the highest excellence, and if she fail, she bids her critics tell her so, and honour her "with truth, if not with praise." Then she dashes into criticism of her own works, and her criticism is, as usual, masterly. The following passage will bear a second or even a third reading. It presents Mrs. Browning's view of art as concerned essentially with reality, not with the fantastic architecture of the brain, even if that architecture is so beautiful as the mythology of Greece, a view which she had already embodied in her noble poem on the gods of Hellas. The passage touches also upon the doctrine of poetic symbolism in its application to the world and all that it contains; every flower, and star, and stream being, for the poet, a word or text in a volume filled with glorious emblems.

> In that descriptive poem called "The Hills"
> The prospects were too far and indistinct.
> 'Tis true my critics said, "A fine view that!"
> The public scarcely cared to climb the book
> For even the finest; and the public's right—
> A tree's mere firewood, unless humanised;
> Which well the Greeks knew when they stirred the bark
> With close-pressed bosoms of subsiding nymphs,
> And made the forest-rivers garrulous
> With babble of gods. For us, we are called to mark
> A still more intimate humanity
> In this inferior nature, or ourselves
> Must fall like dead leaves trodden under foot
> By veritable artists. Earth, shut up
> By Adam, like a fakir in a box
> Left too long buried, remained stiff and dry,
> A mere dumb corpse, till Christ the Lord came down,
> Unlocked the doors, forced open the blank eyes,
> And used His kingly chrisms to straighten out
> The leathery tongue turned back into the throat;
> Since when she lives, remembers, palpitates
> In every limb, aspires in every breath,
> Embraces infinite relations. Now

> We want no half-gods, Panomphœan Joves,
> Fauns, Naiads, Tritons, Oreads, and the rest,
> To take possession of a senseless world
> To unnatural vampire-uses. See the earth
> The body of our body, the green earth
> Indubitably human, like this flesh
> And these articulated veins through which
> Our heart drives blood! There's not a flower of spring
> That dies ere June but vaunts itself allied
> By issue and symbol, by significance
> And correspondence, to that spirit-world
> Outside the limits of our space and time
> Whereto we are bound. Let poets give it voice
> With human meanings; else they miss the thought,
> And henceforth step down lower, stand confessed
> Instructed poorly for interpreters,
> Thrown out by an easy cowslip in the text.
> Even so my pastoral failed; it was a book
> Of surface-pictures—pretty, cold, and false
> With literal transcript—the worse done, I think,
> For being not ill-done. Let me set my mark
> Against such doings, and do otherwise.
> This strikes me. If the public whom we know,
> Could catch me at such admissions, I should pass
> For being right modest. Yet how proud we are,
> In daring to look down upon ourselves!

She proceeds to discuss the question of the fitness of the present age to be poetically treated. "Thinkers scout" our time, and poets abound "who scorn to touch it with a finger-tip." They call it an age of pewter, of scum, of mere transition. All this she declares to be the wrong thinking that makes poor poems, and she illustrates, by a very fine poetical figure, the tendency of the people of each successive age to think their own age trivial.

> Every age,
> Through being held too close, is ill-discerned

> By those who have not lived past it. We'll suppose
> Mount Athos carved, as Persian Xerxes schemed,
> To some colossal statue of a man :
> The peasants, gathering brushwood in his ear,
> Had guessed as little of any human form
> Up there, as would a flock of browsing goats.
> They'd have, in fact, to travel ten miles off
> Or ere the giant image broke on them,
> Full human profile, nose and chin distinct,
> Mouth, muttering rhythms of silence up the sky,
> And fed at evening with the blood of suns ;
> Grand torso,—hand, that flung perpetually
> The largess of a silver river down
> To all the country pastures. 'Tis even thus
> With times we live in,—evermore too great
> To be apprehended near.

She bids poets, if they can sing at all, sing "this live, throbbing age, that brawls, cheats, maddens, calculates, aspires." For her own part, she says that she worked with the true earnestness of the artist. "With no amateur's irreverent haste and busy idleness," did she produce her book. Not failing of recognition, and partially succeeding in what she aimed at, she nevertheless was sad. The womanhood in her called and craved for something more than art,—for affection, for love, for home.

> O supreme Artist, who as sole return
> For all the cosmic wonder of Thy work,
> Demandest of us just a word, a name,
> "My Father!"—Thou hast knowledge, only Thou,
> How dreary 'tis for women to sit still
> On winter nights by solitary fires,
> And hear the nations praising them far off,
> Too far! ay, praising our quick sense of love,
> Our very heart of passionate womanhood,

Which could not beat so in the verse without
Being present also in the unkissed lips,
And eyes undried because there's none to ask
The reason they grow moist.
                              To sit alone,
And think, for comfort, how, that very night,
Affianced lovers, leaning face to face
With sweet half-listenings for each other's breath,
Are reading haply from some page of ours,
To pause with a thrill, as if their cheeks had touched,
When such a stanza, level to their mood,
Seems floating their own thought out—" So I feel
For thee "—" And I, for thee : " this poet knows
What everlasting love is!—how, that night,
A father, issuing from the misty roads
Upon the luminous round of lamp and hearth
And happy children, having caught up first
The youngest there until it shrunk and shrieked
To feel the cold chin prick its dimples through
With winter from the hills, may throw i' the lap
Of the eldest (who has learnt to drop her lids
To hide some sweetness newer than last year's)
Our book and cry, "Ah you, you care for rhymes ;
So here be rhymes to pore on under trees,
When April comes to let you ! I've been told
They are not idle as so many are,
But set hearts beating pure as well as fast :
It's yours, the book ; I'll write your name in it,—
That so you may not lose, however lost
In poet's lore and charming reverie,
The thoughts of how your father thought of *you*
In riding from the town."

Fame—"the love of all"—is, the woman-poet admits, "but a small thing to the love of one." The love of Romney seemed meanwhile to be finally lost to Aurora by his marriage to Lady Waldemar, which she believed to have taken place about this time or soon after. She resolved to leave England and revisit her native Italy, taking Paris in her way. In Paris she meets with Marian Erle. The girl had been subjected to infamous treatment, and, without any fault of hers, had become a mother. The woman to whose care Lady Waldemar had committed her had turned out to be diabolically bad, but there is no reason to suppose that the worst horror in Marian's tragedy had been contemplated by her ladyship. Aurora and Marian go on to Italy in company. The lines descriptive of Aurora's night-watch on deck, as she sails along the Mediterranean coast and looks out for Italy, are, like all the descriptive passages in this book, full of the loveliest poetry.

> I sate upon the deck and watched all night,
> And listened through the stars for Italy.
> Sate silent: I could hear my own soul speak,
> And had my friend,—for Nature comes sometimes
> And says, "I am ambassador for God."
> I felt the wind soft from the land of souls;
> The old miraculous mountains heaved in sight,
> One straining past another along the shore,
> The way of grand dull Odyssean ghosts
> Athirst to drink the cool blue wine of seas
> And stare on voyagers. Peak pushing peak
> They stood: I watched beyond that Tyrian belt
> Of intense sea betwixt them and the ship,
> Down all their sides the misty olive-woods
> Dissolving in the weak congenial moon,
> And still disclosing some brown convent-tower
> That seems as if it grew from some brown rock,—
> Or many a little lighted village, dropt
> Like a fallen star, upon so high a point,
> You wonder what can keep it in its place
> From sliding headlong with the waterfalls
> Which drop and powder all the myrtle-groves
> With spray of silver. Thus my Italy
> Was stealing on us. Genoa broke with day;

> The Doria's long pale palace striking out
> From green hills in advance of the white town,
> A marble finger dominant to ships,
> Seen glimmering through the uncertain gray of dawn.

How Romney follows Aurora and Marian to Italy—how he still proposes to marry Marian—how Aurora and he continue at cross purposes with each other—how Marian declines to accept Romney a second time—and how the cousins at last make it up, and finish the poem with a burst of commonplaces, gloriously versified, about "the love of wedded souls"—my readers must learn for themselves. Perhaps it would be no bad advice to those who wish to make *Aurora Leigh* the means of knowing Mrs. Browning in her strength and not in her weakness, to dip into it here and there, to dwell upon its poetic beauty as distinguished from its qualities as a novel, and thus to get rid of its plot altogether. You cannot read in it too often—you are in no danger of exhausting its treasures; but you may read it too long at a time. There is no end to its good things—its pithy, epigrammatic sayings, its felicities of metaphor and picture.

> Wolff's an atheist;
> And if the Iliad fell out, as he says,
> By mere fortuitous concourse of old songs,
> We'll guess as much, too, for the universe.
> A tree's mere firewood, unless humanised.
> Let us pray
> God's grace to keep God's image in repute.
> Art's the witness of what IS
> Beyond this show. If this world's show were all,
> Mere imitation would be all in Art.

> We should be ashamed to sit beneath those stars,
> Impatient that we're nothing.
>   Art is much, but love is more.
> O Art, my Art, thou'rt much, but Love is more!
> Art symbolises heaven, but Love is God
> And makes heaven.

Here is a metaphysical snatch, in which metaphysics and poetry are so mixed and mingled, and yet so fitly wedded together, that we can hardly tell which is crimson and which cloud:

> No lily-muffled hum of a summer bee
> But finds some coupling with the spinning stars;
> No pebble at your foot but proves a sphere;
> No chaffinch but implies the cherubim:
> And,—glancing on my own thin, veinèd wrist,—
> In such a little tremour of the blood
> The whole strong clamour of a vehement soul
> Doth utter itself distinct. Earth's crammed with heaven,
> And every common bush afire with God:
> But only he who sees, takes off his shoes;
> The rest sit round it, and pluck blackberries,
> And daub their natural faces unaware
> More and more, from the first similitude.

Or take this solemn and profoundly Christian prayer:

> Alas, long-suffering and most patient God,
> Thou need'st be surelier God to bear with us
> Than even to have made us! Thou, aspire, aspire
> From henceforth for me! Thou who hast, Thyself,
> Endured this flesh-hood, knowing how, as a soaked
> And sucking vesture, it would drag us down
> And choke us in the melancholy deep,
> Sustain me, that, with Thee, I walk these waves,
> Resisting!—breathe me upward, Thou for me
> Aspiring, who are the Way, the Truth, the Life,—

> That no truth henceforth seem indifferent,
> No way to truth laborious, and no life,
> Not even this life I live, intolerable !

From these sublime heights, to take farewell of this astonishing poem, we shall descend into the room in which Aurora Leigh and Marian Erle enjoy the woman's treat of having a long look at Marian's baby.

> I saw the whole room, I and Marian there
> Alone.
>   Alone? she threw her bonnet off,
> Then, sighing as 'twere sighing the last time,
> Approached the bed, and drew a shawl away :
> You could not peel a fruit you fear to bruise
> More calmly and more carefully than so,—
> Nor would you find within, a rosier-flushed
> Pomegranate—
>   There he lay, upon his back,
> The yearling creature, warm and moist with life
> To the bottom of his dimples,—to the ends
> Of the lovely tumbled curls about his face ;
> For since he had been covered over-much
> To keep him from the light-glare, both his cheeks
> Were hot and scarlet as the first live rose
> The shepherd's heart-blood ebbed away into,
> The faster for his love. And love was here
> An instant! in the pretty baby-mouth,
> Shut close as if for dreaming that it sucked;
> The little naked feet drawn up the way
> Of nestled birdlings; everything so soft
> And tender,—to the little holdfast hands,
> Which, closing on a finger into sleep,
> Had kept the mould of 't.

In closing the book, I feel that my extracts do it nothing like justice. It is starred with splendours like a clear night in June, or a morning meadow sown with orient pearl.

CONCLUSION.

"I am, of course, not acquainted," I remarked when, many years ago, I first had occasion to print my estimate of Mrs. Browning, "with the works of all great female writers, perhaps not even of many. But as you look towards the brow of a towering mountain, rising far over the clouds, and crowned with ancient snow, you may have an assurance, even though it rises from a plain, or, if amid lower hills, though you have not actually taken the elevation of each, that in height it is peerless. In the poems of Mrs. Browning are qualities which admit of their being compared with those of the greatest men; touches which *only* the mightiest give. These may not come often enough, or they may be too often associated with the spasm of woman's vehemence, to permit her a seat beside those mightiest. With the few sovereigns of literature, the Homers, Shakespeares, Miltons, she will not rank. But in full recollection of Scott's vivacity, and bright, cheerful glow; of Byron's fervid passion and magnificent description; of Wordsworth's majesty; of Shelley's million-coloured fancy; of Coleridge's occasional flights right into the sun-glare; of Bailey's tropic exuberance, and of Tennyson's golden calm; I yet hold her worthy of being mentioned with any poet of this century. She has the breadth and versatility of a man; no sameliness, no one idea, no type character; our single Shakespearean woman. In this I am agreed with by the author of *The Raven*, a critic of great acuteness and originality. 'Woman, sister,' says Thomas de Quincey, 'there are some things which you do not execute as well as your brother, man; no, nor ever will. Pardon me, if I doubt whether you will ever produce a great poet from your choirs, or a Mozart, or a Phidias, or a Michael Angelo, or a great scholar; by which last is meant, not one who depends simply on an infinite memory, but also on an infinite and electrical power of combination, bringing together from the four winds, like the angel of the resurrection, what else were dust from dead men's bones, into the unity of breathing life. If you *can* create yourselves into any of these great creators, why have you not?' Mrs. Browning has exalted her sex; this passage *was* true."

There is, perhaps, more of enthusiasm than of discrimination in these young-mannish sentences. Mrs. Browning I still hold to be, in the full sense of the term, a great poet, but I now see that De Quincey might have maintained the negative on that question with more weighty reasoning than I then surmised; and when I so confidently pronounced Mrs. Browning the greatest of women, fame was but beginning to whisper the name of George Eliot. I would now content myself with saying that, in fervour, melodiousness, and splendour of poetic genius, Mrs. Browning stands, to the best of my knowledge, first among women; that, in tunefulness, the distinctive quality of the poet, George Eliot is greatly her inferior; but that, in knowledge of life, insight into character, comprehensiveness and penetration of thought, and the plastic energy by which the literary artist moulds his figures, she was not the equal of George Eliot.

CHARLOTTE BRONTË AND HER SISTERS.

CHAPTER I.

GENERAL IMPRESSION OF CHARLOTTE BRONTË — THACKERAY'S OPINION OF HER — MRS. GASKELL'S BIOGRAPHY AND MR. WEMYSS REID'S MONOGRAPH — THE JOY OF THE MOORLAND — THE FATHER AND MOTHER OF THE BRONTËS — THE FATHER'S POEMS.

THE main impression derived from the works of Charlotte Brontë or Nicholls—better known a quarter of a century ago as Currer Bell—is that of vivid strength combined with moral vehemence. This is the idea Thackeray felicitously expresses when he calls her "an austere little Joan of Arc marching in upon us, and rebuking our easy lives, our easy morals."

While she lived, very little was known of her history; and the announcement of her death, following swiftly upon that of her marriage, fell upon the public with a suddenness which added poignancy to the pang arising from the knowledge that a genius which, ten years before, had not scaled the horizon, and which had shone for a time with piercing brilliance, was already overtaken by the eclipse of death.

It was in 1855, when the issue of the Crimean war was still undecided, that she died. "Even while the heart of the British nation"—thus I wrote at the time—"is filled to overflowing by one great anguish and one great hope, a thrill of real sorrow will pass to every corner of the land with the tidings that Mrs. Nicholls, formerly Charlotte Brontë, and known to all the world as Currer Bell, is no more. But a few months ago we heard of her marriage. We learned, with a smile of happy surprise, that the merciless derider of weak and insipid suitors had found a lord and master—that the hand which drew the three worshipful ecclesiastics, Malone, Donne, and Sweeting, had been locked at the altar in that of a curate. And already the smile fades away in the sound of her funeral knell, leaving us to reflect, that all of fruit and flower which time might have matured in the garden of her genius has been nipped by the frost of death. There is something which strikes one as peculiarly touching in the death of Currer Bell. She seemed so full of animation, of vigour; life danced in her veins like new wine; all she said was so fresh and stirring; the child-look—taking this for a grand world, worth living in, no place for whining—was still on her face. The brave little woman! in whose works you could not point to a slovenly line, to an obscure or tarrying idea. You thought of her as combining the iron will of her little Jane with the peerless nature of her Shirley, the beautiful pantheress, the forest-born. She could have stood out under the lightning, to

trace, with firm pencil, its zigzags of crackling fire.
And now she, too, is but a few handfuls of white
dust! Her step will never more be upon the loved
wolds of Yorkshire, and the broad moors which she
made classic by her genius.

> Her part in all the pomp that fills
> The circuit of the summer hills
> Is that her grave is green."

Thackeray saw her in London, and the few words
we have from him, whether descriptive of her person,
or characterising the spirit of her books, are deeply
interesting. "Which of her readers," he asks, "has
not become her friend? Who that has known her
books has not admired the artist's noble English, the
burning love of truth, the bravery, the simplicity, the
indignation at wrong, the eager sympathy, the pious
love and reverence, the passionate honour, so to speak,
of the woman?" "I can only say of this lady, *vidi
tantum*. I saw her first just as I rose out of an illness
from which I had never thought to recover. I remember the trembling little frame, the little hand, the
great honest eyes. An impetuous honesty seemed to
me to characterise the woman. Twice I recollect
she took me to task for what she held to be errors in
doctrine. Once about Fielding we had a disputation.
She spoke her mind out. She jumped too rapidly to
conclusions." Her judgment of London celebrities
struck Thackeray as often premature; "but, perhaps,"
he confesses, "the city is rather angry at being
judged." "She gave me the impression of being a

very pure, and lofty, and high-minded person. A great and holy reverence of right and truth seemed to be with her always. Such, in our brief interview, she appeared to me."

The memory of Charlotte Brontë is indissolubly associated with that of her sisters, Emily and Anne. Mrs. Gaskell's biography of Charlotte, an acknowledged masterpiece in that difficult branch of literature, has set before the world in imperishable colours the little Haworth Parsonage, with its neighbouring graves and circling moors, the saturnine father, the unhappy son, and the three shy, pale, plain daughters marked for early death, that belonged to the immortals of the world. "What a story," says Thackeray again, "is that of that family of poets in their solitude yonder on the gloomy northern moors! At nine o'clock at night, Mrs. Gaskell tells us, after evening prayers, when their guardian and relative had gone to bed, the three poetesses—the three maidens, Charlotte, and Emily, and Anne—Charlotte being 'the motherly friend and guardian to the other two'—began, like restless wild animals, to pace up and down their parlour, 'making out' their wonderful stories, talking over plans and projects and thoughts of what was to be their future life."

Perhaps, however, Mrs. Gaskell has conveyed an exaggerated impression of the gloom and desolation of the childhood of the Brontës. Mr. Wemyss Reid, who has made Charlotte Brontë and her sisters the subject of an admirably executed monograph, while acknowledging the great ability and value of Mrs. Gaskell's work, thinks that she has cast the shadow too deeply and too soon over the young Brontës. We have traces, in the earlier part of their lives, of what he justly calls "a wholesome, healthy happiness." No one, I am convinced, will wonder at the fact, who has had any experience of what a high moor on a summer day is to a child. My own first few years, after emerging from infancy, were passed among moors in the north of Scotland, bleaker than it might be easy to find in Yorkshire; and the intense and inexpressible sweetness of roamings among the heather in summer days remains with me to this hour as one of the supreme sensations of my life. This wild joy of the moorland is everywhere traceable in the Brontë books. The very soul of the music that lives, and will live for ever, in the works of the sisters, would have been absent, if they had not heard the song of the winds, and seen the race of the clouds, upon the Yorkshire moors. Mr. Wemyss Reid, therefore, has done good service in counteracting the idea that their life at Haworth was altogether dreary and desolate.

In respect of human companionship, however, the Brontë children were to be pitied. Their mother died when they were tiny things, and their aunt, who came to take care of them, was not fond of children, and had no motherly ways. The servant-of-all-work, Tabby, who assisted their aunt in the housekeeping, was the only other female inmate of the Parsonage; and she, though evidently a rough Yorkshire-woman, had enough kindness of heart to commend her class to Charlotte and Emily, and thus to make the family servants about the most agreeable people in their novels.

The father was peculiar. An Irishman by birth, and rejoicing in the thoroughly Irish name of Prunty —Patrick Prunty—he had cast off his Irish name and called England his adopted country. He was a Tory of the Wellington type; and I have seen—thanks to the courteous suggestion of Mr. Garnett, of the British Museum—three letters, published by him in the *Leeds Intelligencer* newspaper, in January and February, 1829, in which he discusses the question of Roman Catholic Emancipation. Not opposing all concession, he insists that, if Roman Catholics are admitted to the franchise, it will be necessary, in order to secure the Protestantism of the realm, to vest in the King a power "summarily to remove from both Houses of Parliament, and from seats on the judicial bench, all Roman Catholics, when in his judgment they were about to encourage measures subversive of our glorious Constitution in Church and State." This obviously inadmissible and, in fact, childish proposal enables us to gauge his sagacity and information as a politician; and the general cast of his thought on political questions may be further guessed from this incidental utterance: "Our limited Monarchy, which, though not altogether perfect, affords the most rational liberty of any other Government under the sun; and comes, perhaps, as near to perfection as anything that can be devised by, or accommodated to, fallen mortals." This was written before Parliament was reformed, and when pocket boroughs and a good many other things were rotten in the state of England.

Old Brontë is understood to be represented by Helstone, the Tory clergyman in *Shirley*, one of Charlotte's favourite characters. His Toryism was enthusiastically taken up by Charlotte, though I am not so sure as to Emily's political creed. "The election! the election!" wrote Charlotte to a friend in 1835, " that cry has rung even among our lonely hills like the blast of a trumpet. . . . Under what banner have your brothers ranged themselves—the Blue or the Yellow? Use your influence with them, entreat them, if it be necessary, on your knees, to stand by their country and religion in this day of danger!" The vehemently Tory *Blackwood's Magazine* was naturally prized in the parsonage of Haworth, and the good stories it contained, as well as its political articles, were doubtless not without effect on the future novelists. The children were not allowed to associate with the children of the villagers, and grew up shy and sensitive, but not unhappy.

Patrick Brontë's wife, as we learn from Mrs. Gaskell and Mr. Wemyss Reid, was cast in a very different mould from that of her husband. He was tall, strong, full of wiry energy and rugged force, a man against whom Fortune, with all her buffetings, had no chance, who stood the winter of the moors for more than half a century, saw his children die around him, and lived himself to be eighty-five. She was a small woman, of the Cornish type of Celt, frail and fine. Like enough, she may have been "a miracle of symmetry, a miniature of loveliness, all grace summed up and closed in little;" certainly she was a marked contrast to that Irish Hercules, Patrick Brontë. There is no reason to doubt that the tall man loved his delicate and gentle wife. "A few days since" —thus Charlotte writes in 1850—" a little incident happened which curiously touched me. Papa put into my hands a little packet of letters and papers, telling me that they were mamma's, and that I might read them. I did read them, in a frame of mind I cannot describe. The papers were yellow with time, all having been written before I was born. It was strange now to peruse, for the first time, the records of a mind whence my own sprang; and most strange, and at once sad and sweet, to find that mind of a truly fine, pure, and elevated order. They were written to papa before they were married. There is a rectitude, a refinement, a constancy, a modesty, a sense, a gentleness about them indescribable." It may be that some of the finest veining in the genius of the sisters was due to their mother. But we cannot suppose that Brontë treated her with much kindness and sympathy, for this was not in his nature; and in the freakishness of his jealous pride his conduct was sometimes harsh, as when he cut to pieces a dress with which she had been presented. She died before reaching middle age. The children manifestly inherited the low stamina of their mother, as well as their father's fervid temperament and literary ambition.

There is a little volume in the British Museum Library, entitled *The Rural Minstrel: a Miscellany of Descriptive Poems*, which was given to the world by the Rev. Patrick Brontë in 1813. At that date neither Anne, Emily, nor Charlotte was born. Forty-six years later, when all his children were dead, Mr. Brontë published a second volume, also tiny, styled simply *Cottage Poems*. The first was published at Halifax, the second at Bradford. I have glanced over both, and have not seen anything extraordinary in either. There is almost no trace of originality in thought, feeling, or imagery. A strong religious sentiment of the old Evangelical type—the Grimshaw, Toplady, and Wilberforce type—pervades the poems; the Bible is the author's avowed model, authoritative and insuperable, both in matters of thought and of style; Broad Church speculation, High Church enthusiasm, are alike absent. The versification is smooth, and the most observable, perhaps, of the characteristics of the writer is an unaffected, perpetual, child-like delight in the wayside beauties of Nature. He never tires of talking about birds and flowers and dewdrops; and a fresh glimpse now and then shows that he does not always echo the chatter of books, but has cast his own eye lovingly on the things he rhymes about.

> The linnets sweetly sung
> On every fragrant thorn,
> Whilst from the tangled wood
> The blackbirds hailed the morn;
> And, through the dew,
> Ran here and there,
> But half afraid,
> The startled hare.

The first of these stanzas is hopelessly commonplace, but the man who wrote the second must, I think, have watched with patient pleasure the gambollings of half-startled hares. The "ran here and there but half-afraid" is absolutely and exquisitely true to that air of half-domesticated security and familiarity with which a hare will frisk about upon a lawn, whither it has stolen from the adjoining wood or copse, on a clear, warm, dewy evening in June, while overhead the thrush, perched on the highest spray of the larch, is flooding the air with song. I speak from evening observation, but I doubt not it would hold good of early morning. The phenomena that fall to be chronicled about cottage doors were well known to the writer of the following verse, and he would scarcely have placed the accent so nicely on the right spot in the drake, if he had not possessed something of an eye for colour.

> And motley ducks
> Were waddling seen,
> And drake, with neck
> Of glossy green.

We may safely conclude that the vein of poetry which belonged to Charlotte, Emily, and Anne, and of which we have a trace in Branwell, was inherited. Old Brontë was a man of undeveloped genius; and the fact that his genius was undeveloped, will probably account for his unsocial ways, his moody and fitful temper, and his trick of relieving his nervous tension by pistol-shooting. I have seen no reference by the Brontës to their father's poetry, nor does it strike me as unlikely that they may never have read it. He took his meals apart from his children, and though they regarded him with a feeling of respect not unmixed with affection, he was not on terms of sympathetic intimacy with them. Neither Charlotte, Emily, nor Anne ever knew the ecstasy of such a moment as that remembered so vividly by Elizabeth Barrett Browning, when her father looked down upon "the poet at his knee," and rewarded her with a kiss.

CHAPTER II.

*BRANWELL BRONTË—MR. GRUNDY'S REVELA-
TIONS — BRANWELL'S LETTER TO WORDS-
WORTH — CHARLOTTE'S CORRESPONDENCE
WITH SOUTHEY—BRANWELL'S DEATH.*

PATRICK BRANWELL BRONTË, the sole brother of the Brontë sisters, was in his boyhood the hope and darling of the household, but the promise of his early years was lamentably belied, and he died prematurely, an intellectual, as well as moral, wreck. It seems probable that the seeds of a mutinous and wilful disposition soon began to germinate in him, for his father, in a letter quoted by Mrs. Gaskell, refers to him, at a period when he cannot have been more than eight or nine, as "sometimes a naughty boy." A father does not incidentally describe his son in that way without meaning a good deal. Old Brontë mentions that, thinking his children knew more than he had discovered, he put to them certain questions, which they were encouraged to answer by being placed behind a mask. The question addressed to his son was singularly inappropriate to the age of the boy. "I asked Branwell what was the best way of knowing the difference between the intellects of man and woman; he answered, 'By considering the difference between them as to their bodies.'" As Goethe had said almost exactly the same thing, Branwell may be supposed to have picked up the saying in some magazine; but to have even noted such a remark at his age proves him, unless he spoke merely as a parrot, to have been a precocious —perhaps morbidly precocious—boy. There is reason to believe that he possessed a sufficient aptitude for drawing and painting to have made him, under favourable circumstances, an artist of distinction; but a scheme for sending him to study in the Royal Academy miscarried; and his general education appears to have been desultory and imperfect. Probably he read a good many books, and he learned to write in prose and verse with facility. This sufficed to make him a wonder among the rustics, commercial travellers, and small mill-owners of the West Riding, and it is distressing to hear that, when the landlord of the village inn had his room tenanted with travellers or topers, he used to send for young Brontë to talk and drink with them.

Mr. F. H. Grundy, in his recently-published *Pictures of the Past*, after declaring that Branwell "took an unusual fancy" to himself, and that he (Mr. Grundy) "continued, perhaps, his most confidential friend through good and ill until his death," proceeds to expatiate on his "wit, brilliance, attractiveness;" but it would not take much of these qualities to produce an impression on the chance guests or local sots of the

Haworth Black Bull Inn; and nothing could be more stupid than the specimen which Mr. Grundy gives of his friend's conversational performances. The verses which he quotes from Brontë are also excessively poor, nor is there anything remarkable in the extracts from his prose letters. "Remarkable," I mean, in a literary point of view; for as revelations of the writer's moral character, they are remarkably painful. Mr. Grundy talks vaguely of the injustice done to his friend by Mrs. Gaskell, and assumes the part of a vindicator; but the result of his communications, whether in the form of his own remarks or in that of extracts from Branwell's letters, is to convey the impression of a much worse man than we derive from Mrs. Gaskell's biography. Mrs. Gaskell leaves our sentiment of pity comparatively unrestrained in dealing with the sufferings of young Brontë; his self-styled vindicator arouses the sterner sentiments of justice and indignation to contemplate a merited punishment. We used to think of Branwell as a good-natured, weak-willed lad, who, by miscellaneous reading, had turned his mind into a magazine of literary curiosities, who inherited from his father the gift of Hibernian eloquence, who was enthusiastically social, and who thus became first the idol and then the victim of a circle of tipsy villagers. But Mr. Grundy quotes Brontë himself referring to "the grovelling carelessness, the malignant yet cold debauchery, the determination to find how far mind could carry body without both being chucked into hell," which marked his conduct at a time when he had undertaken to discharge the duties of stationmaster on a railway. He threw (Mr. Grundy tells us) all the work on a porter, while he went carousing with brother sots, and " serious defalcations " were the consequence. An inquiry followed; Brontë was acquitted of theft; " but," says his vindicator, " was convicted of constant and culpable carelessness."

In another of his Grundy letters, Brontë avows a breach of trust of a still more dark and treacherous nature. He says that for years he was on terms of disgraceful intimacy with the wife of a gentleman in whose family he acted as tutor. Mr. Wemyss Reid calls attention to a passage in Charlotte Brontë's first novel, *The Professor*, in which this circumstance is alluded to in terms of fervent condemnation. " Limited as had yet been my experience of life, I had once had the opportunity of contemplating, near at hand, an example of the results produced by a course of interesting and romantic domestic treachery. No golden halo of fiction was about this example: I saw it bare and real, and it was very loathsome. I saw a mind degraded by the practice of mean subterfuge, by the habit of perfidious deception, and a body depraved by the infectious influence of the vice-polluted soul. I had suffered much from the forced and prolonged view of this spectacle: those sufferings I did not now regret, for their simple recollection acted as a most wholesome antidote to temptation. They had inscribed on my reason the conviction that unlawful pleasure, trenching on another's rights, is delusive and envenomed pleasure—its hollowness disappoints at the time, its poison cruelly tortures afterwards, its effects deprave for ever."

In his nineteenth year (January, 1837), Branwell Brontë sent a letter to Wordsworth, enclosing a sample of his poetry. It is unmistakable that the adulation of his little circle had already mounted to the lad's brain, and that the conceit and vanity which at this age are of evil augury were in a high state of development. "My aim, sir," he wrote, "is to push out into the open world, and for this I trust not poetry alone—that might launch the vessel, but could not bear her on; sensible and scientific prose, bold and vigorous efforts in my walk of life, would give a farther title to the notice of the world; and then again poetry ought to brighten and crown that name with glory; but nothing of all this can be ever begun without means, and as I don't possess them, I must in every shape strive to gain them. Surely, in this day, when there is not a *writing* poet worth a sixpence, the field must be open, if a better man can step forward." Wordsworth appears to have taken no notice of this letter, and we may pretty confidently conjecture that glancing at the accompanying verses, and finding them utterly void of merit, he put both letter and verses aside, with a smile of serene cynicism at the idea of so paltry a rhymester announcing himself as the probable poet of the future.

A few weeks before Branwell wrote to Wordsworth, Charlotte had written to Southey. Mrs. Gaskell seems to have seen a copy of the letter, for she says that it contained "some high-flown expressions," but she annoyingly withholds it from her readers. She gives us Southey's reply, however, and it is worthy of that Bayard of literary chivalry. He has formed a very different estimate of the poetry of the day from that of the stripling of nineteen, who told Wordsworth that not a writing poet was worth sixpence. "Many volumes of poems," he says, "are now published every year without attracting public attention, any one of which, if it had appeared half a century ago, would have obtained a high reputation for its author." Young Brontë's scornful dismissal of contemporary poetry as beneath notice proves either that he did not know what verse was being published, and therefore spoke with mere random impertinence, or that he had no critical judgment. Since Christopher North was a household word in Haworth Parsonage, and a copious selection from the early poems of Tennyson had been printed in *Blackwood's Magazine* in North's famous critique on Tennyson, the latter seems to be the more probable supposition. The puerile arrogance, which had no effect upon Wordsworth, was likely to be very imposing in the eyes of Brontë's audience in the Black Bull at Haworth; for arrogant depreciation of others will always be accepted by foolish and ignorant persons—that is to say, by a large proportion of mankind—as proof of talent, spirit, and accomplishment.

While writing with the gentlest consideration for his correspondent, Southey advised Charlotte to banish every idea of literature as a profession, and to indulge in poetry only in moments of perfect leisure. "I," he wrote, "who have made literature my profession, and devoted my life to it, and have never for a moment repented of the deliberate choice, think myself, nevertheless, bound in duty to caution every young man who applies as an aspirant to me for encouragement and advice, against taking so perilous a course." In many letters which have found their way into print, Mr. Carlyle has expressed a similar opinion to this of Southey's; and I should think that it would be endorsed by ninety-nine out of every hundred men and women now earning their bread by literature.

After pronouncing somewhat too peremptorily, that "literature cannot be the business of a woman's life, and it ought not to be," Southey proceeds to say that he does not disparage poetry, or forbid its cultivation. "I only exhort you so to think of it, and so to use it, as to render it conducive to your own permanent good. Write poetry for its own sake—not in a spirit of emulation, and not with a view to celebrity; the less you aim at that the more likely you will be to deserve and finally to obtain it. So written, it is wholesome both for the heart and soul. It may be made the surest means, next to religion, of soothing the mind and elevating it. You may embody in it your best thoughts and your wisest feelings, and in so doing discipline and strengthen them."

Charlotte replied to this letter with all the home-bred warmth of feeling, and all the artless simplicity, of an intelligent, good-hearted girl of twenty. "I cannot rest," she says, "till I have answered your letter, even though, by addressing you a second time, I should appear a little intrusive; but I must thank you for the kind and wise advice you have condescended to give me." She sketches her present life and past history with the nicest selection of the essential points, and with self-evidencing fidelity to truth in every touch. "You kindly allow me to write poetry for its own sake, provided I leave undone nothing which I ought to do, in order to pursue that single, absorbing, exquisite gratification. I am afraid, sir, you think me very foolish. I know the first letter I wrote to you was all senseless trash from beginning to end; but I am not altogether the idle dreaming being it would seem to denote. My father is a clergyman of limited, though competent income, and I am the eldest of his children. He expended quite as much in my education as he could afford in justice to the rest. I thought it, therefore, my duty, when I left school, to become a governess. In that capacity I find enough to occupy my thoughts all day long, and my head and hands, too, without having a moment's time for one dream of the imagination. In the evenings, I confess, I do think, but I never trouble any one else with my thoughts. I carefully avoid any appearance of pre-occupation and eccentricity, which might lead those I live amongst to suspect the nature of my pursuits. Following my father's advice—who from my childhood has counselled me, just in the wise and friendly tone of your letter—I have endeavoured not only attentively to observe all the duties a woman ought to fulfil, but to feel deeply interested in them. I don't always succeed, for sometimes when I'm teaching or sewing I would rather be reading or writing; but I try to deny myself, and my father's approbation amply rewards me for the privation. Once more allow me to thank you with sincere gratitude. I trust I shall never more feel ambitious to see my name in print; if the wish should rise, I'll look at Southey's letter, and suppress it. It is honour enough for me that I have written to him, and received an answer. That letter is consecrated; no one shall ever see it but papa and my brother and sisters. Again I thank you."

The *naïveté* of this is delicious. Fancy the future authoress of *Jane Eyre* and *Shirley* schooling herself to find occupation for all her faculties in her needle, and calmly resolving never to think of seeing her name in print. A dozen years after she wrote thus, Charlotte had taken her place with acclamation among the world's great women. The kind-hearted, noble Southey was evidently struck with her letter. He replied promptly and with much cordiality. "Your letter has given me great pleasure, and I should not forgive myself if I did not tell you so.

You have received admonition as considerately and as kindly as it was given. Let me now request that, if you ever should come to these Lakes while I am living here, you will let me see you."

There is one sentence in Branwell Brontë's letter to Wordsworth which has a mournful significance. He has, he says, been writing a poem, in which he has "striven to develop strong passions and weak principles struggling with a high imagination and acute feelings, till, as youth hardens towards age, evil deeds and short enjoyments end in mental misery and bodily ruin." The words are a prophecy of his own fate. I have said that his conduct became such as to merit the sternest reprobation; but his fall was due to his misfortune as well as his fault. We may believe Mrs. Gaskell when she tells us that his impulses were originally praiseworthy, and that he showed strong family affection. What failed him was firm and judicious discipline, and he was in that situation which, beyond all others, makes want of discipline fatal. He was an only son in a family of daughters, brought up by an aunt who made him her favourite. "There are always," says Mrs. Gaskell, " peculiar trials in the life of an only boy in a family of girls. He is expected to act a part in life; to *do*, while they are only to *be;* and the necessity of their giving way to him in some things is too often exaggerated into their giving way to him in all, and thus rendering him utterly selfish." Never does the bitterest cruelty disguise itself in the garb of kindness so signally as when proud parents and loving sisters enfeeble, in a son and brother, that moral will on which depends all stability of character. Never, let me add, was the genial and guardian influence of sound moral conditions, in relation to youthful genius, more pointedly illustrated than by the ruin of the young man, and the emergence into fame of the young women, in this " family of poets."

Branwell went from bad to worse until he fell into the criminal degradation on which Mr. Grundy has cast so dismal a light. From the time when he was dismissed his tutorship, he became a prey to the agonies of remorse alternating with forced outbursts of mirth. He had previously given way to intoxication, he now became an opium-eater. His constitution gradually broke down, and, as the end approached, he proved an inexpressible affliction to his old father and his sisters. "For some time," writes Mrs. Gaskell, "before his death he had attacks of delirium tremens of the most frightful character; he slept in his father's room, and he would sometimes declare that either he or his father should be dead before the morning. The trembling sisters, sick with fright, would implore their father not to expose himself to this danger; but Mr. Brontë is no timid man, and perhaps he felt that he could possibly influence his son to some self-restraint, more by showing trust in him than by showing fear. The sisters often listened for the report of a pistol in the dead of the night, till watchful eye and hearkening ear grew heavy and dull with the perpetual strain upon their nerves. In the morning young Brontë would saunter out, saying, with a drunkard's incontinence of speech, 'The poor old man and I have had a terrible night of it; he does his best—the poor old man! but it's all over with me.'" What tragedy could be more drearily sad than that?

Charlotte and her sisters endured this great calamity with heroic fortitude. When Branwell died, the feelings with which they had regarded him in his boyhood returned, and not an angry syllable escaped from Charlotte's pen when she chronicled the event. "He was perfectly conscious till the last agony came on. His mind had undergone the peculiar change which frequently precedes death, two days previously; the calm of better feelings filled it; a return of natural affection marked his last moments. He is in God's hands now; and the All-Powerful is likewise the All-Merciful. A deep conviction that he rests at last—rests well after his brief, erring, suffering, feverish life—fills and quiets my mind now. The final separation, the spectacle of his pale corpse, gave me more acute, bitter pain than I could have imagined. Till the last hour comes, we never know how much we can forgive, pity, regret a near relative. All his vices were and are nothing now. We remember only his woes." He died in the autumn of 1848.

CHAPTER III.

THE POEMS OF CURRER, ELLIS, AND ACTON BELL.

BRANWELL BRONTË proving a scapegrace, the three sisters, Charlotte, Emily, and Anne, seem to have let him pass beyond the circle of their fellowship, and were drawn into closer and intenser sympathy, into more exclusive and close-knit friendship, among themselves, than could well have linked them together if their brother had continued to occupy the place naturally belonging to him in their love and esteem. "The two human beings," wrote Charlotte, after the deaths of Anne and Emily, "who understood me, and whom I understood, are dead." She does not hint that her brother, who stood next to her in the family, ever understood her. At some indefinite period in their girlhood, which Charlotte leaves us to guess at from the phrase, "very early," the three sisters discovered that they possessed, each and all, the gift of literary expression, and "cherished the dream of one day being authors." There was motherly, managing Charlotte, the eldest; there was modest, nun-like Anne, the youngest; and between the two, different from both, stood the deep-thinking, shy, intense, unsocial Emily, content to be subordinate to Charlotte in all ordinary matters, leaning upon her—Emily was the taller and thinner of the two—in walks, and trusting to her to do all the speaking to strangers, but hiding in her own breast an originality weird and morbid, yet more intrepid, thoroughgoing, and imaginative even than Charlotte's.

The strange girls were not popular with their neighbours. Emily in particular was held by the Haworth people to be forbidding. Their personal appearance —if we may trust Mr. Grundy, and I should think that on such a point, allowing for a dash of flippancy and caricature, we may believe him—was not attractive. "Distant and distrait, large of nose, small of figure, red of hair, prominent of spectacles; showing great intellectual development, but with eyes constantly cast down, very silent, painfully retiring,"—such is his picture of the group. The "eyes constantly cast down" I cannot but think apocryphal; Charlotte at least could hold up her head when she chose; but perhaps the sisters did not experience from the presence of Mr. Grundy that "eye-brightening" influence, which makes "the massed clouds roll" from the brow.

An honest stationer in Haworth gave Mrs. Gaskell a much kindlier account of the Misses Brontë. "They used to buy a great deal of writing-paper," he said; and he would "wonder whatever they did with so much." When out of paper for want of capital —"I was always," he says, "short of that"—he feared their coming, "they seemed so distressed about it." The good-natured fellow would walk ten miles "for half a ream of paper," rather than disappoint them. "I did so like them to come," he goes on, "when I had anything for them; they were so much different to anybody else; so gentle and kind, and so very quiet." He was conscious of no repulsiveness in their demeanour. Charlotte, however, seems to have been more affable than the others. She "sometimes would sit and inquire about our circumstances so kindly and feelingly." We may conclude, therefore, that it was not wholly, if at all, from their unsociable character, but because they lacked sympathetic neighbours, that the Brontë sisters lived so recluse a life at Haworth.

It was a great day for the sisters when, in the autumn of 1845, Charlotte "accidentally lighted on a MS. volume of verse" in Emily's handwriting. "Of course," she says, "I was not surprised, knowing that she could and did write verse. I looked it over, and something more than surprise seized me—a deep conviction that these were not common effusions, nor at all like the poetry women generally write. I thought them condensed and terse, vigorous and genuine. To my ear they had also a peculiar music, wild, melancholy, and elevating." So far as it goes, this is a singularly just critique of Emily's poems; but it does not go beyond the record of a first impression.

Anne, finding that the great critical authority of the household smiled approval on Emily, now announced that she also had composed poems. They were produced, and again the judgment proved favourable. "I thought," says Charlotte, "that these verses too had a sweet, sincere pathos of their own." If to "sweet, sincere pathos" we add unaffected and graceful feeling, and correct, easy, not unmelodious versification, we have almost a sufficient account of Anne Brontë's poems.

The poetical powers of Charlotte seem to have been already known in the household, and the three sisters now formed the project of publishing a selection of their poems. It is a striking illustration of the state of severance and solitude, in relation both to their father and their brother, in which these girls lived, that neither Branwell nor Mr. Brontë was consulted as to the merit of the poems, or taken into the secret of publication. A special pathos is shed upon this state of affairs by the fact that the father had himself, as we saw, published poetry.

But what reader with any tincture of sensibility and imagination can altogether fail to realise the situation of the sisters under these new circumstances? How keen would be the interest imparted to their whole life! How "fluttering-fain," to use a fine imaginative epithet from their father's first volume, would be their hearts, as poem after poem was submitted to the critical conclave for selection or rejection! How their eyes would glisten when they dared to look towards the future, and when hope suffused the horizon with auroral tints of fame, fortune, enlargement—a vision on which they would not trust themselves to dwell often or long, but which was quite sure to present itself at moments to gifted and aspiring women. Their complete isolation would enhance their joy; the moaning of the frozen wind of the moors around their little fire brightening the glow of it upon their faces. Then there was much to be excogitated, many letters to be written. Our good Haworth friend of the limited capital would find his boot-leather sorely taxed. They had an idea that the world looks unfavourably upon writing women, yet shrank from anything like a positive act of falsification, and therefore hunted up three names which no mortal could assign expressly to the one sex or the other—Currer, Ellis, and Acton. The choice could not have been more felicitously mystifying, and the rather common surname Bell would naturally suggest a plebeian father, of high-flying temperament, who had given three out-of-the-way names to his sons. There were publishers to be corresponded with, questions of expense to be considered, the father's surprise, when the postman brought a letter addressed to Currer Bell, Esquire, to be obviated, and at last proofs to be corrected. It is in experiences like these that life becomes precious, that friendship and the affection of close relationship combine to pour the elixir of pure and tingling joy along the veins. In those weeks of cosing and conspiring over their grand ploy, England, we may be sure, did not hold many happier groups than that of the three Brontë sisters.

The volume was published in 1846 by Messrs. Aylott and Jones, London. Its interest depends mainly on the self-portraiture of the authors, of which, indeed, it may be said to consist. Anne's verses exhibit a devout, sincere, and tender nature, chastened by religious melancholy. Her mood, as Charlotte says, was that of "perpetual pensiveness." "The pillar of a cloud glided constantly before her eyes; she ever waited at the foot of a secret Sinai, listening in her heart to the voice of a trumpet, sounding long and waxing louder." Patrick Brontë seems to have been what would now be considered a rigid Calvinist, taking the pessimist rather than the equally logical optimist view of the Augustinian system; and the idea of God as an inexorable Fate cast a deep shadow over the minds of the three sisters, but especially of Anne. It is consoling to learn that, "in her last moments, this tyranny of a too tender conscience was overcome; this pomp of terrors broke up, and, passing away, left her dying hour unclouded." The invincible goodness of her nature, the importunate kindness of her heart, are pathetically shown by her rebellion against that harshest of all dogmas which affirms not only that a large proportion of mankind are consigned to eternal torment, but that it is the duty of humble souls to rejoice in this arrangement. A few stanzas from the poem, which she calls *A Word to the "Elect,"* will explain her position.

> You may rejoice to think *yourselves* secure;
> You may be grateful for the gift divine—
> That grace unsought, which made your black hearts pure,
> And fits your earth-born souls in Heaven to shine.

> But is it sweet to look around, and view
>   Thousands excluded from that happiness
> Which they deserved, at least, as much as you,—
>   Their faults not greater, nor their virtues less?
>
> And, wherefore should your hearts more grateful prove,
>   Because for ALL the Saviour did not die?
> Is yours the God of justice and of love?
>   And are your bosoms warm with charity?
>
> And when you, looking on your fellow-men,
>   Behold them doomed to endless misery,
> How can you talk of joy and rapture then?—
>   May God withhold such cruel joy from me!
>
>   And oh! there lives within my heart
>   A hope, long nursed by me;
>   (And should its cheering ray depart,
>   How dark my soul would be!)
>
>   That as in Adam all have died,
>   In Christ shall all men live;
>   And ever round His throne abide,
>   Eternal praise to give.

The sadness which pervades Anne's poems renders them, however, on the whole, oppressive and unhealthy. Only once do I observe that she breaks into a strain of jubilation, a high wind in a wood dissipating for a moment the gloom of her spirit.

> My soul is awakened, my spirit is soaring,
>   And carried aloft on the wings of the breeze;
> For above and around me the wild wind is roaring,
>   Arousing to rapture the earth and the seas.
> The long withered grass in the sunshine is glancing,
>   The bare trees are tossing their branches on high;
> The dead leaves beneath them are merrily dancing,
>   The white clouds are scudding across the blue sky.

Charlotte's own poems, though much less restricted in idea than those of her youngest sister, are not of much value. Both sisters are accomplished versifiers and have command of clear and vivid words, but both fail in imagination, in variety of colour, and in passion. This, from *Pilate's Wife's Dream*, by Charlotte, is a tolerable stanza, but the piece, as a whole, is disappointing.

> The world advances; Greek or Roman rite
>   Suffices not the inquiring mind to stay;
> The searching soul demands a purer light
>   To guide it on its upward, onward way:
> Ashamed of sculptured gods, Religion turns
> To where the unseen Jehovah's altar burns.

The lines entitled *Preference* are eloquent rather than poetical; they read like an average passage from *Jane Eyre* or *Shirley* finely versified; but they have this potent interest, that they present us with a brilliant sketch, from her own hand, of the kind of man whom Charlotte Brontë, in her years of brightest womanhood, would have loved. She first dismisses the man whom she could not love, telling him not to flatter himself that he has made the least impression.

> Why that smile? Thou now art deeming
>   This my coldness all untrue,
> But a mask of frozen seeming,
>   Hiding secret fires from view.
> Touch my hand, thou self-deceiver;
>   Nay—be calm, for I am so:
> Does it burn? Does my lip quiver?
>   Has mine eye a troubled glow?

She grants no refuge to his *amour propre* in the notion that perhaps, if she will not have him, she will have no one.

> Can I love? Oh, deeply—truly—
> Warmly—fondly—but not thee;
> And my love is answered duly,
> With an equal energy.
> Would'st thou see thy rival? Hasten
> Draw that curtain soft aside,
> Look where yon thick branches chasten
> Noon, with shades of eventide.
> In that glade, where foliage blending
> Forms a green arch overhead,
> Sits thy rival, thoughtful bending
> O'er a stand with papers spread—
> Motionless, his fingers plying
> That untired, unresting pen;
> Time and tide unnoticed flying,
> There he sits—the first of men!
> Man of conscience—man of reason;
> Stern, perchance, but ever just;
> Foe to falsehood, wrong, and treason,
> Honour's shield and virtue's trust.
> Worker, thinker, firm defender
> Of Heaven's truth—man's liberty;
> Soul of iron—proof to slander,
> Rock where founders tyranny.
> Fame he seeks not—but full surely
> She will seek him in his home;
> This I know, and wait securely
> For the atoning hour to come—
> To that man my faith is given.

There is better poetry than this in Charlotte Brontë's prose; but it would be hard to refuse one whose strongest feelings take so naturally and flowingly the garment of verse the name of poet.

I have never changed the opinion, formed and expressed by me many years ago, that the poems of Emily Brontë excel those of her sisters. They are superior in occasional splendour and concentrated force of expression; in serene intensity; in penetration and power of thought. Take as a sample of her gift of expression the following poem,—I omit a few of the stanzas.

STARS.

Ah! why, because the dazzling sun
   Restored our earth to joy,
Have you departed, every one,
   And left a desert sky?
All through the night, your glorious eyes
   Were gazing down in mine,
And, with a full heart's thankful sighs,
   I blessed that watch divine.
I was at peace, and drank your beams
   As they were life to me;
And revelled in my changeful dreams
   Like petrel on the sea.
Why did the morning dawn to break
   So great, so pure a spell;
And scorch with fire the tranquil cheek,
   Where your cool radiance fell?
Blood-red, he rose, and, arrow-straight,
   His fierce beams struck my brow;
The soul of nature sprang, elate,
   But *mine* sank sad and low!
My lids closed down, yet through their veil
   I saw him, blazing still,
And steep in gold the misty dale,
   And flash upon the hill.
Oh, stars, and dreams, and gentle night!
   Oh, night and stars return!
And hide me from the hostile light,
   That does not warm, but burn;
That drains the blood of suffering men;
   Drinks tears, instead of dew;
Let me sleep through his blinding reign,
   And only wake with you!

The second of these verses expresses a thought which certainly is not new, but no thought could be more beautiful or more imaginative; the fifth is superb in its brevity and concentration,—in its burst of colour, its blaze of light: we feel ourselves flooded with the crimson of dawn. Charlotte has once or twice written as finely in prose; never in verse.

Lovely also, with a grave, high, solemn loveliness, especially towards its close, is the poem entitled *A Death Scene*. The lady hangs over her dying lover while the sun is high and the west winds are blowing, and entreats him not to yield to death. But a glance that rebuked her for yielding weakly to her woe, " one mute look of suffering," moved her to repent her prayer. She grew calm. No sign of further grieving stirred her soul. The last hour came.

> Paled, at length, the sweet sun setting;
>   Sunk to peace the twilight breeze:
> Summer dews fell softly, wetting
>   Glen, and glade, and silent trees.
>
> Then his eyes began to weary,
>   Weighed beneath a mortal sleep;
> And their orbs grew strangely dreary,
>   Clouded, even as they would weep.
>
> But they wept not, but they changed not,
>   Never moved, and never closed;
> Troubled still, and still they ranged not—
>   Wandered not, nor yet reposed.
>
> So I knew that he was dying—
>   Stooped, and raised his languid head;
> Felt no breath, and heard no sighing,
>   So I knew that he was dead.

But the most important of Emily Brontë's poems—the most original in thought, the most powerful in imagination, the most intensely sincere and impassioned in feeling—is one too vaguely called *The Philosopher*. It consists of an interchange of confidences between two sages, or two personified moods of the same sage, on the question of questions,—God or no God? The one sage believes; the other, to say the least, hesitates. The second sage has the last word, and this appears to show that the position he takes up is adopted by the author. Let us hear first the believing sage.

> " I saw a Spirit, standing, man,
>   Where thou dost stand—an hour ago,
> And round his feet three rivers ran,
>   Of equal depth and equal flow—
> A golden stream—and one of blood—
>   And one of sapphire seemed to be;
> But when they joined their triple flood
>   It tumbled in an inky sea.
> The Spirit sent his dazzling gaze
>   Down through that ocean's gloomy night;
> Then, kindling all, with sudden blaze,
>   The glad deep sparkled wide and bright—
> White as the sun, far, far more fair
> Than its divided sources were!"

Such is the statement of his experience, such the profession of his faith, by the believer in God. Observe the imaginative grandeur, combined with intellectual subtlety, of the similitude made use of. Every painter knows that the three primitive colours, red, yellow, blue—here represented by blood, gold, and sapphire—yield, when mingled, an "inky," or, at least, brown-black tint. Yet out of those same colours, linked in celestial harmony, arises the pure white light. The seer, the proclaimer of faith in God, avers that, while he looked upon the colours mixing in the blackness of chaos—the blackness of matter—the blackness of an universal inky ocean unvisited by light—he saw a Spirit send from His eye an irradiating beam, which turned blackness into beauty and night into day, kindling the universe with sudden blaze of order, life, and joy. That Spirit was God.

To have devised and worked out a conception like this would have satisfied almost any woman-poet that ever lived; but it is only the prelude to what Emily Brontë has to say. She has uttered the challenge: now for the reply. It is the philosophical sceptic, the representative of earnest doubt, that speaks.

> " And even for that Spirit, seer,
>   I've watched and sought my lifetime long;
> Sought Him in heaven, hell, earth, and air,
>   An endless search, and always wrong.
> Had I but seen His glorious eye
>   *Once* light the clouds that wilder me,
> I ne'er had raised this coward cry
>   To cease to think and cease to be;
> I ne'er had called oblivion blest,
>   Nor, stretching eager hands to death,
> Implored to change for senseless rest
>   This sentient soul, this living breath.
> Oh, let me die !—that power and will
>   Their cruel strife may close;
> And conquered good, and conquering ill,
>   Be lost in one repose ! "

To this Emily Brontë gives no answer. By all rules of interpretation, the speaker must be held to stand for the poet. It seems, therefore, to be Emily Brontë who, deliberately and intensely, but without the remotest suggestion of irreverence, affirms that she has looked for the Spirit announced by the seer who spoke first, and has not seen Him. *One* glimpse, she says, would have been enough, but that one glimpse she did not obtain; and in colossal sincerity, though with unspeakable distress, she turns to the universe, which is for her a grave, and accepts the eternal death that is her portion. Whether it is in the mere dramatic sympathy of an artist that Emily Brontë puts words into the mouth of the philosopher; or whether the words are her own, and reveal a secret that might throw some light on her stern, reserved, ungenial existence, and on the mood of mind in which *Wuthering Heights* was composed;—I shall not undertake to decide.

I confess, however, that I look upon the second of these hypotheses as in a high degree probable. The verses come, if ever verses came, from the heart, and I cannot help thinking that the fire within them searched with its burnings the soul of Emily Brontë. Charlotte, I fancy, never fathomed the depths of her sister's mind. At all events, the girl who wrote these stanzas had uttered the last and deepest word that has been spoken, or can rationally be spoken, by modern doubt. "Show us"—this is the challenge of the Tyndalls, the John Morleys—" any glittering upon

the clouds of nature that proceeds from a Divine
Eye, any force, influence, power, in or upon this
all-comprehending nature, which is not part and
parcel of nature itself, of nature everlastingly self-
produced and self-swallowed, which is in any sense
above or beyond, or dynamically distinguishable from
nature, and with which man can enter into communi-
cation; and we will believe." Thrice blessed are they
who can solemnly, and in all the calmness of intelligent
faith, believe that God *has* given them such a glance
of His eye that they cannot but believe in His
existence; but it may be doubted whether the reason
of their faith admits of being presented in a logically
unassailable form. On the other hand, those who
refuse to believe may be expected to admit that their
negation is purely personal, that they are not justified
in converting it into a positive and generalised statement, and that they ought to weigh fairly, in the
opposite scale, the deliberate assertion of tens of
thousands of the best and wisest representatives of
the species, that God *has* spoken to them. To the
individual testimony, also, must in fairness be added
the testimony of the race, a testimony in which,
Hume being judge, all ages and tribes are unanimous,
a testimony so decisively signalising man as the wor-
shipping animal, the creature that, on nature's highest
pinnacle, opens his eye on God, that Auguste Comte
can find no basis of possible organisation for human
society except a religious basis. Why, if evolution
be true, should the supreme and ultimate fact of

evolution be denied? Why, when man, the Columbus of the universe, has caught sight of the Divine and Eternal continents of spiritual existence, should they be perversely declared to be but sun-gilt mist?

This, however, we may hold with all clearness and decision, that when one does, as Emily Brontë did, and as the poet Cowper still more conspicuously did, thirst after God with genuine and impassioned longing, the hiding of His countenance is but apparent —a physical clouding of the brain—and is not only not identical with, but essentially opposite to, that sensual and self-satisfied atheism, that brutish indifference to ideal aims and disinterested virtues, that rancorous mutiny against law and order, which is moral death.

CHAPTER IV.

WUTHERING HEIGHTS—MR. GRUNDY ON ITS AUTHORSHIP—THE EXTRAORDINARY CHARACTER OF THE BOOK.

THE poems of the Brontë sisters, published anonymously at their own expense, shared the fate which has generally attended books in which the publishers have had no interest. Many anonymous books have succeeded, many books by young and unpractised writers have succeeded, but books published by authors at their own expense are the pariahs of literature. These brave girls, however, were not cast down. "Ill-success," says Charlotte, "failed to crush us: the mere effort to succeed had given a wonderful zest to existence; it must be pursued." They resolved that their next venture should be in prose. Charlotte produced *The Professor*, Anne *Agnes Grey*, the reserved, deep-thoughted, brooding Emily *Wuthering Heights*. Of the first I shall have something to say in connection with Charlotte's last novel, *Villette*. The second I attempted to read, many years ago, but failed. *Wuthering Heights* is one of the most remarkable of all the Brontë books, and derives an interest almost poignantly keen from its relation to the character of Emily Brontë. It must be carefully examined.

Before taking up the book I am forced, not without considerable reluctance, to put out of the way a statement respecting it made by Mr. F. H. Grundy, whose unparalleled "vindication" of poor Branwell Brontë I formerly referred to. Mr. Grundy observes "that the question of the authorship of *Wuthering Heights* has long vexed the critics." This is new to me. When *Wuthering Heights* appeared, many people thought that it was by the author of *Jane Eyre*, which had been published a few months earlier. On this misconception Charlotte wrote as follows:— "Unjust and grievous error! We laughed at it at first, but I deeply lament it now." Such a report would naturally pain the true author, and Charlotte did justice to her sister by saying, with brief precision, "Ellis Bell produced *Wuthering Heights*." Since these words were printed, no critic has been "vexed" by doubt or question as to the authorship of the novel. But Mr. Grundy makes this startling averment: "Patrick Brontë declared to me, and what his sister said bore out the assertion, that he wrote a great portion of *Wuthering Heights* himself. Indeed, it is impossible for me to read that story without meeting with many passages which I feel certain *must* have come from his pen. The weird fancies of diseased genius with which he used to entertain me in our long talks at Luddendenfoot, reappear in the pages of the novel, and I am inclined to believe that the very plot was his invention rather than his sister's."

Mr. Grundy's book was published in 1879. The statements which he imputes to Branwell Brontë cannot have been made less than thirty-one years before that date. Mr. Grundy has lived a roving life, traversing first England and then Australia in the exercise of his profession as an engineer, and it is no discredit to him that his memory should have become confused as to the particulars of conversations that took place, in or before 1848, between him and young Brontë. It would be painful to think that the latter laid claim to the authorship of *Wuthering Heights*, for if he did, he must have spoken falsely. Not a line of his composition, whether in prose or in verse, exhibits a glimpse of such power as appears everywhere in the novel. The negative proof against him is singularly complete and convincing. Neither in his own letters, nor in Mrs. Gaskell's biography, nor in Charlotte's account of the origin of *Wuthering Heights*, is there a trace of evidence that he was ever associated with his sisters in their literary enterprises. We hear of him as having been an usher in a school, a private tutor, a portrait-painter, trying to establish himself at Bradford, all before he was twenty-two. At twenty-two he is at Luddendenfoot, astonishing Mr. Grundy by his conversation, neglecting his duties, carousing with worthless companions, and conducting himself, on the whole, disgracefully. It is hardly conceivable that the drunken station-master should have told Mr. Grundy that he had written part of the novel which, six or seven years later, Emily Brontë was to publish as her own. When Brontë left Luddendenfoot, Mr. Grundy lost sight of him for three years; in Brontë's letters which followed the resumption of their intercourse, and from which Mr. Grundy prints several extracts, there is not a hint that he is author of *Wuthering Heights*, or that he has the slightest knowledge of the literary activity of his sisters. In the interval he had been dismissed in profound disgrace from his second tutorship, and had returned, broken-hearted, to Haworth. At the time when Charlotte, Emily, and Anne were preparing first their poems and then their prose tales for the press, he was sinking into the grave, ruined in body and soul, incapable of mental work of any kind, and no more fit to write *Wuthering Heights* than Homer's *Iliad*. There was thus really no period in his history, so far as I can trace it, at which he could have written any part of *Wuthering Heights*. That book is perfectly homogeneous in thought, feeling, and style, and pointedly evinces itself the work of one mind and one pen. It was produced by Emily Brontë, and by her alone. By a strange and sad caprice of fate, her work was claimed for her sister during her life-time, and for her brother after her death.

Charlotte's criticism of her sister's novel is interesting and able, but somewhat perplexing. She first alleges that the characters delineated in *Wuthering Heights* are true to nature, and then surprises us by the announcement that her sister knew nothing personally about the originals that suggested them. Setting out with the remark that to those who are unfamiliar with "the inhabitants, the customs, the natural characteristics of the outlying hills and hamlets in the West Riding of Yorkshire," the book "must appear a rude and strange production," Charlotte proceeds:—"Men and women, who, perhaps naturally very calm, and with feelings moderate in degree, and little marked in kind, have been trained from their cradle to observe the utmost evenness of manner and guardedness of language, will hardly know what to make of the rough, strong utterance, the harshly-manifested passions, the unbridled aversions and headlong partialities, of unlettered moorland hinds and rugged moorland squires, who have grown up untaught and unchecked, except by mentors as harsh as themselves." This clearly implies that the language, customs, passions, in one word, the character, of the moorland hinds and squires, that figure in *Wuthering Heights*, are looked upon by the writer as correctly depicted. But after stating, in the immediate sequel, that the scenery of *Wuthering Heights* is true to the West Riding—that the book is "moorish, and wild, and knotty as a root of heath,"— that the hills and moors were, to her sister, " what she lived in and by, as much as the wild birds, their tenants, or as the heather, their produce,"—she adds that Emily, after all, knew nothing, except at second-hand, about the moorland hinds and squires. " I am bound to avow"—these are Charlotte's words—" that she had scarcely more practical knowledge of the peasantry

amongst whom she lived, than a nun has of the country
people who sometimes pass her convent gates." Emily,
it seems, was benevolent but not "gregarious," by
which word Charlotte means sociable. She had heard
the histories of the moorland folk, but did not know
them personally. "She could hear of them with
interest, and talk of them with detail, minute, graphic,
and accurate; but *with* them, she rarely exchanged a
word. Hence it ensued that what her mind had
gathered of the real concerning them was too exclusively confined to those tragic and terrible traits of
which, in listening to the secret annals of every rude
vicinage, the memory is sometimes compelled to receive the impress. Her imagination, which was a
spirit more sombre than sunny, more powerful than
sportive, found in such traits material whence it
wrought creations like Heathcliff, like Earnshaw, like
Catherine."

I am unable to believe that Emily Brontë had
derived only from hearsay the knowledge of human
character, and in particular of the language and
manners of the West Riding, which is exhibited in
Wuthering Heights. She shows herself almost as
familiar with the dialect of the West Riding as Scott
does with the broad Scotch of Midlothian farmhouses. Secluded as had been her life, I cannot
doubt that she had seen and talked with peasants
who might have sat for Joseph, with woman-
servants who might have been the original of Zillah,
and with youthful hinds who might have suggested

Hareton Earnshaw. Nor is it credible that the dislike of strangers, the vehemence of language even to cursing, the general shaggy rudeness and roughness and ungeniality, that characterised the household of *Wuthering Heights*, were not suggested by personal observation among the moors of Yorkshire. The truth seems to be that Charlotte gave one aspect of the Yorkshire character, and Emily another. Charlotte showed the brilliant, bright, and brave side of Yorkshire human nature in her Shirley Keeldars and her Robert Moores; Emily, in her Josephs and her Heathcliffs, brought out its capacities for badness, its dark Norse tendency to brooding spite and to implacability of vengeful hate, its proneness to case its natural hardness in spiritual pride and to deepen its natural gloom by superstition. Since the domestic annals of England, whether in Yorkshire or elsewhere, have been made public in the reports of the divorce and police courts, it has been no secret that such things happen as are detailed in the history of the neighbour families of Earnshaw and Linton. I, of course, do not presume to set aside Charlotte Brontë's statement as to the slightness of Emily's intercourse with the people of Yorkshire; but I think that she did not sufficiently take account of the opportunities for observation inevitably occurring to one brought up from infancy in a particular locality, and of the value, even of rare occasions of observation, to so sure an eye, and so tenacious a memory, as Emily's.

The stamp of Emily's genius, branded deep on

Wuthering Heights, is seen chiefly in what I shall call the motivation of the work. The secret of her life, if we may read that secret in the terrible poem which I attempted to analyse, is to be discerned between the lines of the novel. The purport of the poem is that Emily Brontë had searched the universe for God, and that God had never, by so much as one glimpse of His eye, revealed Himself to her. The burden of *Wuthering Heights* is the potency of evil— its potency to pervert good. Old Mr. Earnshaw does a deed of kindness—relieves the helpless, shelters the homeless—and thus brings a fiend in human shape into his house. Emily Brontë, with a strange reserve of power in so young an artist, generally covers up her secret; but she is vividly conscious of her own meaning, and sometimes lets us have more than a hint of it. "It's a cuckoo's, sir," answers Nelly Dean, when Lockwood asks her what is Heathcliff's history. Now the ways of the cuckoo are deeply suggestive. The green-finch builds her nest in the hedge, and lays her eggs; the cuckoo comes and inserts her egg among the rest; and if you go and look six weeks afterwards, you find that the young cuckoo has utterly dispossessed the young finches, by way of thanks to their mother for giving it a warm place, while still unfledged, among her eggs. I have seen the young cuckoo—a huge, hawk-like thing, much larger than the whole nest of the green-finch, out of which and over which it had grown until it no longer lay in it but upon it—and could well believe, from its greedy, voracious look, that it was capable, according to the old couplet quoted in *King Lear*, of biting off the head of its good little foster-mother. This is one of those mysterious facts which are not usually mentioned by preachers when expatiating on the bounty and beneficence of nature, but which, at a time when nature-worship is fashionable, ought not to be overlooked. Heathcliff, the little castaway Lascar, or gipsy, whom Mr. Earnshaw picked out of the gutter in Liverpool and brought home, was the human cuckoo of Wuthering Heights. In like manner, the hospitable deed of Mr. and Mrs. Linton, of Thrushcross Grange, in sheltering Catherine Earnshaw, leading, as it did, to an intimacy between the families of the Heights and of the Grange, brought sorrow and death to their offspring.

Strange and appalling thesis to be expounded by an English girl! In the *Iliad* it is of tyrannic rapacity on the one hand, and proud resentment and moody wrath on the other, that the curse is born whence spring unnumbered woes. In the great Greek tragedies it is sin always that is the fountain-head of sorrow. The Supreme is audaciously defied or outwitted before Prometheus is nailed on his rock. Agamemnon slays Iphigeneia; Clytæmnestra kills the husband who had slain her daughter and his own; Orestes kills the mother who had killed his father. Even when the sin is committed in entire unconsciousness, as when Œdipus kills Laius, the deed itself, viewed objectively, is evil. In the tremendous tragedy of *Lear*, in which the genius of Shakespeare reveals itself in all its characteristic moral intensity, it is from folly and lawless passion—the folly of prodigal and impulsive generosity in the old King and the sin of lawless passion in Gloucester—that the subsequent blighting of the earth and blackening of the heavens proceed. But in *Wuthering Heights* the root of pain and misery is goodness, and the world in which we move seems God-forsaken. And yet—this can, I think, be proved—the tale is told without violation of natural possibility. That is to say, we are always made aware of the means by which good is neutralised or perverted and the triumph of evil prepared. Herein is displayed the consummate skill of the author; while at the same time the main doctrine of the book, that there is no overruling Divine force to be counted on to " make for " righteousness, or for those who work righteousness, is fearfully illustrated.

It is not indeed wholly without glimpses of joy and brightness. Were that so, the gloom would be insufferable. "A good heart will help you to a bonny face, my lad," says one of the characters. There is much tenderness, as well as sense of the wild joy of the moors, in the loving inspection and enumeration of the feathers of moorland birds drawn from her pillow by Cathy Linton on her death-bed. Sometimes the darkness is dispersed, like mist by a sudden burst of sunlight, and the joy breaks out in a loud, ringing, lark-like song of gladness, as in that admirable passage where the younger Cathy gives an account of the dispute which she and her boy-lover had as to the best way of imagining happiness and heaven. "One time," she says, "we were near quarrelling. He said, the pleasantest manner of spending a hot July day was lying from morning till evening on the bank of heath in the middle of the moors, with the bees humming dreamily about among the bloom, and the larks singing high up overhead, and the blue sky and bright sun shining steadily and cloudlessly. That was his perfect idea of heaven's happiness. Mine was, rocking in a rustling green tree, with a west wind blowing, and bright white clouds flitting rapidly above; and not only larks, but throstles, and blackbirds, and linnets, and cuckoos, pouring out music on every side, and the moors seen at a distance, broken into cool, dusky dells; but close by, great swells of long grass undulating in waves to the breeze; and woods, and sounding water, and the whole world awake and wild with joy. He wanted all to lie in an ecstasy of peace; I wanted all to sparkle and dance in a glorious jubilee." It is not, however, too much to say that there is only enough of brightness in *Wuthering Heights* to bring out the gloom of the book in its deepest murky glow.

CHAPTER V.

WUTHERING HEIGHTS — HEATHCLIFF AND CATHY — OLD JOSEPH — ISABELLA — LINTON HEATHCLIFF.

AT the beginning of the tale we have a description of its principal locality : " Wuthering Heights is the name of Mr. Heathcliff's dwelling, 'wuthering' being a significant provincial adjective, descriptive of the atmospheric tumult to which its station is exposed in stormy weather. Pure, bracing ventilation they must have up there at all times ; indeed, one may guess the power of the north wind blowing over the edge, by the excessive slant of a few stunted firs at the end of the house; and by a range of gaunt thorns all stretching their limbs one way, as if craving alms of the sun." The book throughout is written in this style ; simple, terse, idiomatic, perfectly clear, singularly picturesque ; without the French polish that is conspicuous in Charlotte's, but with more of homely pith and forceful ease. That of the gaunt thorns asking alms of the sun is a wonderful piece of imaginative work, to come so easily from the hand of a girl-artist.

Mr. Earnshaw, Squire of Wuthering Heights, had been absent for three days, and arrived about eleven o'clock at night. The children, bent on seeing their presents, had prevailed with their mother to let them sit up for him. He flung himself into a chair, saying he was nearly dead. Opening his great coat, " See here, wife!" he said, "I was never so beaten with anything in my life; but you must e'en take it as a gift of God; though it's as dark almost as if it came from the devil." What they saw was "a dirty, ragged, black-haired child," talking gibberish. Mr. Earnshaw had seen it "starving" in the streets of Liverpool. So it was taken into the family and called Heathcliff. It seemed to be "a sullen, patient child; hardened, perhaps, to ill-treatment." Mr. Earnshaw defended the boy against his son Hindley, who disliked him, and ill-feeling thus crept in between son and father. Heathcliff was quiet and uncomplaining, but insensible to kindness, and profoundly selfish. In addition to his son, Mr. Earnshaw had a daughter Catherine. Wild as a moorland bird, she had a strange witching beauty of her own, and none but she had power over the affections of Heathcliff. They grew up side by side, rambled together on the moors, and learned to love each other with what was less an ordinary passion than an absolute absorption of the life and being of the one into those of the other. I shall quote the account of one of their truant excursions which had important effects. They had been banished from the sitting-room as the evening came on, had escaped to the moors, and took it into their heads to ramble to Thrushcross Grange, several miles away, to see

what the Linton children were doing. The boy
Heathcliff is the speaker, Nelly Dean the listener.

"We ran from the top of the Heights to the park without stopping
—Catherine completely beaten in the race, because she was bare-
foot. You'll have to seek for her shoes in the bog to-morrow. We
crept through a broken hedge, groped our way up the path, and
planted ourselves on a flower-plot under the drawing-room
window. The light came from thence; they had not put
up the shutters, and the curtains were only half closed. Both
of us were able to look in by standing on the basement, and
clinging to the ledge, and we saw—ah! it was beautiful—a splendid
place, carpeted with crimson, and crimson-covered chairs and
tables, and a pure white ceiling bordered by gold, a shower of
glass-drops hanging in silver chains from the centre, and shimmering with little soft tapers. Old Mr. and Mrs. Linton were not
there; Edgar and his sister had it entirely to themselves.
Shouldn't they have been happy? We should have thought
ourselves in heaven! And now, guess what your good children
were doing? Isabella—I believe she is eleven—a year younger
than Cathy—lay screaming at the further end of the room,
shrieking as if witches were running red-hot needles into her.
Edgar stood on the hearth, weeping silently, and in the middle of
the table sat a little dog, shaking its paw and yelping; which, from
their mutual accusations, we understood they had nearly pulled in
two between them. The idiots! That was their pleasure! to
quarrel who should hold a heap of warm hair, and each begin to
cry because both, after struggling to get it, refused to take it. We
laughed outright at the petted things; we did despise them!
When would you catch me wishing to have what Catherine
wanted? or find us by ourselves, seeking entertainment in yelling,
and sobbing, and rolling on the ground, divided by the whole
room? I'd not exchange, for a thousand lives, my condition here
for Edgar Linton's at Thrushcross Grange—not if I might have the
privilege of flinging Joseph off the highest gable, and painting the
house-front with Hindley's blood!"

"Hush, hush!" I interrupted. "Still you have not told me,
Heathcliff, how Catherine is left behind?" "I told you we
laughed," he answered. "The Lintons heard us, and with one
accord they shot like arrows to the door; there was silence, and

then a cry, 'Oh, mamma, mamma! Oh, papa! Oh, mamma, come here. Oh, papa, oh!"' They really did howl out something in that way. We made frightful noises to terrify them still more, and then we dropped off the ledge, because somebody was drawing the bars, and we felt we had better flee. I had Cathy by the hand, and was urging her on, when all at once she fell down. 'Run, Heathcliff, run!' she whispered. 'They have let the bull-dog loose, and he holds me!' The devil had seized her ankle, Nelly: I heard his abominable snorting. She did not yell out—no, she would have scorned to do it, if she had been spitted on the horns of a mad cow. I did, though, I vociferated curses enough to annihilate any fiend in Christendom; and I got a stone and thrust it between its jaws, and tried with all my might to cram it down his throat. A beast of a servant came up with a lantern, at last, shouting, 'Keep fast, Skulker, keep fast.' He changed his tone, however, when he saw Skulker's game. The dog was throttled off; his huge, purple tongue hanging half a foot out of his mouth, and the pendent lips streaming with bloody slaver. The man took Cathy up; she was sick; not from fear, I am certain, but from pain. He carried her in; I followed, grumbling execrations and vengeance. 'What prey, Robert?' hallooed Linton, from the entrance. 'Skulker has caught a little girl, sir,' he replied; 'and there's a lad here,' he added, making a clutch at me, 'who looks an out-and-outer! Very like the robbers were for putting them through the window to open the doors to the gang after all were asleep, that they might murder us at their ease. Hold your tongue, you foul-mouthed thief, you! You shall go to the gallows for this. Mr. Linton, sir, don't lay by your gun.' 'No, no, Robert,' said the old fool. 'The rascals knew that yesterday was my rent-day.' He pulled me under the chandelier, and Mrs. Linton placed her spectacles on her nose, and raised her hands in horror. The cowardly children crept nearer, also, Isabel lisping—'Frightful thing! Put him in the cellar, papa.'"

The implacable hatred with which Heathcliff henceforward regarded Isabella Linton and her brother Edgar may be partly accounted for by the impressions received by him on this occasion. Such a proposal as "Put him in the cellar, papa," made by a little girl,

would strike the boy-prisoner as venomously cruel. It
is important to note this point, for in no respect is
Heathcliff's subsequent conduct quite so diabolical as
in his treatment of Isabella and her child. No com-
mittal to the cellar, however, took place. Cathy was
presently recognised and received into favour, while
Heathcliff was ordered out of the house, to pick his
way back to Wuthering Heights over the moors. "I
refused," he says, "to go without Cathy; he (the man-
servant) dragged me into the garden, pushed the lantern
into my hand, assured me that Mr. Earnshaw should
be informed of my behaviour, and, bidding me march
directly, secured the door again. The curtains were
still looped up at one corner, and I resumed my
station as spy; because, if Catherine had wished to
return, I intended shattering their great glass panes
to a million of fragments, unless they let her out.
She sat on the sofa quietly. The woman-servant
brought a basin of warm water, and washed her feet;
and Mr. Linton mixed a tumbler of negus, and
Isabella emptied a plateful of cakes into her lap, and
Edgar stood gaping at a distance. Afterwards they
dried and combed her beautiful hair, and gave her a
pair of enormous slippers and wheeled her to the fire;
and I left her as merry as she could be, dividing her
food between the little dog and Skulker, whose nose
she pinched as he ate; and kindling a spark of spirit
in the vacant blue eyes of the Lintons—a dim reflection from her own enchanting face. I saw they were
full of stupid admiration; she is so immeasurably

superior to them—to everybody on earth—is she not, Nelly?"

At this time there was evidently much capability of good in Heathcliff. He was a brave boy, and intensely devoted to at least one human being in addition to himself. But Hindley had lately succeeded to his father in possession of Wuthering Heights, and had begun to treat Heathcliff with detestable injustice. His cruelty " was enough to make a fiend of a saint." Heathcliff had been no saint, but the fiendish elements in his nature grew apace under Hindley's nurturing. Catherine, too, had apparently ceased to love the alien, and resolved to bestow herself on Edgar Linton. Heathcliff, in desperation, ran away from Wuthering Heights, and was not heard of for several years. One day he returned, full-grown, and with money in his pockets; but where he had been, or how he had got it, he never told.

I shall now make him stand aside until I have said a word or two on old Joseph, a minor character, but one of the most original in the group, and on some others among the *dramatis personæ*.

"There is a dry saturnine humour," says Charlotte Brontë, "in the delineation of old Joseph." The humour is both saturnine and dry, as compared, for example, with that of Scott in the far more genial and amusing portraiture of the kindred character, Andrew Fairservice; but it is of a rarer quality than Charlotte seems to perceive. There are touches in the delineation of Joseph which recall George Eliot in her raciest mood. He can throw a reflection or a sneer into a metaphoric form so apt, compact, and graphic, that we are reminded of Mrs. Poyser and, still more, of Elspeth Bede. His way of describing one man yielding to temptation administered by another is to say that the first "gallops down t' broad road," while the second "flees afore to oppen t' pikes." He characterises a dainty, proud woman in the following remark: "We wer a'most too mucky to sow t' corn for makking her breead." Have we anything better than that from Mrs. Poyser or Elspeth Bede? Joseph is not consciously a bad man. Nay, he is convinced of his superlative goodness, and belongs to that class, with whom we found Anne Brontë expostulating, who have no manner of difficulty, no weak human experience of imaginative or sympathetic pain, in supposing that an enormous proportion of their race have been marked off for everlasting destruction, while they are themselves the favourites of heaven. He was "the wearisomest, self-righteous Pharisee that ever ransacked a Bible to rake the promises to himself and fling the curses to his neighbours." In the height of a thunderstorm he "swung on to his knees, beseeching the Lord to remember the patriarchs Noah and Lot, and, as in former times, spare the righteous, though He smote the ungodly." "Thank Hivin for all!" said Joseph. "All warks togither for gooid to them as is chozzen, and piked out fro' th' rubbidge!" Joseph was not without a certain dog-like fidelity to the Earnshaw family, but it never interfered with the rooted selfishness of his nature. If we take the bank-notes in the following sentence to symbolise the intense worldliness overlying all that was good in his sentiments and theology, the words will expressively denote the kind of man he was. "He solemnly spread his large Bible on the table, and overlaid it with dirty bank-notes from his pocket-book."

Such characters as Joseph are, I think, uncommon. I have met with but one or two in the course of my life, and of none even of these am I perfectly sure that Joseph can be taken as the accurate representative. I do not doubt, however, that Emily Brontë had some actual Yorkshire peasant in view, and without question the peculiar faults and perversities of Joseph are in minor degree and development not too rare to be worth pointing out and guarding against. If you stand on the seashore when the sky is cloudless, and look towards the sun, you will see the sunbeams falling solely on the line between your eye and the luminary, forming a pathway of light along the waves. If the shore were lined by a million men, only one line, kindled by the beams, would be visible to each of the million. Now Joseph corresponds, in the spiritual province, to one of those men who should allege that there was no sunlight in the air except what reached his own eye. The infinite benevolence is drawn into the focus of his small sect, his still smaller self, and by a strange perversion the affections shrink and shrivel even under that sense of Divine kindness which ought to have warmed, expanded, ennobled them.

In boldness of invention and strength of handling, Joseph is like a grotesque by Michael Angelo; gnarled and knotted as a stunted tree of the moorland; his vinegar face perked into contemptuous rebuke of his fellow-creatures, his brow corrugated in an unhappy grudge that there is so much happiness left in the world. He is, indeed, little more than a sketch; but the sketch, if we had nothing else from her hand, would attest the genius of Emily Brontë.

Nelly Dean, Edgar Linton, and Lockwood, to whom might perhaps be added Zillah, though she is nothing more than an ordinary farm servant with some Yorkshire colour about her, are the neutral-tinted characters in the book, neither specially good nor pointedly bad. Emily Brontë evidently took too dark views of life, and was too ironical in her moods of mind, to rejoice in the delineation of heroes and heroines. *Wuthering Heights* is a novel without a hero, and with but a very marred and faulty specimen of a heroine. Charlotte speaks of the " true benevolence and homely fidelity" of Nelly Dean; but in fact Nelly has generally an eye to the main chance, and only once forgets herself into a display of dangerous anger and courage, on which occasion "a touch on the chest" from Heathcliff silences her, she being, as she explains, " stout, and soon put out of breath." Lockwood is little more than a walking gentleman, but, viewed as a walking gentleman, he is made admirable use of. Not only are his successive visits to the gaunt manor-house on the Heights full of vivid and appropriate interest, and cunningly adapted to awaken the curiosity of the reader, but his reception by the various inmates enables us to realise, as we otherwise could not have done, the peculiar feeling of repulsion and dislike with which the natives of the Yorkshire wilds regard strangers. The moorland creatures have their own quarrels and spites; but with creatures of another kind they admit no converse at all. Not only do Joseph and Heathcliff—who look upon the smooth-spoken, conventional, studiously-polite Lockwood as shaggy mastiffs might on an Italian greyhound—despise and repel him; young Cathy will have nothing at all to say to him. He is outside her circle—outside her sympathy; she answers snappishly when he volunteers the slightest act of interrogative courtesy. It is the instinctive shyness, suspicion, aversion of a kitten spitting at a puppy that wants to be civil.

Edgar Linton is the morally best character in the book. Charlotte well describes him as "an example of constancy and tenderness." He is good, but sheepishly, ineffectually good. We cannot help feeling that Emily Brontë shares the contempt for him which is so intensely felt by Heathcliff, and so thinly disguised by his own wife Catherine. He has none of the mental power that is the fitting accompaniment, and indispensable stay, of goodness of heart. He not only fails to defend himself against Heathcliff, but commits the quite unpardonable oversight of making no provision for his daughter, and thus leaving her an easy prey to the enemy of his house.

Isabella Heathcliff and her son Linton are exceedingly remarkable studies of character. Isabella is feeble and morbid, with sickly propensities and a cold heart. Heathcliff hates her inflexibly from the day when she asks her father to put him into the cellar; and yet, when he has grown up and revealed his badness, she will hanker after him, fall into foolish love with him, perversely, and in spite of all dissuasion, and though he hardly condescends to pretend to care for her, throw herself into his arms. She becomes more rational and human when his cruelty drives her into irrepressible rage, and she escapes from him, to return no more. But we never have much regard for her; only we have a profound sense of her reality, and of the fidelity with which she represents a morbid phase of feminine character.

Her son and Heathcliff's is, as Dobell remarked, unmistakably the offspring of those parents. Half is his and half is hers, and he is worthy of the two. The creature is bad—very bad; physically weak, mentally cross-grained, peevish, ill-conditioned. Terrible, once more, is the suggestion of the subtlety and cruelty, and blind and blank indifference to the production of misery, reigning in nature, which this dark, strange woman, this Emily Brontë, half hides, half reveals, in the character and history of Linton Heathcliff. I am not sure that young Heathcliff is not the most wonderful delineation in the book—more wonderful even than his father or than either of the Catherines. A thin, wavering, gossamer-thread of existence is the boy's at best, and it is soon blown away in the chill wind of death; yet we know him as vividly as we know any character in fiction. We know him not from the outside, but the inside,—not merely the marking of the hands on the clock-face, but the wheels and sources of movement behind. This mode of revealing character, not so much by external incident as by psychological analysis—by taking us, as Shakspeare does in the case of Macbeth, and Hamlet, and Brutus, and Angelo, and Claudio, into the mind—is the most difficult and masterly of all. The whining self-pity, the incapacity to regard any one except in the light of his own interest, the pleased excitement of which he is conscious when his words give pain, manifested by young Heathcliff in conversation with his cousin, Cathy Linton, open to us the very *arcana* of his nature. I must quote a short passage to illustrate these remarks. Nelly Dean details a conversation between Linton Heathcliff and young Cathy. The reader is to recollect that young Cathy's mother had really loved Heathcliff, Linton Heathcliff's father, though she gave her hand to Edgar Linton.

"Yes," said Catherine, stroking his long, soft hair; "if I could only get papa's consent, I'd spend half my time with you. Pretty Linton! I wish you were my brother." "And then you would like me as well as your father?" observed he, more cheerfully. "But papa says you would love me better than him and all the world if you were my wife; so I'd rather you were that." "No;

I should never love anybody better than papa," she returned, gravely. "And people hate their wives sometimes, but not their sisters and brothers; and if you were the latter, you would live with us, and papa would be as fond of you as he is of me." Linton denied that people ever hated their wives; but Cathy affirmed they did, and in her wisdom instanced his own father's aversion to her aunt. I endeavoured to stop her thoughtless tongue. I couldn't succeed till everything she knew was out. Master Heathcliff, much irritated, asserted her relation was false. "Papa told me, and papa does not tell falsehoods," she answered, pertly. "*My* papa scorns yours!" cried Linton. "He calls him a sneaking fool." "Yours is a wicked man," retorted Catherine; "and you are very naughty to dare to repeat what he says. He must be wicked to have made Aunt Isabella leave him as she did." "She didn't leave him," said the boy; "you shan't contradict me." "She did," cried my young lady. "Well, I'll tell *you* something," said Linton. "Your mother hated your father; now then." "Oh!" exclaimed Catherine, too enraged to continue. "And she loved mine," added he. "You little liar! I hate you now!" she panted, and her face grew red with passion. "She did! she did!" sang Linton, sinking into the recess of his chair, and leaning back his head to enjoy the agitation of the other disputant, who stood behind. "Hush, Master Heathcliff!" I said; "that's your father's tale, too, I suppose." "It isn't; you hold your tongue," he answered. "She did, she did, Catherine! she did, she did!"

Cathy, beside herself, gave the chair a violent push, and caused him to fall against one arm. He was immediately seized by a suffocating cough that soon ended his triumph. It lasted so long that it frightened even me. As to his cousin, she wept with all her might, aghast at the mischief she had done, though she said nothing. I held him till the fit exhausted itself; then he thrust me away, and leant his head down silently. Catherine quelled her lamentations also, took a seat opposite, and looked solemnly into the fire. "How do you feel now, Master Heathcliff?" I inquired, after waiting ten minutes. "I wish *she* felt as I do," he replied; "spiteful, cruel thing! And I was better to-day; and there——" his voice died in a whimper. "*I* didn't strike you!" muttered Cathy, chewing her lip to prevent another burst of emotion. He sighed and moaned like one under great suffering, and kept it up for a quarter of an hour—on purpose to distress his cousin, apparently, for whenever he caught a stifled sob from her, he put new pain and pathos into the inflexions of his voice.

This combination of utter weakness with bitter badness is exactly what we should have looked for in the son of Heathcliff and Isabella Linton. And yet, with all his badness, there is in Linton Heathcliff I know not what element of fineness and high breeding. The vase holds poison, but it is a vase of delicate porcelain,—the creature is of demon breed, but, like Caliban, he has melodious tones in him, something almost fascinating, which, under favourable auspices, might have made a dainty gentleman of him, if never a brave, healthy, good man.

CHAPTER VI.

HEATHCLIFF AND CATHERINE—WUTHERING HEIGHTS NOT A WHOLESOME BOOK—EMILY BRONTË AND MR. G. H. LEWES.

WHAT Heathcliff had been about in his absence from Wuthering Heights we are not informed. Emily Brontë shows her unacquaintance with, or, more probably, her contempt for, the resources of professional novelists, by not availing herself of the opportunity of filling half-a-dozen chapters with an account of his adventures. We are permitted, if we like, to suppose that he robbed on the highway; but all we are told is that he returned laden with money. Before he went, it had become the ruling passion of his soul to take revenge on Hindley Earnshaw, and to gratify this passion he now addressed himself. His love for the elder Catherine, Hindley's sister, was as intense as before—more intense it could not have been; but she had, in his absence, become the wife of Edgar Linton. I shall not attempt either to prove it likely that Catherine, loving Heathcliff as she did, would have married Linton in real life, or to show that her marriage is pardonable in art. It was one of those unlikely things which, nevertheless, constantly happen. She was wayward, wilful, fantastically perverse and capricious as it is possible for woman to be; she was little more than a girl. To calculate the proceedings even of a man of genius is impossible, and what is there that a woman of genius—and a vein of fiery genius there certainly was in Catherine—may not do?

Her own account of her motives will, at least, give us some idea of her character. She was not, she explained to Nelly Dean, of the steady-going, respectable, angelic order of women. If the truth must be told, the wild moors were more to her taste than heaven, and she would rather be among the flowers of the dells than bask on meadows of asphodel. "If I were in heaven, Nelly, I should be extremely miserable. . . . . I dreamt once that I was there. . . . . Heaven did not seem to be my home; and I broke my heart with weeping to come back to earth; and the angels were so angry that they flung me out into the middle of the heath on the top of Wuthering Heights, where I woke sobbing for joy." The reader will do well to remember that Emily Brontë could not live away from the moors, could not get her heart to fix with right satisfaction on anything away from the moors. She took an engagement in England; but she pined inconsolably, and, to save her life, they had to bring her back to Haworth. She went with Charlotte to Brussels; but even the excitement of new splendours, new associates, new pursuits, which effectually weaned Charlotte from the nest among the hills, had no power upon Emily. "I've no more business," said Catherine, "to marry Edgar Linton than I have to be in heaven." Heathcliff was the wild Wuthering Heights of her heart, that she loved better than Linton, with his heaven of Thrushcross Grange. Of Heathcliff she said, "He's more myself than I am. Whatever our souls are made of, his and mine are the same; and Linton's is as different as a moonbeam from lightning or frost from fire." Nelly bids her consider how, if these are her feelings, she will be able, when she is Mrs. Linton, to bear separation from Heathcliff. She fiercely exclaims that no separation will be necessary. "Every Linton on the face of the earth might melt into nothing before I could consent to forsake Heathcliff. Oh, that's not what I intend—that's not what I mean! I shouldn't be Mrs. Linton were such a price demanded. He'll be as much to me as he has been all his life-time. Edgar must shake off his antipathy, and tolerate him, at least. He will, when he learns my true feelings towards him." This will seem mere affectation or girlish folly unless we realise the fact, essentially important in order to do justice either to Catherine or to Emily Brontë, that there is no sensual element whatever in Catherine's love for Heathcliff, or in Heathcliff's love for her. It is this which makes the conception of the pair so original—this which proves Emily Brontë to have had transcendent power as an artist. A mere sensual passion between Heathcliff and Cathy would have been as valueless in art as that which vulgarises and defiles the first canto of *Don Juan*. Catherine's idea is that she will love Heathcliff as her soul's friend and brother, while her affection for her husband will remain flawless and unsullied. Aided by Linton—such, she further explains to Nelly, is her hope—she will rescue Heathcliff from the cruelty of Hindley, and put him in the way of rising. Nelly, who speaks for respectable common sense, reprobates such a scheme. But Catherine persists in her self-defence, and tries to explain how she feels about Heathcliff, while avowing that she cannot put the matter into words. "I cannot express it; but surely you and everybody have a notion that there is, or should be, an existence of yours beyond you. . . . If all else perished and *he* remained, *I* should still continue to be; and if all else remained, and he were annihilated, the universe would turn to a mighty stranger: I should not seem a part of it. My love for Linton is like the foliage in the woods: time will change it, I'm well aware, as winter changes the trees. My love for Heathcliff resembles the eternal rocks beneath—a source of little visible delight, but necessary. Nelly, I *am* Heathcliff! He's always, always in my mind: not as a pleasure, any more than I am always a pleasure to myself, but as my own being."

The marriage with Linton took place, and when Heathcliff reappeared, Catherine tried to carry out her plan of having him as her friend on Platonic principles. Heathcliff's love for her was of the same kind as hers for him, and there is not the remotest suggestion—nor does such ever occur to her husband —that she gives Linton more cause for jealousy than she might have done if Heathcliff had been her brother. Heathcliff, indeed, acts infamously, but not in the vulgar way. He gives rein to his hatred for Linton, is utterly regardless of Linton's happiness, and produces a storm of varied agitation in the Thrushcross household, which brings a feverish and nervous illness on Catherine, and finally occasions her death. Heathcliff speaks of his affection for Catherine as Catherine had spoken of hers for him. She is his life, his soul. If she dies, he will live with his soul in the grave. He charges her with having broken his heart and her own in leaving him and marrying Linton. "You loved me—then what *right* had you to leave me?" "Let me alone, let me alone," sobbed Catherine. "If I've done wrong, I'm dying for it. It is enough! You left me, too; but I won't upbraid you. I forgive you. Forgive me." "It is hard to forgive, and to look at those eyes, and feel those wasted hands," he answered. "Kiss me again; and don't let me see your eyes! I forgive what you have done to me. I love *my* murderer—but *yours!* How can I?"

She fainted in Heathcliff's arms, and he placed her in those of her husband, bidding him help her. That night she died. "Next morning—bright and cheerful out of doors—stole softened in through the blinds of the silent room, and suffused the couch and its occupant with a mellow, tender glow. Her brow smooth, her lids closed, her lips wearing an expression of a smile, no angel in heaven could be more beautiful than she appeared."

The death of Catherine must be considered to have driven Heathcliff mad. He could not and would not realise that she had left him, and that he was alone. "Where is she?" he cried, when Nelly Dean told him she was dead; "not *there*—not in heaven—not perished—where? Oh! you said you cared nothing for my sufferings! And I pray one prayer—I repeat it till my tongue stiffens—Catherine Earnshaw, may you not rest as long as I am living! You said I killed you—haunt me, then! The murdered *do* haunt their murderers, I believe. I know that ghosts *have* wandered on earth. Be with me always—take any form—drive me mad! only *do* not leave me in this abyss, where I cannot find you! I cannot live without my life! I cannot live without my soul!" Having uttered these words, Heathcliff dashed his head against the knotted trunk of a tree, and "howled, not like a man, but like a savage beast being goaded to death with knives and spears."

For eighteen years after Catherine's death, he believed himself haunted by her presence. In paroxysms of agonised entreaty he implored her to make herself more sensibly present; and at last his mania rose to such a pitch that he believed she had granted his request, and was near him, generally invisible, but sometimes in visible form. Before entering on this last stage of his malady, he had been atrociously wicked and cruel. He completed the ruin of Hindley by gambling and intoxication, he diabolically ill-treated his own wife and son. Even to young Cathy, the daughter of his Catherine, he acted with revolting cruelty, until the shade or spectre of her mother seemed to arise to protect her. The last phase of his madness was that of tolerance for others and harshness to himself. He went about in a high fever, declining food, and roaming, night and day, on the moors. Then he died, and was buried. But if the dwellers on the moors might be believed, he was not at rest, and was not alone. "That old man," says Nelly Dean, "by the kitchen fire affirms he has seen two on 'em, looking out of his chamber window on every rainy night since his death: and an odd thing happened to me about a month ago. I was going to the Grange one evening—a dark evening, threatening thunder—and, just at the turn of the Heights, I encountered a little boy with a sheep and two lambs before him; he was crying terribly, and I supposed the lambs were skittish, and would not be guided. 'What is the matter, my little man?' I asked. 'There's Heathcliff and a woman, yonder, under t'Nab,' he blubbered, ' un' I darnut pass 'em.' "

Such, in imperfect and sketchy outline, are the main features of this astonishing book. My sketch of its contents does less than justice to the author;

but enough has been said and quoted to convey some idea of *Wuthering Heights*. It is a work of great genius, but of genius reared within sight of graves, and amid the winds and mists of the moorland. The morbid and maddening affection with which Heathcliff and Catherine cling to each other was exactly such an affection, so intense, so unreasonable, so original, as that with which Emily Brontë clung to Haworth. And on Emily, as on Catherine, death descended in the prime of her years. With few changes, the illness and death of Catherine might stand for the illness and death of Emily. The book cannot be pronounced a good or a wholesome book. It exaggerates the evil that is in the world, for it does not show the light in due proportion to the darkness. If Haworth Parsonage, beside its graves, moaned around by the wind of the moors, were all the world, then might the gloom of *Wuthering Heights* be accepted for the atmosphere of the planet. But it is not so; and the best that can be said for the book is that it is the product of marvellous genius that never freely and genially expanded; genius that never rose into the blue sky of hope and joy; genius that seems to have watched, and wailed, and waited for God, and yet never *once* saw His eye light up the "wildering clouds" above and around.

Curiously suggestive, in relation to Emily Brontë, is Charlotte's reference to the late Mr. G. H. Lewes: " I have seen Lewes too. . . . . I could not feel otherwise to him than half sadly, half tenderly—a queer word that last; but I use it because the aspect of Lewes's face almost moves me to tears; it is so wonderfully like Emily—her eyes, her features, the very nose, the somewhat prominent mouth, the forehead; even, at moments, the expression." This is the sole resource we have in realising the face of Emily Brontë, since no portrait except the "rough and common-looking oil-painting," executed by her brother in his boyhood, which Charlotte did not think worth mention when her publishers wanted likenesses of her sisters, was taken of her. That she should have resembled Mr. Lewes, both in features and expression, seems at first surprising. Whether there is, or is not, an art to read the mind's construction in the face, it is certain that, unless what her Yorkshire neighbours alleged as to the moroseness and reserve of Emily Brontë be calumnious, and unless the settled gloom of her writings bears false witness, her disposition and temperament were pointedly in contrast with those of G. H. Lewes, one of the most vivacious, nimble-spirited and happy-spirited of authors. Nevertheless, it is unquestionable that the basis of his entire scheme of thought was the proposition that man has, and can have, no certitude respecting immortality and God. He had travelled to all shrines of wisdom; consulted the sages of antiquity and the philosophers of Europe; listened to Descartes and Leibnitz and Spinoza, to Hume and Kant and Reid, and, lastly, to Comte; and announced to his countrymen, as the result, in lucid English, and with the serene good-humour of perfect assurance, that God, if He did exist, was the unknown X of the universe—beyond reason, beyond faith, beyond possible communion. Whether, in the course of arriving at this conclusion, Mr. Lewes passed through seasons of mental anguish, I cannot tell; but his books are remarkable for their genial vivacity, their sweetness of tone and temper, their almost unparalleled range, not only of tolerance, but of sympathetic and kindly tolerance. Having entirely satisfied himself that there is no Infinite Spirit in the universe corresponding in any sense to the father in a human household, or the king in a nation of men, he betrays no sense of bereavement, gives no sign of sorrow. He does not, indeed, exult; arrogance and scornful flippancy belong to a lower and baser kind of man; but neither is he in the least distressed, and we feel that, if questioned on the point, he would have said that his no-belief was true, and that to dwell with truth must always be better for man than to yield to the most soothing falsehood.

I beg to have it clearly understood that I do not put forward the theory that Emily Brontë was an atheist. Charlotte has let fall no hint to that effect, and if Emily had made up her mind that there is no God, it seems highly improbable that she could have prevented a sister with whom she lived on terms of unusual confidence and affection from having some glimpse of the fact. Charlotte herself was not only a believer in God, but derived perpetual practical sustenance in her daily life and work from reference to a Judge who could not err and a Father who could not misunderstand. When she read the atheistic volume published by Miss Martineau and Mr. Atkinson, she shrank back appalled from the abyss then first opened to her. "Sincerely," she said, "for my own part, do I wish to find and know the Truth; but if this be Truth, well may she guard herself with mysteries and cover herself with a veil. If this be Truth, man or woman who beholds her can but curse the day he or she was born." These words remind one of those in which Sir William Hamilton declares that if atheism were true, the last word of philosophy to man would be the terrific message of the oracle to Œdipus, "May you never know the secret of your birth."

Emily Brontë, as I conceive her character, occupied the position of having sought God and not found Him, but did not proceed to infer that He had never been found, and had no existence. She was oppressed with a sense of the power of evil and the ineffectuality of good, and yearned with inexpressible and agonised earnestness for a clearer discovery of God than she had been able to attain to. She would not use a language she could not verify, or pretend to trace the light of God's eye when she could not see it; but she was solitary and sad, no human being rightly comprehended her, and her writings are a despairing cry to God for light. A universe without God was for her a universe of night and chaos, the wail of infinite bereavement rising from its human habitations. But it

is a highly remarkable circumstance that, with so deep
a similarity, and at the same time so marked a dis-
similarity, in their relation to the fundamental beliefs
of religion, Emily Brontë and G. H. Lewes should
have had the same, certainly uncommon, type of
physiognomy.

CHAPTER VII.

*CHARLOTTE BRONTË ON WUTHERING HEIGHTS
—CHARLOTTE AND EMILY IN BRUSSELS—
CHARLOTTE'S STYLE—THE PROFESSOR—
BELGIAN SCENERY — VILLETTE — THE
SCHOOL SCENES IN JANE EYRE.*

CHARLOTTE BRONTË puts into brilliant and picturesque language a theory, partly explanatory, partly apologetic, on the subject of such literary work as we have in *Wuthering Heights*. "Whether," she says, "it is right or advisable to create beings like Heathcliff, I do not know: I scarcely think it is. But this I know; the writer who possesses the creative gift owns something of which he is not always master—something that, at times, strangely wills and works for itself. He may lay down rules and devise principles, and to rules and principles it will, perhaps, for years lie in subjection; and then, haply without any warning of revolt, there comes a time when it will no longer consent to 'harrow the valleys, or be bound with a band in the furrow'—when it 'laughs at the multitude of the city, and regards not the crying of the driver'—when, refusing absolutely to make ropes out of sea-sand any longer, it sets to work on statue-hewing, and you have a Pluto or a Jove, a Tisiphone or a Psyche, a Mermaid or a Madonna, as Fate or Inspiration direct. Be the work grim or glorious, dread or divine, you have little choice left but quiescent adoption. As for you—the nominal artist—your share in it has been to work passively under dictates you neither delivered nor could question—that would not be uttered at your prayer, nor suppressed nor changed at your caprice." That genius is apt to lay imperative commands on its possessor, and that there is the inspiration of genius in *Wuthering Heights*, I should be the last to dispute; but it were rash to admit that genius is not responsible for its creations. And even if this were granted, it would remain incontrovertible that the characteristic creations of literary genius—the portraits it delights to depict, the scenes it loves to describe, the incidents it habitually invents—are trustworthy indications of the nature of the artist. Even the religious inspiration, which is more intense and transforming in its potency than the literary inspiration, has been held by all wise theologians to irradiate but never to obliterate or misrepresent the natural character. Both the poems and the prose work of Emily Brontë lie in pessimistic shadow as dark and deep as that cast by the storm-clouds on the sea in Turner's murkiest pictures of shipwreck. We ought, indeed, to recollect that she died young; that young persons of genius are apt to lay stress upon the tragic tones in life; that, if she

had lived to be sixty, she might have produced so
many sunny and healthy works, that the grim
grotesque of her 'prentice hand would have been
thrown into the background. Against this, however,
we must in fairness set the fact, that the execution of
Wuthering Heights is singularly mature—the style
such as practised and consummate writers use, the
sentiment free of young-mannish bravura, and, still
more, of young-womanish syllabub. The author never
seems for one moment to lose her self-possession and
self-command. Had Shakespeare written *Lear* before
he was thirty, and died, we should have had a right to
believe that he took a pessimistic view of life ; and of
Emily Brontë we must hold that she was morbidly
pessimistic. "I am oppressed," says Charlotte, after
reading the book anew in 1850 : "the reader is
scarcely ever permitted a taste of unalloyed pleasure ;
every beam of sunshine is poured down through black
bars of threatening cloud ; every page is surcharged
with a sort of moral electricity."

It is, however, the sunny book—above all, it is the
sunny novel—that the world most cordially takes to ;
and we may doubt whether Emily Brontë's name
would ever have obtained a place in the chronicles
of English literature, if the more buoyant and happy
genius of her sister had not fairly scaled the horizon,
and drawn all eyes to the wonder that had appeared
somewhere among the Yorkshire hills.

Mr. Wemyss Reid seems to me to be correct in
deciding that the main determining incident in

Charlotte Brontë's life was not the death of her brother, but her own residence, at two successive periods, in Brussels. When the change—to her immense—from native Yorkshire to the Belgian capital took place, she was twenty-six years old, but had very much to learn. M. Heger, the head of the seminary to which she went as a pupil, declared that she and her sister Emily knew nothing of French. He meant, I presume, that they had no extensive or finely accurate acquaintance with the language, and set about drilling them in the fashion adopted with his advanced French and Belgian pupils. His experience with the sisters was what we should have expected. "Emily," says Mrs. Gaskell, summarising the Belgian headmaster's estimate, "had a head for logic, and a capability for argument, unusual in a man, and rare, indeed, in a woman." He thought Emily abler than Charlotte; but, unfortunately, "a stubborn tenacity of will," "impairing" in his view the force of her genius, rendered her occasionally impervious to his instructions, "where her own wishes, or her own sense of right, was concerned." We may interpret this to mean that she chose to retain in her compositions the idiom of her native English, and in conventional morals her "heretic" and Protestant ideas, rather than to have her forms of expression and her notions of truth passed through M. Heger's mill. The style of Emily Brontë is thoroughly English.

In Charlotte's case M. Heger had not to deplore any tenacity of will resisting his influence. She delighted in feeling herself once more a schoolgirl. "It is natural," she said, "to me to submit, and very unnatural to command." I believe the characterisation to be just. It would be correct also, if applied to Mrs. Barrett Browning, and, I think, though some might dispute the fact, to George Eliot. But there are women to whom it does not apply, women to whom it is unnatural and painful to submit, and natural and pleasant to command. Emily Brontë, I take it, was one of these last. Whether submission would have been so pleasant for Charlotte if M. Heger had not been what he was, may remain a question. Him she describes as "a man of power as to mind, but very choleric and irritable in temperament." The words describe the essential characteristic of Charlotte Brontë's pet hero, be his name Rochester, or be it Moore, or be it Paul Emanuel. A clever man, with strongly-marked features, who is fervently in love with a plain girl, to whom, while he longs to clasp her to his heart, he talks harshly, is the man whom Charlotte Brontë always hero-worships.

Under M. Heger's auspices and instruction, Charlotte learned to write French so well that her English style became thenceforward characteristically French. Her *devoir* on the death of Napoleon is written in French which I may err in pronouncing classic of the best modern French school; but it certainly has a tone and air characteristically French, and yet it reads exactly like a passage from her English prose translated into French. "Napoléon"—this is the opening passage—" naquit en Corse et mourut à Ste. Hélène. Entre ces deux îles rien qu'un vaste et brûlant désert et l'océan immense. Il naquit fils d'un simple gentilhomme, et mourut empereur, mais sans couronne et dans les fers. Entre son berceau et sa tombe qu'y a-t-il? La carrière d'un soldat parvenu, des champs de bataille, un mer de sang, un trône, puis de sang encore, et des fers. La vie, c'est l'arc en ciel; les deux points extrêmes touchant la terre, la comble lumineuse mesure les cieux. Sur Napoléon au berceau une mère brillait; dans la maison paternelle il avait des frères et des sœurs; plus tard dans son palais il eut une femme qui l'aimait. Mais sur son lit de mort Napoléon est seul; plus de mére, ni de frère, ni de sœur, ni de femme, ni d'enfant!! D'autres ont dit et rediront ses exploits, moi, je m'arrête à contempler l'abandonnement de sa dernière heure!"

Did not the writer of this evidently, while writing it, think in French? And did not Charlotte Brontë, when writing in English, write in exactly the same way? In other words, her style was French. In some very important respects no style could be better. It is clear as crystal, pointed as diamond, admirably fitted for rapid and animated narrative, as well as for the description of passion. But I think that, in variety and expressiveness, it is not equal to those English styles which are formed on the best Teutonic models. The ornamental, the fashionable, the courtly, to a great extent also the martial elements in our language, are French; the homelier and the heartier are Teutonic; and striking as is much of the prose written by those of our young authors who have brought French models again into vogue, it cannot vie, in respect of expressiveness, or home-bred tenderness, or Doric simplicity and idiomatic pith and melody, with the prose of Carlyle's early essays, such as that on Burns, or the prose in which George Eliot wrote *Silas Marner*. The culture, both of Carlyle and George Eliot, was mainly German.

Of her experience in Brussels, Charlotte Brontë availed herself in the composition of two novels, her first and her last—*The Professor* and *Villette*. Critics have loudly praised *Villette*, and I do not recollect seeing anything said in commendation of *The Professor;* but I own to finding it a stiffer business to read the later than the earlier book. *The Professor*, I make bold to say, has not received due appreciation. It is by no means a wonderful book, but it has signal merits. Nothing could be more sharp than the chiselling of the characters, which are neither uninteresting nor commonplace, and the story is full of life. Hunsden is unmistakably a first sketch of the Yorke of *Shirley*, and the school scenes, though not so carefully elaborated as those in *Villette*, are, to my thinking, more fresh, and, in general respects, about as good. Frances, of *The Professor*, is perhaps somewhat too commonplace for a heroine : but not even a critic has, to my knowledge, been found who could care for the Lucy Snowe of *Villette*. The following passage will enable us to realise the hopeful and cheerful spirit of Charlotte Brontë's first book, and has a biographical interest as manifestly recalling the impressions with which she first looked upon Belgium.

Belgium! name unromantic and unpoetic, yet name that whenever uttered has in my ear a sound, in my heart an echo, such as no other assemblage of syllables, however sweet or classic, can produce. Belgium! I repeat the word, now as I sit alone near midnight. It stirs my world of the past like a summons to resurrection; the graves unclose, the dead are raised; thoughts, feelings, memories that slept are seen by me ascending from the clods—haloed most of them; but while I gaze on their vapoury forms, and strive to ascertain definitely their outline, the sound which wakened them dies, and they sink, each and all, like a light wreath of mist, absorbed in the mould, re-called to urns, re-sealed in monuments. Farewell, luminous phantoms!

This is Belgium, reader. Look! don't call the picture a flat or a dull one—it was neither flat nor dull to me when I first beheld it. When I left Ostend on a mild February morning, and found myself on the road to Brussels, nothing could look vapid to me. My sense of enjoyment possessed an edge whetted to the finest— untouched, keen, exquisite. I was young; I had good health; pleasure and I had never met; no indulgence of hers had enervated or sated one faculty of my nature. Liberty I clasped in my arms for the first time, and the influence of her smile and embrace revived my life like the sun and the west wind. Yes, at that epoch I felt like a morning traveller who doubts not that from the hill he is ascending he shall behold a glorious sunrise; what if the track be straight, steep, and stony? He sees it not; his eyes are fixed on that summit, flushed already, flushed and gilded, and having gained it, he is certain of the scene beyond. He knows that the sun will face him, that his chariot is even now coming over the eastern horizon, and that the herald breeze he feels on his cheek is opening for the god's career a clear, vast path of azure, amidst clouds soft as pearl and warm as flame. Difficulty and toil were to be my lot; but, sustained by energy, drawn on by hopes as bright as vague, I deemed such a lot no hardship. I mounted now the hill in shade; there were pebbles, inequalities, briars in my path; but my eyes were fixed on the crimson peak above; my imagination was with the refulgent firmament beyond, and I thought nothing of the stones turning under my feet, or of the thorns scratching my face and hands.

I gazed often, and always with delight, from the window of the diligence (these, be it remembered, were not the days of trains and railroads). Well! and what did I see? I will tell you faithfully. Green, reedy swamps; fields fertile, but flat, cultivated in patches that made them look like magnified kitchen-gardens; belts of cut trees, formal as pollard willows, skirting the horizon; narrow canals, gliding slow by the roadside; painted Flemish farmhouses; some very dirty hovels; a grey, dead sky; wet road, wet fields, wet house-tops; not a beautiful, scarcely a picturesque, object met my eye along the whole route; yet to me all was beautiful, all was more than picturesque. It continued fair so long as daylight lasted, though the moisture of many preceding damp days had sodden the whole country; as it grew dark, however, the rain recommenced, and it was through streaming and starless darkness my eye caught the first gleam of the lights of Brussels. I saw little of the city but its lights that night. Having alighted from the diligence, a fiacre conveyed me to the Hôtel de ——, where I had been advised by a fellow-traveller to put up. Having eaten a traveller's supper, I retired to bed, and slept a traveller's sleep.

Charlotte, as we saw, was favourably impressed by M. Heger, and enjoyed life in Brussels; but one thing pained and offended the instincts of her nature so bitterly that she wrote vehemently of it both in her first book and in her last. The " plague-spot of dissimulation," she said, rested upon each and all of those girls who were reared under the influence of Rome and the Jesuits. " Most of them could lie with audacity when it appeared advantageous to do so. All understood the art of speaking fair when a point was to be gained. Backbiting and tale-bearing were universal." On girls from the United Kingdom she was severe enough, but she " could at a glance distinguish the daughter of Albion and nursling of

Protestantism from the foster-child of Rome, the *protégée* of Jesuistry." In making these assertions Charlotte Brontë guards herself against being supposed to speak from prejudice against Popish theology. Her own experience it is that she states, professing her inability to account for the facts except on the supposition that the cause "is to be found in the discipline, if not the doctrines, of the Church of Rome." Between the composition of *The Professor* and that of *Villette*, something like ten years intervened, and during these Charlotte had mingled in the best intellectual society of London; yet in *Villette* the demoralising influences of the Romish discipline are described with a force at least equal to that displayed in the earlier book. "In an unguarded moment," she writes, in the person of her heroine, "I chanced to say that, of the two errors, I considered falsehood worse than an occasional lapse in church attendance." From that time she was differently regarded by the girls. They had told the school authorities what she said, and were instructed to look upon her as dangerous. "Not a soul," she says, "in Madame Beck's house, from the scullion to the directress herself, but was above being ashamed of a lie; they thought nothing of it. '*J'ai menti plusieurs fois*' formed an item of every girl's and every woman's monthly confession: the priest heard unshocked, and absolved unreluctant. If they had missed going to mass, or read a chapter of a novel, that was another thing; these were crimes whereof rebuke and penance were the unfailing meed."

Villette has been lauded to the skies by critics, but the book has never been popular, and its failure as a pecuniary success, in comparison with *Jane Eyre*, was one of the bitterest disappointments of Charlotte Brontë's closing years. There is a tone of remonstrance, nay, of irritation and complaint, in some of her references to the reception of the book; and she says, half-mournfully, half-reproachfully, when commenting on the general verdict, that but two in the world had understood her, and that both were dead. Yet the result was not in the slightest degree astonishing, nor is it easy to believe that, if Charlotte Brontë had given full play to her excellent critical faculty in relation to the matter, she would not have been able to anticipate, if, indeed, she would not have averted, the failure.

She wrote the book, for one thing, and a very important thing, when in bad health and suffering under constant depression. With immense strength of will she performed her task, but the tide of inspiration had ebbed, and she wrote with effort. In the second place, she chose a subject which presented practically insuperable difficulties. " Out of so small a circle of characters," exclaims Mrs. Gaskell, in the plenitude of her admiration, " dwelling in so dull and monotonous an area as a ' pension,' this wonderful tale was evolved ! " Yes. The tale deserves the epithet, wonderful. All honour to the author who wielded the magical wand that " evolved " its scenes and incidents; all credit to the critics who celebrated the feat " with one burst of acclamation." But the great world does not care a straw whether a work of fiction is a miracle of evolution or not, but only whether the thing evolved is an interesting novel. Charlotte Brontë, when writing of Miss Austen, seems to be quite aware that the novelist must have suitable materials if he is to succeed. She complains that, in *Pride and Prejudice*, we have "a carefully-fenced, highly-cultivated garden, with neat borders and delicate flowers; but no glance of a bright, vivid physiognomy, no open country, no fresh air, no blue hill, no bonny beck." And what have we in *Villette?* The routine of what Mrs. Gaskell calls a "pension"—the schoolrooms and dwelling-rooms and fine gardens of an educational establishment in Brussels. It must be confessed that the interest of mankind in education, as a subject of entertainment, is limited. Schoolmasters and schoolmistresses, clever and affectionate pupils, or stupid and heartless, are not capable of being made so interesting to the mass of mankind as more picturesque and open-air personages. And then the charm at which Charlotte so felicitously hints—the charm of blue hill and bonny beck, of woods and moors, and craggy heathery dells—the charm whose fascination is so pervasively felt in *Jane Eyre* and *Shirley*, is absent in *Villette*.

School life, skilfully treated, may, of course, come in admirably in a novel, but it must by no means occupy almost the whole of the three volumes. In *Jane Eyre* the school scenes are telling and effective. Whether it is because the few chapters in which we are introduced to Mr. Brocklehurst and Miss Temple, to Miss Scatcherd and Helen Burns, are written with more subtle and heart-reaching power than the ampler descriptions of school life in *The Professor* and *Villette*, or whether it is simply because they are short, certain it is that they excite a far livelier interest than is awakened by the others. The school-girl, Jane Eyre, is a singularly vivid and accurate miniature likeness of Charlotte herself. The impetuosity with which little Jane resents injustice, whether to herself or to her friends—the fierce haste, for instance, with which she tears from the forehead of Helen Burns, and flings into the fire, the badge of "Slattern"—can hardly fail to remind us of Charlotte's curt and stinging letter to Mr. Lewes, when she thought he had unfairly criticised her, after having made demonstrations of friendliness. "I can be on my guard against my enemies, but God deliver me from my friends!"

In describing Helen Burns, a true effect in pathos is attained, and pathos is rare in Charlotte Brontë's books. "When I should be listening to Miss Scatcherd," says the self-accusing Helen, "and collecting all she says with assiduity, often I lose the very sound of her voice. I fall into a sort of dream. Sometimes I think I am in Northumberland, and that the noises I hear round me are the bubbling of a little brook, which runs through Deepden near our house; —then, when it comes to my turn to reply, I have to be wakened; and, having heard nothing of what was read for listening to the visionary brook, I have no answer ready." The reference to the brooks of Northumberland reminds us that we are in the country; and this is not the only touch of out-of-door and out-of-town fascination that tends to make it pleasanter to read of the Lowood Seminary than of the more imposing one in Brussels. Here is another glimpse of the sylvan surroundings of Lowood :—" April advanced to May. A bright, serene May it was; days of blue sky, placid sunshine, and soft western or southern gales filled up its duration. And now vegetation matured with vigour; Lowood shook loose its tresses; it became all green, all flowery. Its great elm, ash, and oak skeletons were restored to majestic life; woodland plants sprang up profusely in its recesses; unnumbered varieties of moss filled its hollows, and it made a strange ground-sunshine out of the wealth of its wild primrose plants. I have seen their pale gold gleam in overshadowed spots like scatterings of the sweetest lustre."

CHAPTER VIII.

*JANE EYRE—LITTLE JANE AND THE REEDS—
THORNFIELD HALL—FURNITURE FORTY
YEARS AGO—GRACE POOLE—A WINTER
EVENING WALK—MEETING WITH RO-
CHESTER.*

THE *Professor*, though not itself deemed satisfactory, was considered by Messrs. Smith and Elder, the enterprising and sagacious publishers to whom Charlotte Brontë had offered it, to afford evidence that Currer Bell could produce a splendidly successful novel in three volumes. Charlotte's previous efforts had been but enough to awake in her a surmise of her genius, and to accustom her to her tools as a literary artist. She now worked with all her might, heart engaged as well as brain, with that concentrated energy, and that exultation in the outgoing of power, which preclude haste yet secure speed. It is a great mistake to suppose that when artist-work, whether of the pencil or of the pen, is quickly done, it is necessarily hastily done. Haste throws off with slovenly indifference sheet after sheet of heartless and colourless task-work; genius, rejoicing in congenial activity, doing easily what it does consummately well, joins the patient strength of the horse to the wings of a bird, as the wise Greeks signified by their fable of Pegasus. It may safely be said that all art-work which is not, in this sense, quick work, is not supremely excellent. The novel which Charlotte Brontë produced under these circumstances was published in the autumn of 1847, and before the end of the year it had taken its place as one of the most popular novels in the world. To this day it holds, in general estimation throughout Europe and America, the first place among her books. It was cast in the unpromising form of an autobiography of a governess, and named *Jane Eyre*.

The earlier chapters are a model of those preludings which, interesting themselves, ought always to prepare the way for, and to yield complete precedence to, the main interest in a three-volume novel. The heroine, introduced to us in early girlhood, is realised with decisive and errorless touches, few but sufficient. She was one to be vehemently liked by some, to be unaffectedly detested by a much larger number. Abbot, Mrs. Reed's maid, defined her as "a tiresome, ill-conditioned child, who always looked as if she were watching everybody, and scheming plots underhand." Yet all her fault was that she was thoughtful, quiet, gentle, deficient in animal spirits, and plain in feature. She could be interested in books, and loved fairy tales. She had looked for the elves "among foxglove leaves and bells, under mushrooms and beneath the ground-ivy mantling old wall-nooks," and had at length owned "the sad truth that they were all gone out of England." Such a little creature would seem to vulgar worldlings, like Abbot and her coarse, red-faced mistress, to be perpetually asserting a claim to spiritual superiority, and would be hated with the perfect hatred wherewith animals of all species, the human emphatically included, regard creatures that are strange, and alien, and perhaps superior, to themselves.

Villanously ill-treated as our small heroine was by the red-faced Reed and her brute son, John, the author avoids Dickens-ish caricature by letting us see how natural it was for such persons to be rude and cruel to Jane. "I was a discord," writes the latter, commenting on the experiences of her childhood, "in Gateshead Hall; I was like nobody there; I had nothing in harmony with Mrs. Reed or her children, or her chosen vassalage. If they did not love me, in fact, as little did I love them. They were not bound to regard with affection a thing that could not sympathise with one amongst them; a heterogeneous thing, opposed to them in temperament, in capacity, in propensities; a useless thing, incapable of serving their interest, or adding to their pleasure; a noxious thing, cherishing the germs of indignation at their treatment, of contempt of their judgment. I know that had I been a sanguine, brilliant, careless, exacting, handsome, romping child—though equally dependent and friendless—Mrs. Reed would have endured my presence more complacently." And again, with still more pregnant suggestiveness:—" Mrs. Reed, to you I owe some fearful pangs of mental suffering. But I ought to forgive you, for you knew not what you did: while rending my heart-strings, you thought you were only uprooting my bad propensities."

These words convey a most valuable hint to all engaged in the up-bringing of the young. Misunderstandings are easy to produce, hard to destroy. I was once in boyhood driven almost to despair by a teacher, an able man, and not unduly harsh, who quite misunderstood me, and yet, when I reflect on the whole of the circumstances, I cannot fix upon any point in which he was culpable; and I have seen the ablest schoolmaster under whom I ever sat—Dr. Melvin, of Aberdeen—most severely reprimand, in presence of the whole class, a boy who was perfectly innocent of what was imputed to him. "Jane, I don't like cavillers or questioners," said Mrs. Reed, when the little girl objected to be wrongfully accused. But without questioning, nay, ample and fine cross-questioning, the truth is often not to be come at; and of this it is generally impossible for the teacher, compelled to be judge, jury, and, in most cases, sole witness in his own court, to have the advantage. Children, besides, and even boys and girls well-grown, have limited powers of expression, and do not know how to enter upon an explanation. What is wanted is precisely what cannot be had, some mutual friend, with gifts of reconciliation, like those by which, as Macaulay so charmingly describes, Gilbert Burnet removed the misunderstanding that alienated William of Orange from Mary.

From Gateshead Hall Jane was sent to Lowood School. Enough, and not more than enough, is told of her misfortunes and fortunes, the injustice she met with from Mr. Brocklehurst, and the justice done her by Miss Temple; and pathetic and beautiful details are given of her friendship with Helen Burns. Thus prepared, we follow her with stimulated attention when, having plucked up resolution to advertise for a situation, she steps out—a highly unprotected female, aged eighteen, of plain face, tiny figure, strong will, good head, and very limited experience —into the great world. The situation which her advertisement has found for her is that of governess to Adèle Varens, the ward of Edward Fairfax Rochester, Esq., of Thornfield Hall, near Millcote, in a nameless county, which we may identify as Yorkshire. Thornfield Hall was a three-storied house, with picturesque battlements a-top; a rather venerable mansion, but not rising to the dignity of a nobleman's seat. "Its grey front stood out well from the background of a rookery, whose cawing tenants were now"—when Jane looked at them on the morning after her arrival—"on the wing. They flew over the lawn and grounds to alight in a great meadow, from which these were separated by a sunk fence, and where an array of mighty old thorn trees —strong, knotty, and broad as oaks—at once explained the etymology of the mansion's designation.

Farther off were hills; not so lofty as those round Lowood, nor so craggy, nor so like barriers of separation from the living world; but yet quiet and lonely hills enough, and seeming to embrace Thornfield with a seclusion I had not expected to find existent so near the stirring locality of Millcote."

There is one point in the interior arrangements of Thornfield Hall, as described by Charlotte Brontë, which, though unimportant otherwise, has a special interest for those who like to detect in literature the signs of change in social habitude and prevailing taste. It has often been remarked, and the remark seems to me just, that, within the last thirty years, people have become sadder. Ruskin speaks somewhere of the growing incapacity among us to be amused by poor jests. We require more to make us laugh than the mere attempt at a joke which furnishes pretext enough to a happy schoolboy for breaking into a guffaw, or to a healthy milkmaid for showing her white teeth. *Punch* does not make us laugh now as *Punch* used to make people laugh a quarter of a century ago. Leech's faces were always glad, unless marked with vexation about some obvious disaster; Du Maurier's are invariably sad, especially those of his women, except when they are vulgar or ugly. The change is discernible also in the rooms we inhabit. Thirty years ago, the ideal parlour or drawing-room of the middle-class Englishman was one in which the colours were harmoniously bright. In its tones of colour he liked it to approach, as

Furniture Forty Years Ago. 253

nearly as possible, to an apple blossom painted by old William Hunt. Brightness in furniture is now thought by many to betray vulgarity; it is almost as bad form as a loud laugh; the olive greens, the sober greys, the deep-toned reds, in which Mr. Morris has taught us to find a melancholy satisfaction, suggest, however beautiful they may be, a more sombre ideal of domestic felicity. It is curiously interesting, in connection with this change of feeling, that Emily and Charlotte Brontë, both of them what one would call grave and earnest rather than sprightly women, have given us descriptions of rooms, evidently intended by them to be delightful, in which the apple-blossom ideal is realised, and that Charlotte, when her taste presided over the furnishing of a room in Haworth Rectory, was true to the ideal presented in her writings.

When Heathcliff and Cathy look through the window into the domestic heaven of Thrushcross Grange, what they see is thus enthusiastically described by the boy: "Ah! it was beautiful—a splendid place carpeted with crimson, and crimson-covered chairs and tables, and a pure white ceiling bordered by gold, a shower of glass-drops hanging in silver chains from the centre, and shimmering with little soft tapers." When Mrs. Fairfax permits Jane Eyre to look into the drawing-room of Thornfield Hall, what meets her delighted gaze is thus described by the governess: "I thought I caught a glimpse of a fairy palace, so bright to my novice eyes appeared the view beyond. Yet it was merely a very pretty drawing-room, and within it a boudoir, both spread with white carpets, on which seemed laid brilliant garlands of flowers; both ceiled with snowy mouldings of white grapes and vine-leaves, beneath which glowed in rich contrast crimson couches and ottomans; while the ornaments on the pale Parian mantelpiece were of sparkling Bohemian glass ruby-red, and between the windows large mirrors repeated the general blending of snow and fire." "The parlour," writes a visitor to Haworth Parsonage when Charlotte was its mistress, "has been evidently refurnished within the last few years, since Miss Brontë's success has enabled her to have a little more money to spend. The prevailing colour of the room is crimson,"—harmoniously blended, we need not doubt, though this deponent saith not, with white and gold. For my own part, though I unaffectedly enjoy Mr. Morris's best colours, I agree with the simple, cheerful people of the early Victorian era, in thinking that the pleasantest of all family sitting-rooms, especially in the country, is one in which the tone of colour is a delicate harmony of crimson, white, and gold.

We shall not accompany Jane in her tour of discovery, with Mrs. Fairfax for guide, from room to room and story to story, in Thornfield Hall, but the description of the landscape which she saw when she emerged, through a trap-door, upon the roof, is too characteristic of Charlotte Brontë to be omitted:

"I was now on a level with the crow colony, and could see into their nests. Leaning over the battlements and looking far down, I surveyed the grounds laid out like a map: the bright and velvet lawn closely girdling the grey base of the mansion; the field, wide as a park, dotted with its ancient timber; the wood, dun and sere, divided by a path visibly overgrown, greener with moss than the trees were with foliage; the church at the gates, the road, the tranquil hills, all reposing in the autumn day's sun; the horizon bounded by a propitious sky, azure, marbled with pearly white. No feature in the scene was extraordinary, but all was pleasing."

We are bound also to take note of the first introduction of that mystery which plays so important a part in the machinery of *Jane Eyre*. The governess had stepped in again, after looking from the roof; Mrs. Fairfax stayed behind for a moment to fasten the trapdoor; and Jane was alone in the passage leading from the garret staircase. This passage, so near the roof of the house, was "narrow, low, and dim, with only one little window at the far end, and looking, with its two rows of small black doors all shut, like a corridor in some Bluebeard's castle." "While I paced softly on," proceeds Jane, "the last sound I expected to hear in so still a region, a laugh, struck my ear. It was a curious laugh, distinct, formal, mirthless. I stopped; the sound ceased, only for an instant; it began again, louder, for at first, though distinct, it was very low. It passed off in a clamorous peal that seemed to wake an echo in every lonely chamber, though it originated but in one, and I could have pointed out the door whence the accents issued. 'Mrs. Fairfax!' I called out, for I now heard her descending the great stairs, 'did you hear that loud laugh? Who is it?' 'Some of the servants, very likely,' she answered; 'perhaps Grace Poole.' 'Did you hear it?' I again inquired. 'Yes, plainly; I often hear her; she sews in one of these rooms.' The laugh was repeated in its low, syllabic tone, and terminated in an odd murmur. 'Grace!' exclaimed Mrs. Fairfax. I really did not expect any Grace to answer; for the laugh was as tragic, as preternatural a laugh as any I ever heard; and, but that it was high noon, and that no circumstance of ghostliness accompanied the curious cachinnation, but that neither scene nor season favoured fear, I should have been superstitiously afraid. However, the event showed me I was a fool for entertaining a sense even of surprise. The door nearest me opened, and a servant came out,—a woman of between thirty and forty; a set, square-made figure, red-haired, and with a hard, plain face: any apparition less romantic or less ghostly could scarcely be conceived. 'Too much noise, Grace,' said Mrs. Fairfax. 'Remember directions!' Grace curtsied silently and went in."

It is only in the sequel that we appreciate the admirable artfulness of this. Grace Poole, the contradictory creature who is utterly wooden when we get a full sight of her, and becomes so mysteriously and eerily mirthful whenever the door in the long, low, remote passage closes behind her, is a singularly ingenious invention.

Jane, too active-minded to find full occupation for her faculties with her one pupil and Mrs. Fairfax, frequently walked in meditative mood in the weird corridor. "When thus alone," she says, "I not unfrequently heard Grace Poole's laugh : the same peal, the same low, slow ha! ha! which, when first heard, had thrilled me : I heard, too, her eccentric murmurs, stranger than her laugh. Sometimes I saw her: she would come out of her room with a basin, or a plate, or a tray in her hand, go down to the kitchen and shortly return, generally (oh, romantic reader, forgive me for telling the plain truth!) bearing a pot of porter." Was ever mystery more tantalising—more provokingly unpoetical? The reader must recollect that Jane was at this time a girl of eighteen, who had lived for eight years at Lowood school; had she possessed more knowledge of the world, she might have taken a somewhat different view of the enigma connected with Grace Poole.

In spite, however, of Adèle's vivacity, Mrs. Fairfax's judicious observations, and Grace Poole's eccentric merriment, Jane had begun to feel existence too tranquil at Thornfield, when a new chapter opened in her history by the occurrence of an event. Winter had succeeded autumn, and the ground was hard, the air keen, with January frost. Tired of sitting in the library, Jane offered to carry a letter for Mrs. Fairfax to the village of Hay, two miles off. The bracing influence of the sharp Yorkshire air seems to be upon us as we read the description of her walk.

The ground was hard, the air was still, my road was lonely. I walked fast till I got warm, and then I walked slowly to enjoy and analyse the species of pleasure brooding for me in the hour and situation. It was three o'clock; the church bell tolled as I passed under the belfry: the charm of the hour lay in its approaching dimness, in the low-gliding and pale-beaming sun. I was a mile from Thornfield, in a lane noted for wild roses in summer, for nuts and blackberries in autumn, and even now possessing a few coral treasures in hips and haws, but whose best winter delight lay in its utter solitude and leafless repose. If a breath of air stirred, it made no sound here; for there was not a holly, not an evergreen to rustle, and the stripped hawthorn and hazel bushes were as still as the white, worn stones which causewayed the middle of the path. Far and wide, on each side, there were only fields, where no cattle now browsed; and the little brown birds, which stirred occasionally in the hedge, looked like single russet leaves that had forgotten to drop.

This lane inclined up-hill all the way to Hay: having reached the middle, I sat down on a stile which led thence into a field. Gathering my mantle about me, and sheltering my hands in my muff, I did not feel the cold, though it froze keenly; as was attested by a sheet of ice covering the causeway, where a little brooklet, now congealed, had overflowed after a rapid thaw some days since. From my seat I could look down on Thornfield: the grey and battlemented hall was the principal object in the vale below me; its woods and dark rookery rose against the west. I lingered till the sun went down amongst the trees, and sank crimson and clear behind them. I then turned eastward.

On the hill-top above me sat the rising moon; pale yet as a cloud, but brightening momently: she looked over Hay, which, half lost in trees, sent up a blue smoke from its few chimneys; it was yet a mile distant, but in the absolute hush I could hear plainly its thin murmurs of life. My ear, too, felt the flow of currents; in what dales and depths I could not tell: but there were many hills beyond Hay, and doubtless many becks threading their passes. That evening calm betrayed alike the tinkle of the nearest streams, the sough of the most remote.

This is very simple, yet quite masterly, writing. It is like the best parts of Cowper's *Task* with something that reminds you of the minute elaboration of Crabbe or John Clare. There is a crispness in the touch suggestive of frost, when frost is seasonable and not too severe. What a nice precision and judicious parsimony of descriptive features—none of the too-much-ness, the too florid exuberance, of vulgar word-painting! The hedge has its "coral treasures," in hip and haw, though the rose leaves are gone, and the little brown birds are among the branches,—"like single russet leaves!"—though the songs of summer are hushed. And how fine and deep is that poetry of the hill streams! "My ear felt the flow of currents." The poet-woman was with the becks as they stole quietly on, humming their own low, sweet moorland tune, among the dales.

The frost and the silence having brought our nerves into exquisite tension, we are in a condition to be not unpleasantly startled by sound. "A rude noise broke on these fine ripplings and whisperings, at once so far away and so clear; a positive tramp, tramp; a metallic clatter, which effaced the soft wave-wanderings; as, in a picture, the solid mass of a crag, or the rough boles of a great oak, drawn in dark and strong on the foreground, efface the aerial distance of azure hill, sunny horizon, and blended clouds, where tint melts into tint."

A great dog, "a lion-like creature with long hair and a huge head," went careering along; a horse and rider passed; and Jane took a few steps onward towards Hay : but a noise caused her to look back, and she saw that horse and man were down on the ice of the causeway. The dog, barking loudly as dogs will do when circumstances suddenly overtax their canine sagacity, ran instinctively towards Jane as if to summon her assistance. She walked back to the traveller, who was extricating himself from his hazardous situation, and offered help. He limped to the stile on which she had been seated a minute before, and she had time to survey him. " His figure was enveloped in a riding cloak, fur-collared, and steel-clasped ; its details were not apparent, but I traced the general points of middle height, and considerable breadth of chest. He had a dark face, with stern features and a heavy brow; his eyes and gathered eyebrows looked ireful and thwarted just now ; he was past youth, but had not reached middle age ; perhaps he might be thirty-five." After some little colloquy, he accepted Jane's aid to the extent of leaning on her shoulder, as he halted on his sprained foot towards his horse ; he then rode off, and she went on her way. " The incident," she writes, " had occurred, and was gone for me ; it *was* an incident of no moment, no romance, no interest in a sense ; yet it marked with change one single hour of a monotonous life. My help had been needed and claimed ; I had given it ; I was pleased to have done something ; trivial, transitory though the deed was, it was yet an active thing, and I was weary of an existence all passive. The new face, too, was like a new picture introduced to the gallery of memory; and it was dissimilar to all the others hanging there : firstly, because it was masculine; and, secondly, because it was dark, strong, and stern." On returning to Thornfield Hall, she found that the rider was her employer, Mr. Rochester.

CHAPTER IX.

*JANE AND ROCHESTER—JANE'S PICTURES—
CHARLOTTE BRONTË'S IMAGINATION—THE
MERMAID—THE NEREIDES—ROCHESTER'S
SELF-DESCRIPTION—THE MYSTERY—RO-
CHESTER'S PLEA.*

FEW characters, if any, in modern fiction, have been so much discussed as that of the hero of *Jane Eyre*. My own estimate of Edward Fairfax Rochester has long been formed, but it will be more satisfactory to my readers that the facts on which a just estimate must be based should be fairly set before them than that I should begin with a statement of my own opinion.

On the evening of the day after his arrival at Thornfield, Rochester conversed at some length with Jane. We shall take a few words from their colloquy. "'You have been resident in my house three months?' 'Yes, sir.' 'And you came from——?' 'From Lowood school in ——shire.' 'Ah! a *charitable concern*. How long were you there?' 'Eight years.' 'Eight years! you must be tenacious of life. I thought half the time in such a place would have done up any constitution! No wonder you have rather the look of another world. I marvelled where you had got that sort of face. When you came on me in Hay Lane last night, I thought unaccountably of fairy tales, and had half a mind to demand whether you had bewitched my horse : I am not sure yet. Who are your parents?' 'I have none.' '*Nor ever had, I suppose; do you remember them?*' 'No.'"

I put into italics that remark of Rochester's which must, I think, have grated on the ear, or rather on the heart, of the reader. It is entirely decisive as to the fact that Rochester had not the intuitions of a gentleman. "A charitable concern!" he says. The girl had just told him she had been trained in it. Noah Claypole called Oliver Twist "Vurkus." Rochester did not, like Claypole, wish to wound the person he addressed ; but if he had not been characterised by that defect of sensibility which Ruskin rightly pronounces the infallible note of vulgarity, he would instinctively and instantaneously have placed his recollection of the nature of the Lowood foundation under the strictest guard of silence, and hastened on without letting Jane detect, even by a glance of his eye, what he had been thinking of. There was a lack of delicacy in the blunt cross-questioning about Jane's parentage, but this was a venial offence compared with the other. In his second conversation with Jane, Rochester took occasion, à *propos* of his disliking the prattle of children, to inform her that he was an "old bachelor." The sequel proves that this was a lie,— not a quite unqualified lie, but a statement which, in any court of justice, would be characterised as the real thing. Rather unmanageable items these, to reconcile with the character of a hero,—a piece of rudeness of which no one could be guilty who had the sympathetic nerve of a gentleman, and a fib!

We shall return to the character of Rochester, but I must here make him stand aside for a moment, in order that the attention of the reader may be given to a passage, occurring in connection with one of these early conversations between **Jane and her master,** which is specially illustrative of Charlotte Brontë's imaginative genius. I refer to the description of three of Jane's water-colour pictures, as they were placed before the critical eye of Rochester.

> The first represented clouds low and livid, rolling over a swollen sea; all the distance was in eclipse; so, too, was the foreground; or, rather, the nearest billows, for there was no land. One gleam of light lifted into relief a half-submerged mast, on which sat a cormorant, dark and large, with wings flecked with foam: its beak held a gold bracelet, set with gems, that I had touched with as brilliant tints as my palette could yield, and as glittering distinctness as my pencil could impart. Sinking below the bird and mast, a drowned corpse glanced through the green water; a fair arm was the only limb clearly visible, whence the bracelet had been washed or torn.
>
> The second picture contained for foreground only the dim peak of a hill, with grass and some leaves slanting as if by a breeze. Beyond and above spread an expanse of sky, dark blue as at twilight; rising into the sky was a woman's shape to the bust, portrayed in tints as dusk and soft as I could combine. The dim forehead was crowned with a star; the lineaments below were seen as through the suffusion of vapour; the eyes shone dark and wild; the hair streamed shadowy, like a beamless cloud torn by storm or by electric travail. On the neck lay a pale reflection like moonlight; the same faint lustre touched the train of thin clouds from which rose and bowed this vision of the Evening Star.

The third showed the pinnacle of an iceberg piercing a polar winter sky : a muster of northern lights reared their dim lances, close serried, along the horizon. Throwing these into distance, rose, in the foreground, a head—a colossal head, inclined towards the iceberg, and resting against it. Two thin hands, joined under the forehead, and supporting it, drew up before the lower features a sable veil; a brow quite bloodless, white as bone, and an eye hollow and fixed, blank of meaning but for the glassiness of despair, alone were visible. Above the temples, amidst wreathed turban folds of black drapery, vague in its character and consistency as cloud, gleamed a ring of white flame, gemmed with sparkles of a more lurid tinge. This pale crescent was 'The likeness of a Kingly Crown;' what it diademed was 'the shape which shape had none.'"

Chapters—books, I daresay—have been written to discuss and define the nature of imagination; but the main and central application of the term is that which rests upon the idea of eyesight. Imagination is the soul's eye. In its highest power, however, it is creative in a sense in which the bodily eye, except for diseased persons or fantastic philosophers, never is. The vision of the external world rolls into the bodily eye, unbidden; not at all created, and very slightly modified, by the eye that sees; but the imagination, working, indeed, with materials furnished in their originals by perception, bodies out visions which have no counterpart in the external world. These are produced by the poet and the artist, and demand a higher form of mental operation than any that is engaged in by the man of science. The imaginative power displayed in inventing and describing Jane's pictures gives Charlotte Brontë a better title to the name of poet than anything in her verses. The passage seems to me to transcend anything that has been done, either in verse or prose, by George Eliot. Only Mrs. Browning, among Englishwomen of literary genius, has surpassed these word-paintings.

Perhaps still finer illustration of the power in question than is afforded by the three pictures which Jane Eyre placed before Rochester, may be found in some passages occurring in *Shirley*. They are brief, and admit of being easily separated from the context. It will be unnecessary to quote more than two. The first appears in a conversation between Shirley Keeldar, the heroine of the novel, and her friend Caroline Helstone, on the subject of a voyage which they propose taking to the Arctic regions.

"I suppose you expect to see mermaids, Shirley?" "One of them at any rate. I do not bargain for less; and she is to appear in some such fashion as this. I am to be walking by myself on deck, rather late of an August evening, watching and being watched by a full harvest-moon; something is to rise white on the surface of the sea, over which that moon mounts silent, and hangs glorious. The object glitters and sinks. It rises again. I think I hear it cry with an articulate voice: I call you up from the cabin: I show you an image, fair as alabaster, emerging from the dim wave. We both see the long hair, the lifted and foam-white arm, the oval mirror brilliant as a star. It glides nearer; a human face is plainly visible; a face in the style of yours, whose straight, pure (excuse the word, it is appropriate)—whose straight, pure lineaments paleness does not disfigure. It looks at us, but not with your eyes. I see a preternatural lure in its wily glance: it beckons. Were we men we should spring at the sign, the cold billow would be dared for the sake of the colder enchantress; being women, we stand safe, though not dreadless. She comprehends our unmoved gaze; she feels herself powerless; anger crosses her front; she cannot charm, but she will appal us; she rises high, and glides all revealed, on the dark wave-ridge. Temptress-terror! monstrous likeness of ourselves! Are you not glad, Caroline, when at last, and with a wild shriek, she dives?"

The other passage is suggested by the contraband reading of the schoolboy, Martin Yorke, who likes better to con fairy tales when the lingering light of sunset blends with the first beams of the moon, than to explore the mysteries of Latin grammar. The few lines descriptive of the vision of the fairy queen are unimportant, but we may as well take them for what Charlotte Brontë doubtless intended them to be, a kind of introduction to the more original bit of imaginative work that succeeds.

He reads: he is led into a solitary mountain region; all round him is rude and desolate, shapeless, and almost colourless. He hears bells tinkle on the wind; forth-riding from the formless forms of the mist, dawns on him the brightest vision—a green-robed lady, on a snow-white palfrey; he sees her dress, her gems, and her steed; she arrests him with some mysterious question; he is spell-bound, and must follow her into Fairyland.

A second legend bears him to the sea-shore; there tumbles in a strong tide, boiling at the base of dizzy cliffs; it rains and blows. A reef of rocks, black and rough, stretches far into the sea; all along, and among, and above these crags, dash and flash, sweep and leap, swells, wreaths, drifts of snowy spray. Some lone wanderer is out on these rocks, treading, with cautious step, the wet, wild sea-weed; glancing down into hollows where the brine lies fathom-deep and emerald-clear, and seeing there wilder, and stranger, and huger vegetation than is found on land, with treasure of shells—some green, some purple, some pearly—clustered in the curls of the snaky plants. He hears a cry. Looking up, and forward, he sees, at the bleak point of the reef, a tall, pale thing—shaped like man, but made of spray—transparent, tremulous, awful: it stands not alone; they are all human figures that wanton in the rocks—a crowd of foam-women—a band of white, evanescent Nereides.

That Mermaid is, so far as I know, an entirely original conception. Despite the presence of the mirror, she is not in the least like the lady of marine tradition who combs her locks with a golden comb, as Heine makes his witch of the Loreley do; nor has she any resemblance to the Sirens of the old Sicilian shore. She is born of the imagination of Charlotte Brontë, and is invested with a new and strange mystery as a temptress of women; not impassioned, but wily and cold, incarnating the treachery, and the wild gleaming perilous beauty, and the cruel power, of the Northern sea. How finely in keeping is it that such a creature should appear when the pale moon is rising into the steely sky, and the cold glitter of its beam lends a more witching whiteness to arm and bosom as she "glares appalling from the ridge of the wave!"

The description, in the second passage, of the broken sea on a craggy shore beneath high cliffs, with interposed hollows, rock-protected, where the salt water lies in crystalline clearness, shows how carefully Charlotte Brontë had noted the scenery of the English seashore on her visits to Scarborough and Filey; but in the personification of the filmy foam-wreaths, wavering in the wind, as evanescent Nereides, there is a far more subtle and plastic power than that of mere observation, a power essentially identical with that of the poet and the creative artist. And while the imagination, in its plastic, form-giving energy, calls into visible shape the Mermaid or the Nereid, the imagination, in its revealing, penetrating, and sympathetic energy, enables us to realise how, in a distant age, the legend of the

Mermaid or the Nereid arose. Charlotte Brontë, with her quick eye and kindling sympathy, as she looked at the wind-shaken foam beneath Yorkshire cliffs, felt as the early Greek felt when he first saw, in the wavering spray of the Ægean, the white draperies of the daughters of Nereus. Thus treated, old legends are never dead; the fossil tradition is re-inspired with life, and we know how our remote ancestors first learned to believe in it. And now let us return to Edward Fairfax Rochester.

He was, we found, an imperfect character, his imperfection including a vulgar callousness of feeling and a disregard of truth. The author, however, is careful to inform us that his imperfection was not without excuse. He had suffered wrong. His elder brother had prejudiced his father against him. His father, anxious that he should be rich, had co-operated with his brother in placing him in " what he considered a painful position, for the sake of making his fortune." The nature of the injury is not, at this stage, disclosed ; but " his spirit could not brook what he had to suffer." His misfortune had caused him to lead " an unsettled kind of life," and since the death of his brother, when he became master of Thornfield, he had hardly stayed at the place for a fortnight together. In his wanderings he had acquired the habit of brooding on his sorrows, and his conversation with Jane was strongly tinged with egotism. "' Criticise me,' he said to her once ; ' does my forehead not please you?' He lifted up the sable waves of hair which lay horizontally over his brow, and showed a solid enough mass of intellectual organs, but an abrupt deficiency where the suave sign of benevolence should have risen. 'Now, ma'am, am I a fool?' 'Far from it, sir. You would, perhaps, think me rude if I inquired in return whether you are a philanthropist?'" No, he is not a "general philanthropist." He does not like children or old women; but "I bear," he says, "a conscience," and "I once had a kind of rude tenderness of heart."

This looks much like the kind of man who, by the lords of creation, wherever they do congregate—in college hall, or club dining-room—is unanimously voted a bore and prig. There is a fine stagy sadness about him, and he looks not ill. "He rose from his chair, and stood, leaning his arm on the marble mantelpiece. In that attitude his shape was seen plainly, as well as his face; his unusual breadth of chest disproportionate almost to his length of limb. I am sure most people would have thought him an ugly man; yet there was so much unconscious pride in his port, so much ease in his demeanour, such a look of complete indifference to his own external appearance, so haughty a reliance on the power of other qualities, intrinsic or adventitious, to atone for the lack of mere personal attractiveness, that, in looking at him, one inevitably shared the indifference, and, even in a blind, imperfect sense, put faith in the confidence."

If men would call this a strutting coxcomb, there are few women who would not be touched by his melancholy charm. The reader has probably been already reminded of the Byronic hero—the Giaour, the Corsair, the Childe, Lara, Manfred—who awoke such a *furore* of sympathetic admiration two or three generations back. Byron, at bottom one of the shrewdest men of the world, appreciated the theatricality of his own stock character, and laughed ironically when a young American hero-worshipper, Coolidge by name, betrayed symptoms of disappointment at not finding his lordship attired in wolfskin breeches and answering in fierce monosyllables, on the model of his typical hero. When Moore, however, sketched the character in its generic traits, Byron did not half like his friend's wit.

> The sallow, sublime, kind of Werter-faced man,
> With moustachios that gave, what we read of so oft,
> The dear Corsair-expression, half-savage, half-soft.

Rochester, proceeding with his autobiographical confidences to Jane, informs her that he is not a villain, but " a trite, common-place sinner, hackneyed in all the poor, petty dissipations with which the rich and worthless try to put on life." He detects in her, he says, a capacity of listening to him, not with malevolent scorn, but with "innate sympathy," and he opens his heart to her in return. " 'You would say, I should have been superior to circumstances; so I should; but you see I was not. When fate wronged me, I had not the wisdom to remain cool. I turned desperate ; then I degenerated. . . . Dread remorse when you are tempted to err, Miss Eyre. Remorse is the poison of life.'" She suggests that repentance is its cure; but he will not listen to so commonplace a prescription. He has one of his own. A notion, he says, has flitted across his brain. "'I believe it was an inspiration rather than a temptation: it was very genial, very soothing—I know that. Here it comes again. It is no devil, I assure you; or, if it be, it has put on the robes of an angel of light. I think I must admit so fair a guest when it asks entrance to my heart.'" Jane warns him that it may be an angel of darkness, but he refuses to believe her. "'Not at all,' he exclaims; 'it bears the most gracious message in the world: for the rest, you are not my conscience-keeper, so don't make yourself uneasy. Here, come in, bonny wanderer!' He said this as if he spoke to a vision, viewless to any eye but his own; then, folding his arms, which he had half extended, on his chest, he seemed to enclose in their embrace the invisible being. 'Now,' he continued, again addressing me, 'I have received the pilgrim—a disguised deity, as I verily believe. Already it has done me good: my heart was a sort of charnel; it will now be a shrine.'"

The whisper of hope and healing from heaven, or the muttered temptation from hell—for it is not on the surface discernible which of these it may be—which Rochester expected to turn his heart from a charnel into a shrine, was, in more prosaic language, the suggestion that he should marry Jane. What stands in the way he will not tell her; but readers doubtless suspect that it is something connected with

Grace Poole. A succession of incidents, devised and described with an ingenuity, a felicity, an intensity, unsurpassed in the whole range of fictitious literature, perplexes us with a sense of the mystery. One night Jane, startled from sleep, hears close to her room door the laugh which had surprised her in the corridor, finds presently that the curtains and bed-clothes of Rochester's bed had been set on fire, and barely succeeds in extinguishing the flames and saving his life. He refers her to Grace Poole as the source of the mischief. On another night the silence is rent by a terrific shriek; a visitor sleeping on the same story with Grace Poole has been murderously attacked; and Jane holds the basin while Rochester sponges away the blood and restores the rescued victim to consciousness. This operation is performed in a room into which another room opens, and from this inner room Jane hears " a snarling, snatching sound, almost like a dog quarrelling." It need scarcely be said that she was perplexed. "What crime," she speculated, "was this, that lived incarnate in this sequestered mansion, and could neither be expelled nor subdued by the owner? What mystery that broke out, now in fire and now in blood, at the deadest hour of night? What creature was it, that, masked in an ordinary woman's face and shape, uttered the voice, now of a mocking demon, and anon of a carrion-seeking bird of prey?" Once more—this time, also, in the dead of night—Jane Eyre was awakened by the presence of the mystery. In the description of what followed, taken in connection with the subsequent explanation of it, Charlotte Brontë has succeeded in creating the emotion of terror as effectually as Edgar Poe ever did in those weird and awful tales in which he concentrated the whole force of his genius upon the production of that particular emotion. Jane details the circumstances to Rochester, most imaginatively leading up to the climax of horror by an account of the troubled dreams which had been previously vexing her sleep. I include in my quotation the closing sentences of this "preface."

"I heard the gallop of a horse at a distance on the road; I was sure it was you; and you were departing for many years, and for a distant country. I climbed the thin wall with frantic, perilous haste, eager to catch one glimpse of you from the top; the stones rolled from under my feet, the ivy branches I grasped gave way, the child clung round my neck in terror, and almost strangled me; at last I gained the summit. I saw you like a speck on a white track, lessening every moment. The blast blew so strong, I could not stand. I sat down on the narrow ledge; I hushed the scared infant in my lap; you turned an angle of the road; I bent forward to take a last look; the wall crumbled; I was shaken; the child rolled from my knee, I lost my balance, fell, and woke."

" Now, Jane, that is all." "All the preface, sir; the tale is yet to come. On waking, a gleam dazzled my eyes; I thought—oh, it is daylight! But I was mistaken; it was only candle-light; Sophie, I supposed, had come in. There was a light on the dressing-table, and the door of the closet, where, before going to bed, I had hung my wedding dress and veil, stood open; I heard a rustling there. I asked, 'Sophie, what are you doing?' No one answered; but a form emerged from the closet; it took the light, held it aloft, and surveyed the garments pendent from the portmanteau.* 'Sophie! Sophie!' I again cried, and still it was silent. I had risen up in bed, I bent forwards: first, surprise, then

---

* I quote from the illustrated edition of 1875. It is not easy to see how garments could be pendent from a portmanteau.

bewilderment, came over me, and then my blood crept cold through my veins. Mr. Rochester, this was not Sophie, it was not Leah, it was not Mrs. Fairfax; it was not—no, I was sure of it, and am still—it was not even that strange woman, Grace Poole." "It must have been one of them," interrupted my master. "No, sir, I solemnly assure you to the contrary. The shape standing before me had never crossed my eyes within the precincts of Thornfield Hall before; the height, the contour, were new to me." "Describe it, Jane." "It seemed, sir, a woman, tall and large, with thick and dark hair hanging long down her back. I know not what dress she had on : it was white and straight; but whether gown, sheet, or shroud, I cannot tell." "Did you see her face?" "Not at first. But presently she took my veil from its place; she held it up, gazed at it long, and then she threw it over her own head, and turned to the mirror. At that moment I saw the reflection of the visage and features quite distinctly in the dark oblong glass." "And how were they?" "Fearful and ghastly to me—oh, sir, I never saw a face like it. It was a discoloured face—it was a savage face. I wish I could forget the roll of the red eyes and the fearful blackened inflation of the lineaments." "Ghosts are usually pale, Jane." "This, sir, was purple; the lips were swelled and dark; the brow furrowed; the black eyebrows widely raised over the bloodshot eyes! Shall I tell you of what it reminded me?" "You may." "Of the foul German spectre—the Vampire." "Ah! What did it do?" "Sir, it removed my veil from its gaunt head, rent it in two parts, and flinging both on the floor, trampled on them." "Afterwards?" "It drew aside the window-curtain and looked out; perhaps it saw dawn approaching, for, taking the candle, it retreated to the door. Just at my bedside the figure stopped; the fiery eye glared upon me—she thrust up her candle close to my face, and extinguished it under my eyes. I was aware her lurid visage flamed over mine, and I lost consciousness : for the second time in my life—only the second time—I became insensible from terror."

The peculiar and penetrating horror of this apparition is derived from the subsequent discovery that it was no ghost that appeared to Jane, but a fierce and dangerous maniac. The spectral woman was, of course, Rochester's wife, and he led Jane to the altar without correcting his early statement to her that he was a bachelor. He had been married to his maniac wife when he was very young, through the influence of a mercenary father and a heartless brother. How far was he justifiable in attempting to marry again while she was alive? In order to do Charlotte Brontë justice, and to obviate all doubt that we have the character of Rochester fully and favourably presented to us, we shall take his plea from his own lips, as he stated it to Jane one lovely morning in the garden, when the air was fragrant with sweet-brier, and bright with apple-blossom.

"Now, my little friend, while the sun drinks the dew—while all the flowers in this old garden awake and expand, and the birds fetch their young ones' breakfast out of the cornfield, and the early bees do their first spell of work—I'll put a case to you, which you must endeavour to suppose your own; but first, look at me, and tell me you are at ease, and not fearing that I err in detaining you, or that you err in staying." "No, sir; I am content." "Well, then, Jane, call to your aid your fancy;—suppose you were no longer a girl, well reared and disciplined, but a wild boy, indulged from childhood upwards; imagine yourself in a remote foreign land; conceive that you there commit a capital error, no matter of what nature or from what motives, but one whose consequences must follow you through life and taint all your existence. Mind, I don't say a *crime;* I am not speaking of shedding of blood or any other guilty act, which might make the perpetrators amenable to the law: my word is *error*. The results of what you have done become in time to you utterly insupportable; you take measures to obtain relief; unusual measures, but neither unlawful nor culpable. Still you are miserable; for hope has quitted you on the very confines of life; your sun at noon darkens in an eclipse, which you feel will not leave it till the time of setting. Bitter and base associations have become the sole food of your memory; you wander here and there, seeking rest in exile:

happiness in pleasure—I mean in heartless, sensual pleasure—such as dulls intellect and blights feeling. Heart-weary and soul-withered, you come home after years of voluntary banishment; you make a new acquaintance—how or where no matter; you find in this stranger much of the good and bright qualities which you have sought for twenty years, and never before encountered; and they are all fresh, healthy, without soil and without taint. Such society revives, regenerates; you feel better days come back—higher wishes, purer feelings; you desire to recommence your life, and to spend what remains to you of days in a way more worthy of an immortal being. To attain this end, are you justified in overleaping an obstacle of custom—a mere conventional impediment, which neither your conscience sanctifies, nor your judgment approves?"

He paused for an answer, and what was I to say? Oh, for some good spirit to suggest a judicious and satisfactory response! Vain aspiration! The west wind whispered in the ivy round me; but no gentle Ariel borrowed its breath as a medium of speech; the birds sang in the tree-tops, but their song, however sweet, was inarticulate. Again Mr. Rochester propounded his query, "Is the wandering and sinful, but now rest-seeking and repentant, man justified in daring the world's opinion, in order to attach to him for ever this gentle, gracious, genial stranger, thereby securing his own peace of mind and regeneration of life?" "Sir," I answered, "a wanderer's repose or a sinner's reformation should never depend on a fellow-creature. Men and women die; philosophers falter in wisdom, and Christians in goodness. If any one you know has suffered and erred, let him look higher than his equals for strength to amend, and solace to heal." "But the instrument —the instrument! God, who does the work, ordains the instrument. I have myself—I tell it you without parable—been worldly, dissipated, restless man; and I believe I have found the instrument for my cure in ——." He paused; the birds went on carolling, the leaves lightly rustling.

Shall we pronounce Rochester a true hero, or a theatrical scamp, or something between the two? The question is too important to be answered in the fag end of a chapter.

CHAPTER X.

*CHARLOTTE BRONTË'S DEFENCE OF JANE EYRE
—ROCHESTER AN EGOIST—THE PRECISE
CHARGES AGAINST JANE EYRE—JANE'S DIS-
APPOINTMENT—ROCHESTER'S LAST WORD—
JANE IN EXTREMIS—OUR VERDICT ON THE
AUTHOR.*

THE force of Rochester's plea for himself might be enhanced if we in imagination accompanied him and Jane, and the clergyman and clerk, and Mr. Mason, who interrupted the marriage ceremony, from the altar to the room in which his maniac wife was confined. But this is happily not necessary. Rochester had been grievously sinned against—cajoled in his youth into marriage with one of "a mad family, idiots and maniacs through three generations;" his wife was a drunkard, and worse, before she became a raging lunatic, and nothing could be more hideously infra-human than her final state. He "meant," therefore, to use his own words, "to be a bigamist," and he "entrapped," or did his best to entrap, "into a feigned union," a girl of eighteen, whose residence under his roof, in capacity of governess, gave him his opportunity. *Voilà*, the plain facts.

Rochester's plea was not universally sustained by the readers of *Jane Eyre*. To the second edition of the book Charlotte Brontë affixed a preface, in which she took to task " the timorous or carping few " who pronounced its tendency questionable, its morality doubtful. Her unfavourable critics are therein described as persons " in whose eyes whatever is unusual is wrong; whose ears detect in each protest against bigotry—that parent of crime—an insult to piety, that regent of God on earth." Rather hard measure to deal out to the unfavourable critics, one must admit. She suggests to them " certain obvious distinctions," reminds them of "certain simple truths." We are bound to bestow upon these our best attention. The following is her statement of them:—
" Conventionality is not morality. Self-righteousness is not religion. To attack the first is not to assail the last. To pluck the mask from the face of the Pharisee is not to lift an impious hand to the crown of thorns. These things and deeds are diametrically opposed: they are as distinct as is vice from virtue. Men too often confound them : they should not be confounded ; appearance should not be mistaken for truth ; narrow human doctrines, that only tend to elate and magnify a few, should not be substituted for the world-redeeming creed of Christ. There is—I repeat it—a difference ; and it is a good, and not a bad action, to mark broadly and clearly the line of separation between them. The world may not like to see these ideas dissevered, for it has been accustomed to

blend them; finding it convenient to make external show pass for sterling worth—to let white-washed walls vouch for clean shrines. It may hate him who dares to scrutinise and expose—to rase the gilding, and show base metal under it—to penetrate the sepulchre, and reveal charnel relics; but hate as it will, it is indebted to him. Ahab did not like Micaiah, because he never prophesied good concerning him, but evil; probably he liked the sycophant son of Chenaanah better; yet might Ahab have escaped a bloody death, had he but stopped his ears to flattery, and opened them to faithful counsel."

These diamond-pointed sentences afford the most humorously-beautiful illustration known to me in literature of that style of argument which is ungallantly, and perhaps unjustly, called lady's logic. With charming coolness—with winning and child-like *naïveté*—Charlotte Brontë begs the whole question, and assumes what she is bound to prove. No sane man, from Nova Zembla to Cape Comorin, from Pekin to Birmingham, could confound the things she distinguishes, or dispute the truths she enunciates. But when all these generalities have been admitted and put aside, the question remains, whether Rochester is a legitimate hero, and whether the ethical foundations of the novel are sound. The preliminary flourish of the advocate is extremely fine—but she commits the slight mistake of not following it up by any argument whatever—of not once referring to the facts in evidence. We must repair her omission, remarking

that the advocate must be held to plead not only her
hero's cause, but her own. She unquestionably be-
speaks the admiration of the reader for Rochester.
This is on the face of the novel. He is made
attractive. Courage, firmness, manliness, ardour,
talent, soldierly frankness, are his characteristics,
and he rides his black horse Mesrour like a prince.

Looking searchingly then into Rochester's plea,
what better, let us ask, is he at bottom than an
egoist? In his selfishness he does not scruple to lie.
He has not resolutely adjusted himself to the melancholy circumstances which have darkened his life, but
has drawn a veil over them; and he attempts, though
it be by criminal means, to evade the misfortune under
which he has fallen. His own word "entrap" applies
strictly to his conduct in relation to Jane, for if he
intended to make of her a friend and nominal wife, he
ought to have let her know precisely how matters
stood, and to have obtained her consent or refusal.
But the darkest symptom in Rochester's case is one
which Charlotte Brontë must, I fear, be held not only
to condone, but to enter in mitigation of his offence. I
allude to his suggestion as to the religious elevation of
his motives in deceiving Jane. What he says about
receiving a heavenly visitant into his breast when the
idea occurs to him of marrying the governess, about
knowing that his "Maker sanctions" what he does,
and so forth, is cant. A ruggedly honest man,—a
healthily strong man,—though he might be passion-
driven into crime, would not fall into sickly self-

deception like this. The personage who, with a wife in the garret, snivels about little Jane being the instrument ordained by Providence to work out his reformation, must have a vein of rather malignant humbug in him. Heep's parade of his 'umbleness, Pecksniff's advertisement of his generosity, are superficial weaknesses compared with the rooted falseness of cant like this. I should not call Rochester a scoundrel or a worthless fellow, but he falls below the lowest standard of a heroic character. Yet he is the hero of this book; and so attractive is he made—so effectually are his bad elements masked in his fascinating qualities—that, of the tens of thousands of girls who have hung enraptured over the pages of *Jane Eyre*, I should doubt whether one of a thousand has not fallen in love with Rochester. Thackeray took it for many years as his mission to castigate those writers of fiction who arrayed vice in the attractiveness pertaining legitimately to virtue. The representative of such writers he found in the author of *Pelham* and *Ernest Maltravers*, and no one, I think, has ventured to maintain that his censure was wholly unjust or uncalled for; but the subtly seductive and cunningly masked badness of Rochester is fitted to exert a far deadlier influence than that of the gorgeous voluptuaries whom one smiles at in those romances that carried the name of Bulwer over the world.

Let it not, however, be supposed that I charge Charlotte Brontë with what Scotch lawyers would call homologating Rochester. She does not take him over as all right, and cover him with the mantle of her approval. We cannot make her answerable for more than Jane's estimate of Rochester—for the treatment which, first and last, he obtains at Jane's hands; but she is assuredly answerable for this. Jane, it is true, does not take Rochester at his own valuation. She starts back so soon as she knows what he has prepared for her; declines to exculpate him; promptly leaves his house. Her previous conduct had not been faultless, but neither had it been gravely censurable. She had not been duly respectful to herself, duly sensible of her dignity as a teacher, of her rights as a woman and a lady; but she was very young, and she came from Lowood school, where she had been accustomed to answer "Yes, sir," "No, sir," to the portentous Mr. Brocklehurst. It was a more serious offence to the right instincts of a woman, that she should listen to Rochester's unedifying account of his Parisian experiences. No man perfectly entitled to the name of gentleman would have stained the imagination of a girl in that way; no woman entitled to the name of lady would have permitted her imagination to be so stained. Charlotte Brontë had no such sense of delicacy, in man or woman, as was possessed by Miss Austen, greatly more original and potent as I hold her genius to have, on the whole, been than that of her matronly and sweet-minded predecessor. But Jane stops short of actual degradation. When the catastrophe comes, she is true to herself, and in her inflexible resistance to Rochester we see how, under like circumstances, Charlotte, the intrepid little Yorkshire-woman, would have acted. Jane had loved Rochester with all the energy of her keen brain and virgin heart. He had seemed to be lifting her into exquisite bliss. The extent of her distress when the shock arrived we are enabled to realise when we accompany her into her room after the clergyman and the lawyer have left Thornfield Hall. She bolts her door, takes off her marriage dress, and, in the consciousness that the place she had been about to occupy is already occupied by a hideous maniac, begins to think. The passage in which her reflections and feelings are expressed is another of those that mark Charlotte Brontë as a poet and great literary artist. Its imagery—in particular its brief, superb contrast of wintry grief with summer gladness—is unsurpassable.

> Jane Eyre, who had been an ardent, expectant woman—almost a bride—was a cold, solitary girl again: her life was pale; her prospects were desolate. A Christmas frost had come at Midsummer; a white December storm had whirled over June;[*] ice glazed the ripe apples, drifts crushed the blowing roses; on hayfield and cornfield lay a frozen shroud; lanes which last night blushed full of flowers, to-day were pathless with untrodden snow; and the woods, which twelve hours since waved leafy and fragrant as groves between the tropics, now spread waste, wild, and white as pine-forests in wintry Norway. My hopes were all dead,—struck with a subtle doom, such as, in one night, fell on all the first-born in the land of Egypt. I looked on my cherished wishes, yesterday so blooming and glowing; they lay stark, chill, livid

---

[*] " Seek roses in December, ice in June."—*Byron*.

corpses that could never revive. I looked at my love; that feeling which was my master's—which he had created; it shivered in my heart like a suffering child in a cold cradle; sickness and anguish had seized it; it could not seek Mr. Rochester's arms—it could not derive warmth from his breast. Oh, never more could it turn to him, for faith was blighted—confidence destroyed! Mr. Rochester was not to me what he had been; for he was not what I had thought him. I would not ascribe vice to him; I would not say he had betrayed me; but the attribute of stainless truth was gone from his idea; and from his presence I must go; *that* I perceived well. When?—how?—whither? I could not yet discern; but he himself, I doubted not, would hurry me from Thornfield. Real affection, it seemed, he could not have for me; it had been only fitful passion: that was baulked; he would want me no more. I should fear even to cross his path now: my view must be hateful to him. Oh, how blind had been my eyes! How weak my conduct!

My eyes were covered and closed; eddying darkness seemed to swim round me, and reflection came in as black and confused a flow. Self-abandoned, relaxed, and effortless, I seemed to have laid me down in the dried-up bed of a great river; I heard a flood loosened in remote mountains, and felt the torrent come; to rise I had no will, to flee I had no strength. I lay faint; longing to be dead. One idea only still throbbed life-like within me—a remembrance of God; it begot an unuttered prayer. These words went wandering up and down in my rayless mind, as something that should be whispered; but no energy was found to express them: " Be not far from me, for trouble is near; there is none to help."

It was near; and as I had lifted no petition to heaven to avert it —as I had neither joined my hands, nor bent my knees, nor moved my lips—it came: in full, heavy swing the torrent poured over me. The whole consciousness of my life lorn, my love lost, my hope quenched, my faith death-struck, swayed full and mighty above me in one sullen mass. That bitter hour cannot be described; in truth, " the waters came into my soul, I sank in deep mire; I felt no standing, I came into deep waters; the floods overflowed me."

It was now that the fiercest trial of her virtue began. While she shook like a reed under the stress of her anguish, she found herself again in the presence of Rochester. He was contrite; he spoke in the tone of one who was broken-hearted. "Jane, I never meant to wound you thus. If the man who had but one little ewe lamb that was dear to him as a daughter, that ate of his bread and drank of his cup, and lay in his bosom, had by some mistake slaughtered it at the shambles, he would not have rued his bloody blunder more than I now rue mine. Will you ever forgive me?" She forgave him; but repelled him decisively when he attempted to caress her, reminding him that he had a wife, and stating her determination to leave him. Thereupon he entered more explicitly than he had ever done before on an explanation of his circumstances, insisting that, whatever might be his position in the eye of human law, he was, in the sight of God, divorced from his wedded wife. It was not only that he had been grossly deceived before the marriage, or that she had been intolerable afterwards; she had, he said, conducted herself so as to entitle him to a legal divorce; but "the doctors now discovered that *my wife* was mad —her excesses had prematurely developed the germs of insanity." Legal proceedings, therefore, could not be resorted to.

Whether Rochester was right or wrong in thus defining his position before the law may be open to question. The prevailing impression, at the time when *Jane Eyre* was written, undoubtedly concurred with the view he takes of his case; but, since then, events have taken place which suggest a doubt whether he might not have obtained legal relief. A poor man, it is too true, who was forced to maintain a lunatic wife in an asylum, and who applied for a divorce on account of her unfaithfulness before madness had ensued, was driven, almost with hootings, from the judgment-seat; but when a rich man, a man of title, applied for a divorce on exactly the same grounds, he found English law not inexorable to a petition that aristocratic blood might be warded from taint. Rochester was a rich man and of an old family, and he might possibly have found the aristocratic luxury called justice not so unobtainable as he thought. All this, however, was unknown to Charlotte Brontë when she published *Jane Eyre*. She had a right to represent her hero as barred from proceedings against his wife.

Rochester next describes to Jane how the misery of his indissoluble connection drove him almost to suicide. Then a new hope awoke within him. "That woman," whispered the new hope, "who has so abused your long-suffering, so sullied your name, so outraged your honour, so blighted your youth, is not your wife—nor are you her husband. See that she is cared for as her condition demands, and you have done all that God and humanity require of you." He was then in the West Indies. Animated with his new purpose, he sailed for Europe, immured his wife in Thornfield Hall under the charge of Grace Poole, set out for the Continent, and "pursued wanderings as wild as those of the March-spirit." What he sought for was a woman to whom he could tell all, who might take his own view of his position, "understand" him and "accept" him. He found that his ideal woman could not be discovered. He had recourse to unideal women—much the reverse of ideal. They did not answer. Returning to his native country "in a harsh, bitter frame of mind, the result of a useless, roving, lonely life," he met little Jane on the frost-bound highway. "When once I had pressed the frail shoulder, something new —a fresh sap and sense—stole into my frame." He dwells with glowing tenderness upon the incidents of their life in Thornfield Hall, and brings his whole tale to a climax of entreaty. "Jane, you understand what I want of you? Just this promise—' I will be yours, Mr. Rochester.'" She had now heard not only his plea, but his proposed application of its ethical principles to the circumstances of his position: her reply was brief, clear, and right. "Mr. Rochester, I will *not* be yours."

"Jane," recommenced he, with a gentleness that broke me down with grief, and turned me stone-cold with ominous terror—for this still voice was the pant of a lion rising—"Jane, do you mean to go one way in the world, and to let me go another?" "I do." "And now?" softly kissing my forehead and cheek. "I do"—extricating myself from restraint rapidly and completely. "Oh, Jane, this is bitter! This—this is wicked. It would not be wicked to love me." "It would to obey you." A wild look raised his brow—crossed his features: he rose; but he forebore yet. I laid my hand on the back of a chair for support: I shook, I feared—but I resolved. "One instant, Jane. Give one glance to my horrible life. When you are gone all happiness will be torn away with you. What, then, is left? For a wife I have but the maniac upstairs: as well might you refer me to some corpse in

Jane in Extremis.

yonder churchyard. What shall I do, Jane? Where turn for a companion, and for some hope?" "Do as I do: trust in God and yourself. Believe in heaven. Hope to meet again there." ." Then you will not yield?" "No." "Then you condemn me to live wretched, and to die accursed?" His voice rose. "I advise you to live sinless; and I wish you to die tranquil." "Then you snatch love and innocence from me? You fling me back on lust for a passion—vice for an occupation?" "Mr. Rochester, I no more assign this fate to you than I grasp at it for myself. We were born to strive and endure—you as well as I: do so. You will forget me before I forget you." "You make me a liar by such language: you sully my honour. I declared I could not change: you tell me to my face I shall change soon. And what a distortion in your judgment, what a perversity in your ideas, is proved by your conduct! Is it better to drive a fellow-creature to despair than to transgress a mere human law—no man being injured by the breach?—for you have neither relatives nor acquaintances whom you need fear to offend by living with me." This was true; and while he spoke my very conscience and reason turned traitors against me, and charged me with crime in resisting him. They spoke almost as loud as Feeling: and that clamoured wildly. "Oh, comply!" it said. "Think of his misery; think of his danger—look at his state when left alone; remember his headlong nature; consider the recklessness following on despair—soothe him; save him; love him; tell him you love him and will be his. Who in the world cares for *you?* or who will be injured by what you do?"

Still, indomitable was the reply—"*I* care for myself. The more solitary, the more friendless, the more unsustained I am, the more I will respect myself. I will keep the law given by God, sanctioned by man. I will hold to the principles received by me when I was sane and not mad—as I am now. Laws and principles are not for the times when there is no temptation: they are for such moments as this, when body and soul rise in mutiny against their rigour; stringent are they; inviolate they shall be. If at my individual convenience I might break them, what would be their worth? They have a worth—so I have always believed; and if I cannot believe it now, it is because I am insane—quite insane: with my veins running fire, and my heart beating faster than I can count its throbs. Preconceived opinions, foregone determinations, are all I have at this hour to stand by: there I plant my foot."

19

So she conquered. Simple, sound—the very foundations of human society—the adamant on which the pillars of the household and of the State alike rest—are these principles of morality: and they did not fail her. Rochester was an egoist, but one of a high order: we should utterly misconceive his character, as imagined by Charlotte Brontë, if we thought him capable, even though he might threaten it, of resorting to violence. He was vanquished, and sank into silence. Jane left Thornfield, and did not again look into the face of Rochester till she could respond honourably to his love. The worst charge, therefore, which we can bring against Charlotte Brontë in relation to this novel is that she casts too great a charm over Rochester, not that she does not discern him to be blameworthy. The length to which he protracted his persecution of Jane was, next to his hypocrisy, the worst thing in his conduct. No man could have a right to bait and badger a woman like that; and if Jane had been a little more strong and a little more proud, she would never have favoured him with another look of her face. Am I right here, ladies?

CHAPTER XI.

WOMEN'S RIGHTS—THE ETHICS OF ABNEGATION —MR MEREDITH ON EGOISM—THACKERAY'S MORAL ANALYSIS—JANE LEAVES THORNFIELD—THE REST OF THE BOOK.

IT is worth while, in these days of vociferous debate concerning the place of women in the social system, when perfect equality between men and women is indignantly claimed as a right, or asserted as a fact, by a thousand voices, to take note of Jane Eyre's mode of allusion to Rochester's career of dissipation during his wife's lunacy. She does not quite approve of his successive *liaisons*, but her rebuke is the mildest of upbraiding glances. "Jane," he says, pausing in his narrative, "I see by your face you are not forming a very favourable opinion of me just now. You think me an unfeeling, loose-principled rake, don't you?" "I don't like you," she replies, "so well as I have done sometimes, indeed, sir. Did it not seem to you in the least wrong to live in that way? . . . You talk of it as a mere matter of course." "It was with me," he somewhat jauntily answers: "and I did not like it. It was a grovelling fashion of existence; I should never like to return to it." Jane continues to look grave. She will not sanction his proceedings. But it seems never to have occurred to Charlotte Brontë, as a possible way of viewing the case, that Jane might have said to him, "Now suppose, Mr. Rochester, that *I* had conducted myself as you have done, and had then bestowed on you so frank a series of confidences as you have bestowed upon me, how would you have taken it? and, in particular, how would you have been affected by the concluding expression of superlative affection for yourself? Would you have accepted this last with gratitude and ecstasy, or repelled it with anger and contempt?" This is what it must come to if women are to teach men to do justice to women not only by precept but by example.

Morality is, after all, a commonplace affair,—commonplace as the beaten road through the treacherous morass. Right and wrong are seldom difficult to discriminate, though it is not seldom difficult to do the one and refrain from doing the other. As Pope shrewdly suggests, the energy that might concentrate itself on doing the right is apt to be attenuated into ingenuity to devise excuses for doing the wrong. Mr. Carlyle has been vehement beyond tolerance of ears polite in his contempt for the modern notion that duty can arrange a compromise with voluptuous ease. Not moral heroism only; but the honesty, the habit of painful persistent work, the manly acceptance of loss, of misfortune, of failure, of irremediable wrong, without mutinous infraction of the divine-human laws of society: all these, which are the very stuff of virtue and the soul of nations, would perish if Rochester's practical ethics found universal favour. Abnegation is not easy,—but it cannot be dispensed with for all that. Call it, in the dialect of self-sufficient humanism, conscious submission to necessity; call it, in the language of old-world reverence, bowing of the back to the burden providentially laid upon it,—the thing, once for all, cannot, unless man degrades into a beast, become obsolete.

The root of Rochester's moral malady is his egoism, and Charlotte Brontë fails chiefly, not in perceiving the fact of his wrongness, for she does that, but in analysing it. Mr. George Meredith, in his remarkable novel *The Egoist*, furnishes so masterly an example of the kind of analysis which ought to have been applied to Rochester, that I am glad to be able to refer to it. Sir Willoughby Patterne is a self-worshipper of the most elaborate get-up. He has an income of fifty thousand pounds drawn from land; his family is old enough to give him a pretence for pride of birth; he is naturally "anything but obtuse," and has had every advantage of education; he is handsome in figure, good-looking in face, imposing in manner, and has been nurtured in the idolatry of his mother and aunts. Such a man is the most eligible match in his county. Clara Middleton, an exceedingly beautiful girl, attracts

his attention, accepts his hand, and fancies herself as
happy as all the world believes her to be enviable. He
cants to her about ideals, and about ethereal separation from the world. She is, however, affectionate and
sincere, and while Sir Willoughby discourses of the
felicities that await her and him, it gradually dawns
upon her that there is a hollowness at the man's
heart; that he is like a cathedral whose painted
windows are lit up, not with God's sunlight from
without, but with a strange and sickly light derived
from the lamp which perpetually burns in its centre at
the shrine of self. In fact, he is an egoist; and when
this word is accidentally uttered by some one in her
hearing, she mentally fixes upon it as the title that
befits and explains him. In place of the vague warmth
of admiration with which she had previously regarded
him, there steals over her an absolute horror at the
idea of becoming his wife.

Rochester's egoism is of a different kind from that of
Sir Willoughby Patterne. It has less of the element
of aristocratic pride, more of the element of passion.
Mr. George Meredith's egoist is incapable of loving any
one so ardently as Rochester loves Jane. But love that
is altogether noble dwells first and supremely on the happiness of the loved one; and it cannot be maintained
for a moment that Rochester is primarily swayed by
what is due to Jane. Of himself he always talks; he
does not implore permission to make her happy, but
beseeches her to confer happiness on him. The test
of noble and knightly passion is that it exults in

conferring joy, and that the "chord of self," struck by it, passes in music "out of sight." The egoism of passion, however, is more human and morally hopeful than the egoism of vanity and of worldly pride.

The man to treat Rochester with unique felicity would have been Thackeray. The performance would have been a faultless masterpiece of moral vivisection. That combination of insight into human nature and experience of human life, with the finest irony, which distinguished the great censor and humorist, is exactly what was required for the problem. Thackeray's irony, never cruel, never Swiftian, yet irresistible in its sharpness and fineness, would have played like a tongue of lambent, finely-laughing fire upon Rochester's views of self-reformation, upon his edifying aspirations after goodness, his generous readiness to make Jane's fall the instrument of his spiritual elevation, his self-pitying sentimentalism. But while Thackeray would have left us under no mistake as to what he thought of Rochester's heroism, he would probably have represented Jane as no less fascinated and subdued by him than Charlotte Brontë shows her to have been. It is a Chorus we want to the play, after the fashion of the Greek drama, and this part of Chorus might have been taken with unsurpassable effect by Thackeray. The brief snatches of comment that he could have thrown in while he made Rochester tell his own story, would have had a still more delicate aroma of humour than those with which he satirises the pretensions of Barry

Lyndon. He would not have made Rochester either quite a coxcomb or quite a histrio, but he would have brought out in vivid and piquant relief the lurking ingredients of coxcomb and histrio which Charlotte Brontë's hand—perhaps because it was a woman's hand—does not disclose to us.

Miss Martineau, who doubtless had the information from head-quarters, tells us that Charlotte Brontë, as she proceeded with the novel, became intensely interested in the fortunes of her heroine, whose smallness and plainness corresponded with her own. When she brought little Jane to Thornfield her enthusiasm had grown so great that she could not stop. She went on "writing incessantly for three weeks." At the end of this time she had made the minute woman conquer temptation, and, in the dawn of the summer morning, leave Thornfield. It was in the dead of winter that the great agitation of Jane's life had begun with the arrival of Rochester. The morning was now lovely with the streaks of sunrise, and the grass was bright with dew; but the icy sharpness of that winter evening had been sweeter to Jane than this balmy summer morn. "I looked neither to rising sun, nor smiling sky, nor wakening nature. He who is taken out to pass through a fair scene to the scaffold, thinks not of the flowers that smile on his road, but of the block and axe-edge; of the disseverment of bone and vein; of the grave gaping at the end: and I thought of drear flight and homeless wandering—and, oh! with agony I thought of what I left. I could not help it." She pictured to herself Rochester, sleepless, watching the dawn. She trembled lest, on discovering her flight, he might sink into self-abandonment and ruin. Under the inexorable rule of duty, her emotions chafed and fretted like fiery horses against the curb, lashing out in their rebellious desire for freedom. "Birds began singing in brake and copse; birds were faithful to their mates; birds were emblems of love. What was I? In the midst of my pain of heart and frantic effort of principle, I abhorred myself. I had no solace from self-approbation; none even from self-respect. I had injured—wounded—left my master. I was hateful in my own eyes. Still I could not turn nor retrace one step. God must have led me on. As to my own will or conscience, impassioned grief had trampled one and stifled the other. I was weeping wildly as I walked along my solitary way; fast, fast I went like one delirious." This is imagined with superb power and, I have no doubt, with substantial fidelity to truth; but the phenomena chronicled are those of the surface—those which a spectator would have seen—those of which Jane herself was distinctly conscious; and beneath all these was the great deep of Jane's spiritual nature, unagitated by the surface waves, resting on the immovable foundations of the world, the changeless laws of rectitude, morality, religion.

After Jane left Thornfield "the rest of the book," says Miss Martineau, "was written with less vehemence, and with more anxious care; the world adds, with less vigour and interest." Miss Martineau seems, though she does not actually say so, to agree with the world; and I certainly do. Jane's experiences between the time of her departure from Thornfield and her return to Rochester at Ferndean Manor would form an excellent one-volume tale; but, in relation to the main interest and plan of this book, they are what magazine editors call padding. And their style has that elaborate perfection—that "anxious care," as Miss Martineau well words it—which shows that the fires of imagination had subsided. I should say that, on the whole, the part of *Jane Eyre* which comes between the heroine's meeting with Rochester and her departure from Thornfield is more deeply imbued with the genius and imagination of Charlotte Brontë than anything else she has written. In fidelity of characterisation,—in consistency of thought, feeling, speech, conduct, mood, even caprice,—Rochester is as fine a piece of artistic portraiture as we have from Miss Austen, Thackeray, or Scott. But on that matter Mr. Swinburne has sufficiently enlarged.

CHAPTER XII.

M. PAUL EMANUEL—THE PROFESSOR IN CLASS —THE BRONTË LOVERS.

THERE is one of her characters which some might aver to be executed with more consummate skill than Rochester, and which, whether superior or inferior, is so differently handled that it may be profitable, as well as interesting, to compare the two. I allude to Paul Emanuel, professor in the Villette Seminary, and lover of Lucy Snowe. Rochester is the more imaginatively conceived portrait; M. Paul has the closer resemblance to a living man. It might, indeed, be argued, though I should not care to maintain the position dogmatically, that Paul Emanuel is too much an individual to attain high perfection as a figure in a work of art. It is with the type, not the individual, or at least with the type *in* the individual, that art concerns itself. The particulars specified regarding him have the air, indefinable yet unmistakable, of literal facts. But it is a special note of Charlotte Brontë's work that both Rochester and Paul Emanuel have harsh and repulsive, as well as attractive, qualities. Charlotte Brontë never forgets to give " the bitter of the sweet" and the sweet of the bitter, in her characteristic heroes. Rochester is imperious, abrupt, almost rude, and it is plain that Jane likes the element of austerity in her "master." Emanuel is choleric, arbitrary, eccentric, even cruelly harsh. When his temper is ruffled, he makes all who come near him the victims of his petulant fury. An illustrative passage will enable my readers to know what I mean better than any words of mine. Emanuel had just delivered to Lucy Snowe a letter, which suggested to him that he had a rival in her affections, handing it to her with "a look of scowling distrust." She retired with the letter, and presently returned.

> When I re-entered the schoolroom, behold M. Paul raging like a pestilence! Some pupil had not spoken audibly or distinctly enough to suit his ear and taste, and now she and others were weeping, and he was raving from his estrade almost livid. Curious to mention, as I appeared, he fell on me. " Was I the mistress of these girls? Did I profess to teach them the conduct befitting ladies?—and did I permit and, he doubted not, encourage them to strangle their mother-tongue in their throats, to mince and mash it between their teeth, as if they had some base cause to be ashamed of the words they uttered? Was this modesty? He knew better. It was a vile pseudo-sentiment—the offspring or the forerunner of evil. Rather than submit to this mopping and mowing, this mincing and grimacing, this grinding of a noble tongue, this general affectation and sickening stubbornness of the pupils of the first class, he would throw them up for a set of insupportable *petites maitresses*, and confine himself to teaching the A B C to the babies of the third division."
>
> What could I say to all this? Really nothing; and I hoped he would allow me to be silent. The storm recommenced. "Every answer to his queries was then refused? It seemed to be considered in *that* place—that conceited boudoir of a first class, with its pretentious bookcases, its green-baized desks, its rubbish

of flower-stands, its trash of framed pictures and maps, and its foreign *surveillante*, forsooth!—it seemed to be the fashion to think *there* that the Professor of Literature was not worthy of a reply! These were new ideas; imported, he did not doubt, straight from 'la Grande Bretaigne'—they savoured of island insolence and arrogance." Lull the second—the girls, not one of whom was ever known to weep a tear for the rebukes of any other master, now all melting like snow-statues before the intemperate heat of M. Emanuel: I not yet much shaken, sitting down, and venturing to resume my work. Something—either in my continued silence or in the movement of my hand, stitching—transported M. Emanuel beyond the last boundary of patience. He actually sprang from his estrade. The stove stood near my desk; he attacked it; the little iron door was nearly dashed from its hinges, the fuel was made to fly. "*Est-ce que vous avez l'intention de m'insulter?*" said he to me, in a low, furious voice, as he thus outraged, under pretence of arranging, the fire.

It was time to soothe him a little. "Mais, monsieur," said I, "I would not insult you for the world. I remember too well that you once said we should be friends." I did not intend my voice to falter, but it did: more, I think, through the agitation of late delight than in any spasm of present fear. Still there certainly was something in M. Paul's anger—a kind of passion of emotion— that specially tended to draw tears. I was not unhappy, nor much afraid, yet I wept. "Allons, allons!" said he presently, looking round and seeing the deluge universal. "Decidedly I am a monster and a ruffian. I have only one pocket-handkerchief," he added, "but if I had twenty, I would offer you each one. Your teacher shall be your representative. Here, Miss Lucy." And he took forth and held out to me a clean silk handkerchief. Now, a person who did not know M. Paul, who was unused to him and his impulses, would naturally have bungled at this offer—declined accepting the same—et cetera. But I too plainly felt this would never do: the slightest hesitation would have been fatal to the incipient treaty of peace. I rose and met the handkerchief halfway, received it with decorum, wiped therewith my eyes, and, resuming my seat, and retaining the flag of truce in my hand and on my lap, took especial care during the remainder of the lesson to touch neither needle nor thimble, scissors nor muslin. Many a jealous glance did M. Paul cast at these implements; he hated them mortally, considering sewing a source of distraction from the attention due to himself. A very eloquent lesson he gave, and very kind and friendly was he to the close. Ere he had done, the clouds were dispersed and the sun shining out—tears were exchanged for smiles.

Capricious, whimsical, subject to sudden gusts of irrational anger, Professor Emanuel had the faculty of diffusing an immense deal of discomfort among his fellow-creatures. *They* had the irritation—the annoyance even to tears—of the stormy gusts; and *he* reaped the advantage of finding his sunshine, when he chose to smile, more highly prized, more sweetly felt, than if no bad weather had preceded it. He could be kind; his heart was not "ossified;" nay, "in its core was a place tender beyond man's tenderness, a place that humbled him to little children, that bound him to girls and women." This made amends for "many a sharp snap and savage snarl." "Naturally a little man, of unreasonable moods," he resembled Napoleon in his "shameless disregard of magnanimity." He detested learned women. A "woman of intellect" was, he thought, "a luckless accident, a thing for which there was neither place nor use in creation, wanted neither as wife nor worker." He was, withal, forgiving to the vanquished, and though lacking magnanimity in trifles, was "great in great things." Sharing Dr. Johnson's capricious temper, he was, like Johnson, a succourer of poor and unpleasant creatures who had no other friend, and had on hand Mother Walravens, Father Silas, Mrs. Agnes, "and a whole troop of nameless paupers." He had been constant to a youthful love

—" one grand love, born so strong and perfect, that it had laughed at Death himself, despised his mean rape of matter, clung to immortal spirit, and, in victory and faith, had watched beside a tomb twenty years." Why is it that all the heroes—all the admired men and accepted lovers—of Charlotte Brontë are choleric, moody, masterful, and are obviously felt by her to be, for that reason, the more enchanting?

The tartness—to use a somewhat indefinite term—of Charlotte Brontë's lovers is, to the best of my knowledge, a thing peculiar to the Brontë genius. Except Emily and Charlotte Brontë I do not know any writer who imputes asperity to love-making and captivating gentlemen. The author of the old ballad, *Burd Helen*, whose name is, I suppose, unknown, occurs to me as having approached the Brontë practice more clearly than most, and Chaucer, I have no doubt, could have accurately analysed the charm of Rochester's imperiousness, and shown its root in the nature and social habits of women and of men. Helen in the ballad is atrociously ill-used by her lover, being forced by him to follow a-foot, clinging to his saddle-bow, as he rides on his journey by moorland waste and haggard stone; he refuses to take her up, but lets her still drag on at his horse's side, even when they must ford " Clyde water," which rolls full in flood " from bank to brae." But we are relieved, or half relieved, at length, by finding that he has only been testing her affection, and that, when he proves it sufficiently, he accepts and returns it. Chaucer represents patient Grisildis as suffering exquisite mental torment from the man she loves, yet never faltering in her devotion. But Chaucer is careful to announce his own disapproval of Lord Walter's conduct, and to exhort wives not to be so meek as Grisildis, but always to give the husband back his own with usury. In the prenuptial period, Lord Walter had been gentleness itself.

Probably enough, it is due to my lack of information, but I cannot, I repeat, recall any lover, outside the Brontë books, who, in the time of courtship, when desirous of presenting himself in the most attractive guise to the lady, is so blunt and peremptory as Rochester, or so snappish as Paul Emanuel. In Charlotte's other great novel she adheres to her practice. Both Robert Moore and Louis Moore in *Shirley* are stern, commanding men, with something of the soldier, something even of the drill-sergeant, in them. And Shirley Keeldar herself has the Brontë contempt for soft lovers. "Pah!" she says, "my husband is not to be my baby. I am not to set him his daily lesson and see that he learns it, and give him a sugar-plum if he is good, and a patient, pensive, pathetic lecture if he is bad." The love-lorn Louis understood the woman he had to deal with. "I scared her," he remarks, in describing what is generally held to be the delicate process of eliciting from a lady a confession of affection. "I scared her; that I could see; it was right; she must be scared to be won." He scared her so effectually that she "trembled." The more she trembled the more commanding he became. "My pupil!" he said.

" My master!" she replied in accents fainter. After one or two other passes of amatory fence, " Am I to die without you," he cries, " or am I to live for you?" " Do as you please," she answers; " far be it from me to dictate your choice." " You shall tell me with your own lips, whether you doom me to exile, or call me to hope." " Go, I can bear to be left." " Perhaps, I too *can* bear to leave you ; but reply, Shirley, my pupil, my sovereign—reply." This is peremptory enough, so she answers, " Die without me, if you will. Live for me, if you dare." Of course he tells her that he dares to be her accepted lover, addressing her by the endearing term of " leopardess." " You name me leopardess? remember the leopardess is tameless." " Tame or fierce," he answers, " wild or subdued, you are *mine*." " I am glad I know my keeper," she says, with the smile of acceptance on her lip, " and am used to him. Only his voice will I follow; only his hand shall manage me ; only at his feet will I repose."

Neither in Shakespeare nor in Goethe, neither in Schiller nor in Byron, neither in Fielding nor in Scott, neither in Thackeray nor in Dickens, neither in Mr. Trollope nor in George Eliot, do I find acid mixed with sweetness in love-making as it is mixed in the love-making of the Brontë novels. Heathcliff, in his boyish time, when the fine and manly ingredients in his nature have not yet become malignant, is a rough and saucy lover ; nor would the wild, wayward, witching Cathy have endured him if he had been a soft and sighing swain. When Shakespeare introduces Richard the Third wooing Anne, an express opportunity is afforded him for representing the lady as impressed by the hardness of Richard's character, and as influenced by the force—even though the harsh force—of one born to be a king. Had Charlotte Brontë designed and executed the scene, she would certainly have made Richard cast over Anne the glamour of his imperious strength, and shown her fluttering into his arms like a bird sinking fascinated into the jaws of a snake. Shakespeare's Richard is subtle, insinuating, sophistical, wily, but he studiously disguises his harshness. King Henry, making love to the Princess of France, with the garlands of Agincourt on his brow, is a less masterful lover than Louis Moore extorting an avowal of regard from the splendid heiress whose tutor he has been. Egmont is all softness to Clärchen—Faust to Margaret. And so on *ad infinitum*.

If it were in a merely whimsical and fantastic spirit that Charlotte Brontë assigned to her lovers a gift of government and faculty of sarcasm distinguishing them from all other lovers,—if they were extravagant or untrue to nature as well as unique,—the originality with which she is to be credited on their account would be little worth. Stupidity, affectation, conceit, impudence, strong drink, opium, are all prolific sources of originality. But the distinctive charm of the acid in the Brontë love-making is connected with broad and well-established facts of human nature, and is neither fantastic nor far-fetched. Amiability is apt to be insipid—is always insipid when it is monotonous and constant. Flavour in fruit or wine is hopelessly destroyed by excess of sweetness. Smiling innocence is oftener complimented than liked, and Byron—who, one would think, had never suffered much from amiability, whether as exhibited by himself or his friends or foes—expresses sceptical wonder how the grand old gardener and his wife could have found it agreeable in Eden. The Brontë sisters had an exceptionally keen and clear, but hardly exaggerated, perception of this general fact. Sugary people they regarded with aversion—the remark is illustrated by their delineation of pleasant women as well as of pleasant men; and they instinctively shrank from sugary love-making. Little Jane, Shirley, and Lucy Snowe are women of great strength of character, and Caroline and Polly are not without decision. Mr. Linton's well-meaning friendliness does not save him from Emily Brontë's scorn, and the weak Mr. Sympson in *Shirley* is the most despicable of all Charlotte's characters. Manliness, intellectual power, caustic piquancy of conversation, are qualities universally popular, and the Brontë sisters discerned that they are not suspended, and do not cease to be charming, though people are in love.

But there is a still more specific element in the fascination of Rochester and his peers than that dependent on the general interest of vigorous and pithy character. Charlotte Brontë unmistakably intends that a sense of the dominance and control exercised by her lovers shall

be intensely delightful to the women who are loved.
There is no term of endearment applied by Jane to
Rochester which seems to have so exquisite a charm
for her as "master." Shirley, the proud, rich, wild,
brilliant Shirley, exults, as we saw, in the thought
that she has found her "keeper," the man who can
"manage" her. A deep swell of hero-worshipping
enthusiasm—an enraptured recognition that the man
worthy to be a woman's lover is worthy also to be her
lord—passes through the whole of Charlotte Brontë's
writings. Imbecility in the form of a man is indeed
only the more contemptible for having degraded the
temple it usurps; but a man of true nobility, a man
whose patent is stamped by Almighty God, is for her
the king of the world. "I tell you," exclaims Shirley,
"when they *are* good, they are the lords of the creation
—they are the sons of God. Moulded in their
Maker's image, the minutest spark of His spirit lifts
them almost above mortality. Indisputably a great,
good, handsome man is the first of created things."
Keen as is her assertion of every claim that she
believes capable of being justly preferred on behalf
of her sex, Charlotte Brontë has not a shred of
sympathy with those who maintain the absolute
equality of men and women. This cannot, I think,
be reasonably disputed. Not only are we made to
feel that Jane and Shirley and Lucy Snowe would
be defrauded of their intensest joy in loving if they
did not feel that their lovers were their masters, but
we are expressly informed, through the lips of Shirley,

when Caroline asks her whether man must indeed be acknowledged woman's superior, that such is Charlotte Brontë's opinion. "I would scorn," Shirley answers, "to contend for empire with him. I would scorn it. Shall my left hand dispute for precedence with my right? shall my heart quarrel with my pulse? shall my veins be jealous of the blood which fills them? . . . . Nothing ever charms me more than when I meet my superior, one who makes me sincerely feel that he is my superior." "Did you ever meet him?" asks Caroline. "I should be glad to see him any day," she replies; "the higher above me, so much the better; it degrades to stoop, it is glorious to look up." When Shirley did see her lover, it was the very elixir of her joy that he could rule her. In her love, as in that of all Charlotte Brontë's heroines, there was a "delicious pride," but a "more delicious humility."* I presume that the ladies and gentlemen who are at present conspicuous by their advocacy of "women's rights" would hesitate to admit that their contention involves a denial of the superiority assigned to men by Shirley; but I believe that the main drift of their movement is practically its denial; and I hold further that, though all the enactments which give power to men as compared with women were swept from the Statute Book—a consummation to which I should offer no resistance—every woman supremely in love would, all the same, feel the crown of her joy to be in self-surrender. Mrs. Browning

* This antithesis, however, is not quoted from Charlotte Brontë.

attests this as well as Charlotte Brontë. It is woman who is addressed in the words,—

> Thou shalt be served thyself by every sense
> Of service which thou renderest.

I have no doubt, however, that there are women whom it would not be safe to woo in the fashion of the Brontë lovers—some who would have resented Rochester's behaviour if he had ordered them about so bluntly as he ordered Jane Eyre, and who would have found nothing attractive in M. Emanuel's irascibility and caprice.

CHAPTER XIII.

MR. DONNE'S EXODUS—SHIRLEY THE AUTHOR'S MOST CHARACTERISTIC BOOK—ROBERT'S PROPOSAL—MERCENARY MARRIAGE—A DAY WITH SHIRLEY—LANDSCAPE GLIMPSES—THE DUTY OF ENDURANCE.

ENTERTAINING for great and good men an impassioned and frankly expressed admiration, Charlotte Brontë treats feeble and bad men with unrelenting scorn, and shows us, in an entirely characteristic passage, how, in her opinion, a spirited Yorkshire girl might put down a coarse and self-obtruding clergyman. The occurrence described took place in the grounds of Fieldhead, Miss Keeldar's residence. The Rev. Mr. Donne is the first speaker.

"Ahem!" he began, clearing his throat evidently for a speech of some importance. "Ahem! Miss Keeldar, your attention an instant, if you please." "Well," said Shirley, nonchalantly, "what is it? I listen: all of me is ear that is not eye." "I hope part of you is hand also," returned Donne, in his vulgarly presumptuous and familiar style, "and part purse: it is to the hand and purse I propose to appeal. I came here this morning with a view to beg of you——" "You should have gone to Mrs. Gill; she is my almoner." "To beg of you a subscription to a school. I and Dr. Boultby intend to erect one in the hamlet of Ecclefigg, which is under our vicarage of Whinbury. The Baptists have got possession of it; they have a chapel there, and we want to dispute the ground." "But I have nothing to do with Ecclefigg: I possess no property there." "What does that signify? You're a Churchwoman, ain't you?" "Admirable creature!" muttered Shirley, under her breath; "exquisite address! fine style! What raptures he excites in me!" Then aloud, "I am a Churchwoman, certainly." "Then you can't refuse to contribute in this case. The population of Ecclefigg are a parcel of brutes— we want to civilize them." "Who is to be the missionary?" "Myself, probably." "You won't fail through lack of sympathy with your flock." "I hope not—I expect success; but we must have money. There is the paper—pray give a handsome sum."

When asked for money, Shirley rarely held back. She put down her name for £5. After the £300 she had lately given, and the many smaller sums she was giving constantly, it was as much as she could at present afford. Donne looked at it, declared the subscription "shabby," and clamorously demanded more. Miss Keeldar flushed up with some indignation and more astonishment. "At present, I shall give no more," said she. "Not give more? Why, I expected you to head the list with a cool hundred. With your property, you should never put down a signature for less." She was silent. "In the south," went on Donne, "a lady with a thousand a-year would be ashamed to give £5 for a public object." Shirley, so rarely haughty, looked so now. Her slight frame became nerved; her distinguished face quickened with scorn. "Strange remarks!" said she: "most inconsiderate! Reproach in return for bounty is misplaced." "Bounty! Do you call five pounds bounty?" "I do; and bounty which, had I not given it to Mr. Boultby's intended school, of the erection of which I approve, and in no sort to his curate, who seems ill-advised in his manner of applying for, or rather extorting, subscriptions— bounty, I repeat, which, but for this consideration, I should instantly reclaim."

Donne was thick-skinned; he did not feel all or half that the tone, air, glance of the speaker expressed; he knew not on what ground he stood. "Wretched place—this Yorkshire," he went on. "I could never have formed an idear of the country had I not seen it; and the people—rich and poor—what a set! How *corse* and uncultivated! They would be scouted in the south." Shirley leaned forwards on the table, her nostrils dilating a little, her taper fingers interlaced and compressing each other hard. "The rich," pursued the infatuated and unconscious Donne, "are a parcel of misers—never living as persons with their incomes ought to live: you scarsely—(you must excuse Mr. Donne's pronunciation, reader; it was very choice; he considered it genteel, and prided himself on his southern accent; northern ears received with singular sensations his utterance of certain words)—you scarsely ever see a fam'ly where a propa carriage or a regla butla is kep; and as to the poor—just look at them when they come crowding about the church-doors on the occasion of a marriage or a funeral, clattering in clogs; the men in their shirt-sleeves and wool-combers' aprons, the women in mob-caps and bedgowns. They pos'tively deserve that one should turn a mad cow in amongst them to rout their rabble-ranks—he! he! What fun it would be!"

"There, you have reached the climax," said Shirley quietly. "You have reached the climax," she repeated, turning her glowing glance towards him. "You cannot go beyond it; and," she added with emphasis, "you *shall* not, in my house." Up she rose. Nobody could control her now, for she was exasperated. Straight she walked to her garden gates, wide she flung them open. "Walk through," she said, austerely, "and pretty quickly, and set foot on this pavement no more." Donne was astounded. He had thought all the time he was showing himself off to high advantage, as a lofty-souled person of the first *ton;* he imagined he was producing a crushing impression. Had he not expressed disdain of everything in Yorkshire? What more conclusive proof could be given that he was better than anything there? And yet here he was about to be turned like a dog out of a Yorkshire garden! Where, under such circumstances, was the "concatenation accordingly"? "Rid me of you instantly—instantly!" reiterated Shirley, as he lingered. "Madam—a clergyman! Turn out a clergyman?" "Off! Were you an archbishop, you have proved yourself no gentleman, and must go. Quick!" She was quite resolved; there was no trifling with her. Besides, Tartar was again rising; he perceived symptoms of a commotion; he manifested a disposition to join in. There was evidently nothing for it but to go, and Donne made his exodus, the heiress sweeping him a deep curtsey as she closed the gates on him.

The book, *Shirley*, from which this admirable piece

of life-comedy is taken, though not marked by the sustained intensity of imaginative power which characterises the central portion of *Jane Eyre*, is in some respects the finest of all Charlotte Brontë's novels. There is more ease in it—more freedom and variety—than in *Jane Eyre*, and it is less laborious and didactic than *Villette*. In none of Charlotte Brontë's books are there more fresh and lovely glimpses of landscape; and the heroines, Shirley and Caroline, so felicitously contrasted, so finely harmonised, so perfectly life-like, are embodiments of the pride and love with which she regarded the girls of England and, above all, the girls of Yorkshire.

In *Shirley* we see Charlotte Brontë in her ordinary mood, the mood in which she most broadly, simply, unconstrainedly reveals herself. Her genius shows its strength most decisively in *Jane Eyre*. Her most mature philosophy and her most carefully elaborated style are to be found in *Villette*. The former was written under high pressure, her feelings greatly excited, her genius making its critical, dead-lift attempt to establish a reputation; the latter was also composed with conscious, painful effort, under a sense of duty. *Shirley* was written under more ordinary circumstances, in the natural outflow of sympathy and imagination. The shadow of death falls upon the page at the beginning of the third volume, written when the grave had just closed upon Emily and Anne; but the spirit of the book is cheerful. Upon none of her characters does

Charlotte Brontë lavish such glad enthusiasm as upon Shirley Keeldar and Caroline Helstone. They are English girls, and Charlotte Brontë, having lived in a Continental school, cherished a firm persuasion of the superior worth and attractiveness of the girls of England. They are Yorkshire girls, and Charlotte Brontë, though she loved England well, loved Yorkshire better, and was almost fiercely proud of the stalwart lads and brave and bonny lasses of the dales and moors. There is also, to my thinking, a natural fitness in the circumstance that, in a woman's novel, the chief part among the characters is played by women. Rochester might have given his name to the book in which he figures almost as well as the little governess; but neither of the Moores is half so prominent in the *Shirley* group of personages as Shirley herself. Louis Moore, who holds technically the place of hero as the accepted lover of the heroine, is hardly heard of until the third volume; and his brother Robert, though we see him sooner, stands third in the order of interest, Shirley and Caroline being first and second. Women, though they may write passionately and splendidly about men, write, nevertheless, most congenially, and with greatest reality and accuracy of knowledge, about women. There is, accordingly, I repeat, more ease in *Shirley*, more free and natural and brilliant play of the author's faculties, than in her other books. In it, also, more than elsewhere, have we her idea of women's rights and wrongs. It was published about eighteen months after *Jane Eyre*.

There is almost no plot, but the story is sufficiently well planned to secure for the reader the interest of mild surprise. The question—all-important from the novelist's specific point of view—who is to marry the heroine, is made adequately perplexing throughout the first and second volumes. Every one supposes that Robert—also called Gerard—Moore will marry Shirley, and yet no unfair means are made use of to convey that impression to the reader. Nothing could be more natural, yet nothing more dramatic, than the interview between Robert and Shirley, witnessed by Caroline; and Robert's account to his friend Yorke of his proposal to Shirley is quite masterly, alike in invention, in humour, in truth to human nature in general, and in exactitude of correspondence with the characters of Moore and of Shirley in particular. The passage, however, must be read to be appreciated. I abridge some of the sentences, yet it is so long that I can quote but part.

"Yorke, if I got off horseback, and laid myself down across the road, would you have the goodness to gallop over me—backwards and forwards about twenty times?" "Wi' all the pleasure in life, if there were no such thing as a coroner's inquest." "Hiram Yorke, I certainly believed she loved me. I have seen her eyes sparkle radiantly when she has found me out in a crowd; she has flushed up crimson when she has offered me her hand, and said, 'How do you do, Mr. Moore?' My name had a magical influence over her; when others uttered it she changed countenance—I know she did. She pronounced it herself in the most musical of her many musical tones. She was cordial to me; she took an interest in me; she was anxious about me; she wished me well; she sought, she seized every opportunity to benefit me. I considered, paused, watched, weighed, wondered; I could come to but one conclusion—this is love. I looked at her, Yorke; I saw in her youth and a species of beauty. I saw power in her. Her wealth offered me the redemption of my honour and my standing. I owed her gratitude. Young, graceful, gracious—my benefactress, attached to me, enamoured of me—I used to say so to myself; dwell on the word; mouth it over and over again; swell over it with a pleasant, pompous complacency—with an admiration dedicated entirely to myself, and unimpaired even by esteem for her; indeed, I smiled in deep secrecy at her *naïveté* and simplicity, in being the first to love, and to show it. That whip of yours seems to have a good heavy handle, Yorke; you can swing it about your head, and knock me out of the saddle, if you choose. I should rather relish a loundering whack."

"Tak' patience, Robert, till the moon rises, and I can see you. Speak plain out;—did you love her or not? I should like to know; I feel curious." "Sir—sir—I say—she is very pretty, in her own style, and very attractive. She has a look, at times, of a thing made out of fire and air, at which I stand and marvel, without a thought of clasping and kissing it. I felt in her a powerful magnet to my interest and vanity: I never felt as if nature meant her to be my other and better self. When a question on that head rushed upon me I flung it off, saying brutally, I should be rich with her, and ruined without her; vowing I would be practical, and not romantic." "A very sensible resolve! What mischief came of it, Bob?"

"With this sensible resolve, I walked up to Fieldhead one night last August: it was the very eve of my departure for Birmingham,—for—you see—I wanted to secure fortune's splendid prize: I had previously dispatched a note, requesting a private interview. I found her at home, and alone. She received me without embarrassment, for she thought I came on business; *I* was embarrassed enough, but determined. I hardly know how I got the operation over; but I went to work in a hard, firm fashion,—frightful enough, I daresay. I sternly offered myself—my fine person—with my debts, of course, as a settlement. It vexed me; it kindled my ire, to find that she neither blushed, trembled, nor looked down. She responded: 'I doubt whether I have understood you, Mr. Moore.' And I had to go over the whole proposal twice, and word it as plainly as A B C, before she would fully take it in. And then, what did she do? Instead of faltering a sweet Yes, or maintaining a soft, confused silence (which would have been as good), she started up, walked twice fast through the room, in the way that *she* only does, and no other woman, and ejaculated, 'God bless me!' Yorke, I stood on the hearth, backed by the mantelpiece; against it I leaned, and prepared for anything—everything. I knew my doom, and I knew myself. She stopped and looked at me. 'God bless me!' she pitilessly repeated, in that shocked, indignant, yet saddened accent. 'You have made a strange proposal—strange from *you;* and if you knew how strangely you worded it, and looked it, you would be startled at yourself. You spoke like a brigand who demanded my purse, rather than like a lover who asked my heart.' I looked at her, dumb and wolfish: she at once enraged and shamed me. 'Gerard Moore, you know you don't love Shirley Keeldar.' I might have broken out into false-swearing; vowed that I did love her; but I could not lie in her pure face Besides, such hollow oaths would have been vain as void: her female heart had finer perceptions than to be cheated into mistaking my half-coarse, half-cold admiration, for true-throbbing, manly love. 'What next happened?' you will say, Mr. Yorke. Why, she sat down in the window-seat, and cried. She cried passionately: her eyes not only rained, but lightened. They flashed, open, large, dark, haughty, upon me: they said—'You have pained me; you have outraged me; you have deceived me. . . . . You— once high in my esteem—are hurled down; you—once intimate in my friendship—are cast out. Go!'"

Do we not feel, as we read, that this passage was written with all Charlotte Brontë's heart, and not only with all her heart, but with all her conscience? She lived much in the sense of duty, and no part of her duty as a novelist did she more vividly conceive, or more fervently grasp, than that of guarding the sacredness of passion. True affection was in her view an indispensable element in the right formation of the marriage tie; and her frame quivered with indignation, her pen emitted lightnings, when selfishness and worldliness tried to pass off some desecrating sem-

blance of true love for the genuine feeling. With
intense emphasis she would have echoed Tennyson's
anathema on "the social lies that warp us from the
living truth." And it was a great occasion for her
when she could punish the hypocrisy that mimicked
love, in the person of Robert Moore, an able, successful, upright man, quite as high-minded as the average
of his sex, and hardly conscious that, with his tradesman's instinct, he was perverting and profaning, in his
proposal to Shirley, the very idea of marriage. Charlotte had inherited from her father a jealousy of the
trading fraternity. She thought that, in the French
war, if the landed gentry had allowed them, the
merchants of England would have sold her honour for
an extension of their markets. "During the late war"
—these are her words—"the tradesmen of England
would have endured buffets from the French on the
right cheek and on the left; their cloak they would
have given to Napoleon, and then have politely offered
him their coat also, nor would they have withheld
their waistcoat if urged; they would have prayed
permission only to retain their one other garment, for
the sake of the purse in its pocket." We need not inquire whether this censure is altogether just in an historical point of view; Charlotte Brontë was, at all events,
right in sharply resenting the intrusion of mercantile
calculation into the sphere and function of the affections.

It is, perhaps, worthy of remark—though the matter
is not of much moment—that, at the time when she
wrote *Shirley*, Charlotte Brontë was timorously

anxious to disguise the fact that she was a woman. Some of the rugged strength, verging on coarseness, in the conversation between Moore and Yorke, may have been intended to countenance the notion that Currer Bell was a man. But if this motive was present with her, it did not drive her to extravagance; possibly it may have assisted her in sympathetically realising how a man would feel under the circumstances described by Moore. In that invitation of Moore's to Yorke to give him a loundering whack with his whip, there is a subtly imaginative, a veritably Shakespearian, penetration into the feelings of a proud man who has made an immense fool of himself. The power displayed in the whole passage strikes me as amazing. I know no woman novelist, not even George Eliot, who has quite equalled it; and yet George Eliot, as she shows in such a passage as that describing the fight between the young squire and Adam Bede, can see very far into the heart of the male creature.

But the view presented of Shirley Keeldar in this passage may convey to the reader a one-sided idea of her character. Capable she indeed was of scorn and severity, but she was not without more maidenly qualities. Let us look at her in a softer aspect.

> She takes her sewing occasionally; but, by some fatality, she is doomed never to sit steadily at it for above five minutes at a time. Her thimble is scarcely fitted on, her needle scarce threaded, when a sudden thought calls her upstairs. Perhaps she goes to seek some just-then-remembered old ivory-backed needle-book, or older china-topped workbox, quite unneeded, but which seems at the moment indispensable; perhaps to arrange her

hair, or a drawer which she recollects to have seen that morning in a state of curious confusion ; perhaps only to take a peep from a particular window at a particular view, whence Briarfield Church and Rectory are visible, pleasantly bowered in trees. She has scarcely returned, and again taken up the slip of cambric or square of half-wrought canvas, when Tartar's bold scrape and strangled whistle are heard at the porch door, and she must run to open it for him. It is a hot day ; he comes in panting. She must convey him to the kitchen, and see with her own eyes that his water-bowl is replenished. Through the open kitchen door the court is visible, all sunny and gay, and peopled with turkeys and their poults, peahens and their chicks, pearl-flecked guinea fowls, and a bright variety of pure-white, and purple-necked, and blue and cinnamon-plumed pigeons. Irresistible spectacle to Shirley ! She runs to the pantry for a roll, and she stands on the door-step scattering crumbs. Around her throng her eager, plump, happy, feathered vassals. John is about the stables, and John must be talked to, and her mare looked at. She is still petting and patting it, when the cows comes in to be milked; this is important ; Shirley must stay and take a review of them all. There are, perhaps, some little calves, some little new-yeaned lambs—it may be twins, whose mothers have rejected them. Miss Keeldar must be introduced to them by John—must permit herself the treat of feeding them with her own hand, under the direction of her careful footman. Meantime, John moots doubtful questions about the farming of certain " crofts," and " ings," and " holms," and his mistress is necessitated to fetch her garden-hat—a gipsy-straw—and accompany him, over stile and along hedge-row, to hear the conclusion of the whole agricultural matter on the spot, and with the said " crofts," " ings," and " holms " under her eye. Bright afternoon thus wears into soft evening, and she comes home to a late tea, and after tea she never sews. After tea Shirley reads, and she is just about as tenacious of her book as she is lax of her needle. Her study is the rug, her seat a footstool, or perhaps only the carpet at Mrs. Prior's feet; there she always learned her lessons when a child, and old habits have a strong power over her. The tawny and lion-like bulk of Tartar is ever stretched beside her ; his negro muzzle laid on his fore paws, straight, strong, and shapely, as the limbs of an Alpine wolf. One hand of the mistress generally reposes on the loving serf's rude head, because if she takes it away he groans and is discontented.

21

Caroline Helstone is more regularly beautiful and more nearly common-place than Shirley. Every curve in her girlish figure is graceful, her skin delicate and of lovely colour; her brown hair falls about her neck in picturesque profusion, her fine eyes are "gifted at times with a winning beam that stole into the heart, with a language that spoke softly to the affections." Intelligent and gentle, she was no sooner known than liked by the more sprightly heiress, and an intimate friendship grew up between them. In their talks, they furnish Charlotte Brontë with an opportunity for airing her opinions upon various questions, chiefly that of the social position, duties, claims, and sufferings of women; in their walks, they lend her occasion for introducing those landscape glimpses which greatly enhance the charm of the novel. "Glimpses" they are rather than elaborate views—hence perhaps some part of their fascination; we catch sight of them as we pass, wishing always at the moment that we could see more of them, yet aware that the novelist does well to keep her word-pictures strictly subordinate to her story. The girls agree upon it that "England is a bonny island," and that "Yorkshire is one of her bonniest nooks." When they halt on the brow of the Common, we peep over their shoulders and look down "on the deep valley robed in May raiment; on varied meads, some pearled with daisies, and some golden with king-cups." The spring verdure smiled in clear sunlight, emerald and amber gleams playing over it. "On Nunnwood—the sole remnant of antique British forest in a region whose lowlands were once all sylvan chase, as its highlands were breast-deep heather—slept the shadow of a cloud; the distant hills were dappled, the horizon was shaded and tinted like mother-of-pearl; silvery blues, soft purples, evanescent greens and rose-shades, all melting into fleeces of white cloud, pure as azury snow, allured the eye as with a remote glimpse of heaven's foundations." Caroline promises to take Shirley into the pleasantest places in the old forest. "I know where wild strawberries abound; I know certain lonely, quite untrodden glades, carpeted with strange mosses, some yellow as if gilded, some a sober gray, some gem-green. I know groups of trees that ravish the eye with their perfect, picture-like effects: rude oak, delicate birch, glossy beech, clustered in contrast; and ash trees stately as Saul, standing isolated, and superannuated wood-giants clad in bright shrouds of ivy." Do not the words gleam like jewellery, set in silver and fine gold?

Almost invariably these limnings from Nature are as remarkable for fidelity as for beauty. In fact, I can recall but one instance in which I doubt the correctness of the delineation. It occurs in the following sentence, descriptive of moonlight. "Tree and hall rose peaceful under the night sky and clear full orb; pearly paleness gilded the building; mellow brown gloom bosomed it round; shadows of deep green brooded above its oak-wreathed roof." So far as my own observation—and it has been somewhat careful—enables me to speak, moonlight shows no colour except in the sky. Wet roofs gleam brightly in strong moonshine, but no shadow cast by the moon can be discriminated as green. It is perhaps legitimate, however, for the word-painter to derive more colour from association of ideas than the painter with pigments can dare to transfer from palette to canvas. Generally speaking, Charlotte Brontë's descriptions are photographically and more than photographically, to wit sympathetically and lovingly, correct. "It was a peaceful autumn day. The gilding of the Indian summer mellowed the pastures far and wide. The russet woods stood ripe to be stripped, but were yet full of leaf. The purple of heath-bloom, faded but not withered, tinged the hills. The beck wandered down to the hollow, through a silent district; no wind followed its course, or haunted its woody borders. Fieldhead gardens bore the seal of gentle decay. On the walks, swept that morning, yellow leaves had fluttered down again. Its time of flowers, and even of fruits, was over; but a scantling of apples enriched the trees; only a blossom here and there, expanded pale and delicate amidst a knot of faded leaves." Miss Martineau speaks of Wilson's descriptions as bringing the scents of the moorland into the sick-room; I can aver that the preceding words, at that particular point where the scantling of apples and the blossoms lingering here and there among the leaves are mentioned, have produced in me what seemed the actual physical sensation of being in a country garden amid faint scents of apples. References abound in *Shirley* to the wind, whether the storm wailing and raging about the hall at midnight, or the gale filling the vault of the clear moonlit sky with silver-hued, swift-sailing clouds. " No Endymion will watch for his goddess to-night: there are no flocks out on the mountains; and it is well, for to-night she welcomes Æolus."

There is a great deal of ethical teaching in this book; but it is thrown in so skilfully that, like the descriptions of scenery, it never suggests the idea of padding. The main precept which, here and elsewhere, Charlotte enforces, is that of entire, unquestioning submission to the inevitable. The Arabian prophet was not more sternly resolute in enjoining submission to fate. " Take the matter as you find it. Ask no questions; utter no remonstrances. It is your best wisdom. You expected bread, and you have got a stone; break your teeth on it, and don't shriek because the nerves are martyrised. You held out your hand for an egg, and fate put into it a scorpion. Show no consternation: close your fingers firmly upon the gift; let it sting through your palm. Never mind. In time, after your hand and arm have swelled and quivered long with torture, the squeezed scorpion will die, and you will have learned the great lesson how to endure without a sob." This is the ethical lesson which Charlotte Brontë never tires of enforcing, but necessity generally takes, for her, the form not of a dead, inexorable fate, but a Father-God.

CHAPTER XIV.

THE BRONTË GENIUS—RETROSPECT—INFLUENCE OF SCOTT AND WILSON—LOVE OF SCOTLAND—M. HEGER'S INFLUENCE—CHARLOTTE'S IDEA OF LOVE—THE YORKSHIRE SCHOOL OF LITERATURE—THE DEATHS OF EMILY AND ANNE—THE MARRIAGE AND DEATH OF CHARLOTTE.

IT is seldom that the critic has so enticing a bit of work cut out for him as is afforded by the Brontë literature, and in particular by Charlotte Brontë. The mysterious thing called genius, of which critics ought to feel themselves the humble ministers and hierophants, has not often lent himself so kindly to scientific inquisition. The celestial spark, the immortal germ, can in this instance be traced in its origin, followed in its development, estimated in its fruits.

An eccentric Irish lad, his brain full of Calvinistic theology, his heart of stiff old Tory pride and not ungenerous prejudice, with thin but genuine melodies, like tinklings of sheep bells, ringing in his head, comes to Yorkshire, divests himself of his Irish name, Prunty, apparently also of all Irish national feeling, marries a Cornish girl, frail but fine, and is found, about the time of the passing of the Reform Bill, a widower, with one son and three daughters, clergyman of Haworth, a poor sequestered parish, high up among the clouds and moors of Yorkshire. From Patrick Prunty, self-named Bronti or Brontë, his daughter Charlotte and her sisters derived that "very fiery particle" of genius which all his children seem to have possessed. The one son led those who knew him in early boyhood to believe in his splendid abilities; but he was so soon and so utterly wrecked, morally and mentally, that were it not for his relationship to his sisters, his name would not for an hour have escaped oblivion. The moral conditions with which girls are environed in England never vindicated themselves so impressively as in the contrast presented by the unredeemed and heart-rending failure of Branwell Brontë and the noble success of his sisters. Those passions which, under due governance of moral law, might have been impelling forces to bear him to honour and fame, became fiends that tare him as he wallowed foaming. This is the grand lesson of his life; and it is one worthy of being laid stress upon; for there are some in these days who would sneer down, as Philistinism and bad form, that reverence for moral law which has characterised the sovereigns of literature generally, and most conspicuously of all, the sovereigns of that literature whose highest thrones are occupied by Milton and Shakespeare.

As a Tory, old Brontë may be credited with a double measure of that enthusiasm for Scott which was at its height when his daughters were passing from childhood into girlhood. The poems and novels of Scott and *Blackwood's Magazine* were the delight of the "family of poets" of Haworth Parsonage. Under the auspices of Scott and Wilson, Scotland became dear to Charlotte Brontë—a circumstance otherwise natural, for Scotland and Yorkshire have varied and close affinities, and the vernacular of the latter is almost the same as the tongue of Burns. She preserved throughout life an affectionate feeling towards the northern part of the United Kingdom, in striking contrast with the bitter, cold, and grudging spirit with which the London schools, whether of poetry or of science, have always regarded Scotland. A visit to that country, after she had become famous, did not destroy her prepossession in its favour. The very names of Melrose and Abbotsford were to her "music and magic." "My dear sir," she wrote to a London friend, "do not think I blaspheme when I tell you that your great London, as compared to Dunedin, 'mine own romantic town,' is as prose compared to poetry, or as a great rumbling, rambling, heavy epic, compared to a lyric, brief, bright, clear, and vital as a flash of lightning. . . . . You have nothing like Arthur's Seat, and, above all, you have not the Scotch national character; and it is that grand character, after all, which gives the land its true charm, its true greatness." Scott's delineations of the peasants and freebooters of Scotland may have encouraged Charlotte Brontë to attempt a similar portraiture of the people of Yorkshire; and from no author could she have caught the contagion of an impassioned joy in forest, moor, and stream, more genially than from Wilson.

But it was France that lighted the torch of her genius. After being partly educated in England, and serving some time, with indomitable energy, as a governess, she went to Brussels, and came under the influence of M. Heger. He saw the powers of her mind, encouraged her in composition, taught her to sharpen and burnish her French *devoirs*, and thus prepared her to make her *début* as an English author in one of the most nervous, terse, and brilliant styles in the whole range of English prose—a style with no fault except a certain uniformity, a too sustained alertness and trenchancy,—a style quite perfect as a music of battle and of march, but far less adapted than some styles, notably than the style of Thackeray, to express the sauntering moods, to suit the meditative hours, that will not fail to occur in our earthly pilgrimage. One cannot think without a smile of the immense part played by M. Heger and her Brussels residence in the history of Charlotte Brontë. Choleric yet good-hearted, highly intelligent yet not without moodiness and whimsicality, M. Heger displayed that "*force du caractère recouvrant une vibrante tendresse*," that combination of masculine strength with feminine tenderness, which M. Eugene Forçade, in his admirable critique on *Shirley*, declares to be irresistibly attractive to women, and which is the keynote of all Charlotte Brontë's characteristic heroes. In her first and last books—the *Professor* and *Villette*—the scene is principally laid in a Brussels school; and in *Shirley* she puts Flemish blood into the veins of the brothers Moore, and avails herself of the opportunity thus offered her of airing her French. In *Villette* there is more French than belongs legitimately to an English novel.

It is beautiful, however, to see how the genial, brave, and healthy nature of our Yorkshire girl takes what is good, and rejects all that is evil, in the influence of the Continent and of France. Like a fair flower, she draws from the morass its richness, turns it into petals of loveliest form, lifts them to be bathed in the colours of heaven, and lets the poison alone. It is a marvellously stupid and superficial mistake to suppose that Charlotte Brontë assails English marriage, or any of the ideas characteristically attached to marriage in England. What she assails, both in *Jane Eyre* and in *Shirley*, is loveless marriage, lucre-made. What she denounces is the laying of young hearts on the altar of the god of this world. "See him," she makes Shirley say, describing to a wretched worldling the activity of his base divinity, "busied at the work he likes best—making marriages. He binds the young to the old, the strong to the imbecile. He stretches out the arm of Mezentius, and fetters the dead to the living. In his realm there is hatred—secret hatred; there is disgust—unspoken disgust; there is treachery—family treachery; there is vice—deep, deadly, domestic vice. In his dominions, children grow unloving between parents who have never loved; infants are nursed on deception from their birth: they are reared in an atmosphere corrupt with lies. Your god rules at the bridal of kings—look at your royal dynasties! Your deity is the deity of foreign aristocracies—analyse the blue blood of Spain! Your God is the Hymen of France—what is French domestic life? All that surrounds him hastens to decay; all declines and degenerates under his sceptre. *Your* god is a masked death." Marriage without affection was in her eyes desecration; but she shrank with equal aversion, and with still more vehement contempt, from the degraded feelings that are too often passed off for love in the literature and on the stage of France. "When I see or hear either man or woman," she writes, "couple shame with love, I know their minds are coarse, their associations debased. . . . In their dense ignorance they blaspheme living fire, seraph-brought from a Divine altar. They confound it with sparks mounting from Tophet." She refers with bitter scorn to those who mistook the sympathetic intensity of her descriptions of spiritual passion for sympathetic intensity of an ignobler sort.

I have spoken of Emily Brontë as a woman of, in some sense, more wonderful and original genius than that of her sister. Charlotte has not left anything evincing such subtle, far-brought, and magical power as the group of Heathcliff and Cathy, nor had her intellectual glance, in the last resort, the same penetrating finality as Emily's; and she herself agreed with all the best judges in awarding the palm of poetic superiority to Ellis Bell. Nevertheless, it is Charlotte that must be pronounced, on the whole, the chief of the sisters, the head of this unique and most interesting Yorkshire school of literature, a school that may outlive English as a spoken language, and that was founded, established, and closed by three provincial governesses, the oldest of whom died before forty. Charlotte stands between Emily and Anne, the mean between two extremes. Emily was hard— too hard. In her books and in her life she lacked expansion and geniality. She was unhealthy, with deficient stamina, a circumstance quite compatible with spasmodic and contracted strength. She has left little, and that little imperfect; and yet it may be doubted whether, if she had lived, she would have done much more or much better; for there is hardly a trace of youngness in her work. Anne, though also a woman of unquestionable genius, fell short in force. Her verses are, indeed, of great value; they express, with faultless simplicity, clearness, tenderness, feelings absolutely sincere, and as pure as the waters of a mountain spring; but both her thoughts and her feelings were limited in range. Charlotte had ten times the power of Anne, and her nature was more healthy and genial, her culture more comprehensive, than Emily's. On the whole, therefore, we must, I repeat, assign her the first place among the sisters.

As the Norwich school of painters, old Crome,

Cotman, and their few brothers of genius, made the low, dune-bordered shores, and windy downs, and lingering rivers, and bits of tufted woodland, that form the scenery of Norfolk, memorable in art, so the Brontë sisters drew the eyes of all the world towards their native Yorkshire. It is a rugged land, inhabited by a proud, independent, sturdy, and strong-brained race, with rather a grating edge towards strangers, and marked individuality of character. Emily Brontë's old Joseph will vie with the peasants of Scott; and a French critic remarked that, after reading *Shirley*, one could swear that he had lived in the world of Yorkshire. Keen-witted, observant, sarcastically contemptuous of sentiment, but at heart true and kind, the Yorkes and Helstones of *Shirley*, as well as a number of peasants and mechanics, are speaking portraits from the West Riding. Eugene Forçade amusingly describes the Yorke children as a half-dozen "*d'enfans terribles qui sont le plus bizarre échantillon d'éducation presbytèrienne, solitaire, egoïste, spontanée, qu'eût pu rêver Jean-Jaques.*"

Were it but for this realisation of a type of character belonging to a territory as large as that of ancient Attica, Charlotte Brontë would take precedence of Miss Austen. Mr. G. H. Lewes who, like Macaulay, overrated that celebrated novelist, wrote advising Charlotte to follow the counsel shining out of his idol's "mild eyes," which counsel he summed up in the formula, "to finish more and be more subdued." In reply she commented politely, but with pungent effect, both upon the precept given and the example suggested. "When authors write best," she says, "or at least when they write most fluently, an influence seems to awaken in them, which becomes their master—which will have its own way—putting out of view all behests but its own, dictating certain words, and insisting on their being used, whether vehement or measured in their nature; new-moulding characters, giving unthought-of turns to incidents, rejecting carefully-elaborated old ideas, and suddenly creating and adopting new ones. Is it not so? And should we try to counteract this influence? Can we, indeed, counteract it?" There is, of course, but one answer to these weighty and pertinent questions. Charlotte Brontë was not only right in maintaining against Mr. Lewes that authors ought to listen to the voice of their genius and obey it—to nurse their fire instead of subduing it—but expressed the prime canon of all criticism, when criticism attempts to direct the artist. To advise the writer to subdue his fire is to give him the counsel by which Meer Jaffier ruined Surajah Dowlah at Plassy, namely, to call off his force in the crisis of the battle.

Turning to the subject of Miss Austen, Charlotte professes herself "puzzled" by her critic's enthusiasm. She had sent for *Pride and Prejudice*, which Mr. Lewes extolled above any of the Waverley novels. "And what," she proceeds, "did I find? An accurate daguerreotyped portrait of a common-place face; a carefully-fenced, highly-cultivated garden, with neat borders and delicate flowers; but no glance of a bright, vivid physiognomy, no open country, no fresh air, no blue hill, no bonny beck. I should hardly like to live with her ladies and gentlemen, in their elegant but confined houses." Admiration for George Sand she can (she says) understand, for whatever Sand's defects, she has grasp of mind, sagacity, profundity. But "Miss Austen is only shrewd and observant." This is true, and nearly the whole truth. Miss Austen has inexpressible and inestimable delicacy of sentiment. Her heroines possess a sweetness all their own, a melodious tenderness and sense and goodness which make their way into our heart of hearts, and remain there for ever. Her old admirals, too, and her clergymen and young naval officers are singularly true to life. But she has no invention, no incident. Her characters walk out in pairs, like boarding-school girls (only that one in each pair is a gentleman and a lover), drive in phaetons, "taäke their regular meals," consult for weeks about private theatricals, and live, on the whole, about as quietly as tulips in a Dutch garden. Now, it is a universal truth in criticism that great passion and great thought require a framework of great incident for their display. The works of Homer and of Shakespeare—the two greatest delineators of passion and character—are as great in incident as in knowledge of human nature. Void of invention, void of imagination, depending solely on her observation and her sentiment, Miss Austen belongs distinctively to the minor schools of literary art; Charlotte Brontë, gifted, as *Jane Eyre* and *Shirley* conclusively prove, with both, is a sister, though perhaps a little sister, of the great imaginative story-tellers of the world—Homer and Scott, Sophocles and Shakespeare. The same honour belongs, I think, to George Eliot, who knows the worth of incident, and certainly stands higher than Charlotte Brontë in reach of thought and variety of power, but has never equalled her in the dewy brilliance, the felicitous splendour, of a few passages, and cannot, at her best, describe scenery with the witching charm and freshness of the Yorkshire girls. George Eliot has suffered from science, that cold Siren on whose breast Goethe laid his head, until he was gradually transformed from the inspired poet of *Faust*, part first, into the droning professor of *Faust*, part second.

There is a tragedy, it has been said, in every deathbed, and Æschylus might be searched for more moving sadness than that of the deaths of the poetic women of Haworth Parsonage. Almost immediately after Branwell's death Emily became ill, and though the mind remained clear and the will adamantine, the body yielded fast to consumption. Towards the end of November, 1848, the deep, tight cough, the panting breath, "the hollow, wasted, pallid aspect," told her sisters that she was dying. But she would see no "poisoning doctor;" when one came, she refused to let him enter her presence; and when Charlotte wrote down her symptoms and, without telling her, sent them to a London physician, she would not take his medicine. She seemed to defy death. "From the trembling hand, the unnerved limbs, the fading eyes, the same service was exacted as they had rendered in health." She was, however, dying rapidly, and though she forced herself to her tasks, her interest in everything around her was vanishing with her hold upon life. Charlotte went out and searched the cold December moors for a lingering spray of heather, and took it in to Emily. But it was too late. "The flower was not recognised by the dim and indifferent eyes." So died, at twenty-seven, without a glimpse of the fame that awaited her, the authoress of *Wuthering Heights* and of that poem of which the main burden is the life-long hiding of God's face from one of His creatures, who had yearned vehemently to behold it. Of hope or of heaven there does not appear to have been one syllable uttered by Emily Brontë throughout her illness. They laid her under the pavement of Haworth Church. Her "fierce, faithful bull-dog," to which Emily had been very kind, howled pitifully at her chamber door for many days.

Anne's death was very different. She had been taken to Scarborough, one of the brightest spots in England, and it was the month of May. On the last Sunday of her life, "the evening closed in with the most glorious sunset ever witnessed. The castle on the cliff stood in proud glory gilded by the rays of the declining sun. The distant ships glittered like burnished gold; the little boats near the beach heaved on the ebbing tide, inviting occupants. Anne was drawn in her easy-chair to the window to enjoy the scene. Her face became illumined almost as much as the glorious scene she gazed upon. Little was said, for it was plain that her thoughts were driven by the imposing view before her to penetrate forwards to the regions of unfading glory." Next day she gently asked her physician how long she had to live, bidding him not fear to speak truly, for she did not fear to die. He told her that death was at the door. She looked serene and undistressed. Clasping her hands, she invoked a blessing on Charlotte and on a friend who waited on her. "Be a sister in my stead. Give Charlotte as much of your company as you can." She thanked them both for their kindness to her. The restlessness of death came upon her, and they carried her to the sofa. "Soon all will be well," she said, "through the merits of our Redeemer." Passing through the gates of death, she still had comfort for her sister. "Take courage, Charlotte; take courage." Then, "calmly and without a sigh," she fell asleep. God had not hidden His countenance from Anne Brontë.

Charlotte returned to the lonely parsonage. She leant upon God, and He did not fail her; but the solitude was deep. "The great trial," she writes to a friend, "is when evening closes and night approaches. At that hour we used to assemble in the dining-room —we used to talk. Now I sit by myself—necessarily

I am silent." On windy nights, in the wailing of the gale in the churchyard and about the parsonage, she fancied she heard the spirits of her sisters trying to reach her. Balmy days came, and the sun of May lighted the moors, making them "green with young fern and moss, in secret little hollows," but to her they were very desolate—"a wilderness, featureless, solitary, saddening. My sister Emily," she goes on, "had a particular love for them, and there is not a knoll of heather, not a branch of fern, not a young bilberry-leaf, not a fluttering lark or linnet, but reminds me of her. The distant prospects were Anne's delight, and when I look round, she is in the blue tints, the pale mists, the waves and shadows of the horizon." Is there any poetry lovelier or sadder than that?

Life, however, was not yet over for Charlotte. With heroic resolution she stood to her work, habitually dwelling upon the thought of Divine help. "The strength," she had formerly said, in the simple and intense faith of that Calvinism which she learned from her father, and which runs through her books and letters, "the strength, if strength we have, is certainly never in our own selves; it is given us." A change came over her life when, in 1854, she was married to a man she wholly loved. Her friends "thought of the slight astringencies of her character, and how they would turn to full ripe sweetness in that calm sunshine of domestic peace." Her look brightened. She was sensible of a new warmth at her heart on hearing a villager describe her husband, Mr. Nicholls, as a "consistent Christian and a kind gentleman," which "high but simple eulogium" she could, she said, echo. She and her father and her husband, who was her father's curate, lived in the old parsonage on the high moor, the graves around it, the stars above. Her happiness endured but for a few months. With the prospect before her of becoming a mother, she found her health give way. True to her religious principles, she endured all with unflinching patience. At last, awaking from long stupor, she saw from the surrounding faces that she was dying. "Oh!" she said, faintly, "I am not going to die, am I? He will not separate us; we have been so happy." I pity those who trace in these words any spirit of irreverence. They seem to me as consistent with sincere and profound and affectionate regard for God, as the burst of tears of a glad child, when told by its parent to put down its playthings and go to bed, is consistent with filial love. But more touching words have seldom been uttered. Charlotte Brontë died as she had lived, a godly and honourable woman, one of whom England and the world may be proud.